Sociology for Midwives

Sociology for Midwives

By

Carol Kingdon

QUAY
BOOKS

A division of MA Healthcare Ltd

Quay Books Division, MA Healthcare Ltd, St Jude's Church, Dulwich Road, London SE24 0PB

British Library Cataloguing-in-Publication Data
A catalogue record is available for this book

© MA Healthcare Limited 2009
ISBN-10: 1-85642-339-5
ISBN-13: 978-1-85642-339-7

Printed in the UK by Ashford Colour Press, Gosport, Hants, PO13 0FW

In memory of Andy Barnard

CONTENTS

ABOUT THE AUTHOR

Carol Kingdon is a sociologist who has worked alongside midwives for over a decade. She is currently employed as a Research Fellow in the Women, Infant and Sexual Health (WISH) Research Group at the University of Central Lancashire. In addition to her research commitments she regularly teaches sociology, feminist theory and research methodology to pre- and post-registration midwives.

ACKNOWLEDGEMENTS

I am indebted to Andy Barnard who first introduced me to sociology as an A-level student, and to everyone who taught me at Staffordshire University (1992-1995), the University of Warwick (1995-1996) and Lancaster University (2001-2007). In particular, Gayle Letherby, Ellen Annandale, Vicky Singleton and Maureen McNeil each shaped my interest in the field of pregnancy and childbirth in important ways. Equally, this book would not have been possible without the insight of my midwifery colleagues at Liverpool Women's NHS Foundation Trust and the University of Central Lancashire, especially Lisa Baker and Tina Lavender. I am also grateful to Maria Anguita at Quay Books for her support. Last but by no means least, I must acknowledge the contribution of my husband, Martin Flanagan, who has been there for me throughout this process.

FOREWORD

Sociology challenges our every day assumptions; it helps improve our understanding about how society works and gives an insight into individual and group interactions. Midwives need knowledge and skills to assist them to provide woman-centred, evidence-based and culturally relevant care that considers sociological factors and issues. The sociological concept of the 'medicalisation of childbirth' is a good example of how our actions are influenced by the structural characteristics of our society, yet we create and adjust those structural characteristics in our actions.

In a British society it is clearly apparent that the role of a midwife represents an established occupational structure, with clear expectations and how to behave being key determinants of the profession. This fits in with the International Confederation of Midwives (ICM) definition of a midwife. However this is not the case worldwide. It is important to recognise and understand the social implications of illness and health inequalities and how these impact on women's lives, and the need for midwives to consider social risks as well as physical risks when caring for women.

The family is the primary focus of human socialisation and development, and midwives have a fundamental role to play in supporting new and existing families.

Similarly, the mass media can play an important role in influencing knowledge and attitudes towards pregnancy and birth, but there appears to be limited evidence relating to women's responses to media representation of childbirth. This indicates that there is an urgent need to undertake research to address this deficit. Also, midwives should be encouraged to think about the ways in which our bodies are shaped by social influences and the increasing demands to have a perfect body, which makes women susceptible to the likelihood of cosmetic surgery following childbirth.

This book focuses on sociological theories, concepts and issues that are very relevant to midwifery care and practice. No assumptions of any previous knowledge of sociology are made, and it introduces the subject of sociology and the key figures that have helped develop sociology as a discipline. Both classical and contemporary theories are discussed and some examples that midwives can relate to are given. It makes clear distinctions between the concepts of society and culture, and the role of the midwife is explored with a specific focus on what being a midwife means.

Dr Mary Steen
Reader in Midwifery and Reproductive Health, University of Chester

CHAPTER 1

Introducing sociology

Midwifery training in the UK has become embedded within a model of higher education that emphasises the study of academic subjects alongside the development of vocational knowledge and practical competencies. Sociology has been part of the pre-registration undergraduate midwifery curriculum since the 1990s. Nevertheless, a survey of pre- and post-registration midwifery education providers reports that whilst those responsible for teaching sociology to midwives value the subject, they acknowledge many students either find it 'difficult' or simply 'just common sense' (Church and Earle, 2006). This raises important questions about how sociology is currently perceived and understood by midwives.

This book aims to change midwives' views of sociology for the better. It is primarily written for pre-registration midwives. However, it should also be of relevance to practising midwives studying for postgraduate courses or with a general interest in the field. No previous knowledge of sociology is assumed. The main body of the book focuses on substantive issues relevant to midwives, and the purpose of this chapter is to offer an accessible introduction to the subject of sociology and its relevance to midwifery practice. This chapter also lays the foundations for the rest of the book by introducing some key figures in the development of sociological theory, key concepts and key debates. The sociological concepts introduced are not simply common sense, but neither are they difficult to grasp and some terms may already be familiar. Wherever possible I have tried to avoid the use of unnecessary jargon and words highlighted in bold can also be found in the glossary at the end of the book.

It is my intention that this chapter serves to capture midwives' interest. I also hope that it will enable readers to begin to think more critically about how societies operate and to question their own taken-for-granted assumptions and beliefs. This is because learning sociology requires individuals to take a step back from their own personal interpretations of the world, to look anew at the social influences that shape our lives (Giddens, 1989). Sociology is more than a discipline concerned with social issues, injustices and inequality; it challenges our everyday assumptions to advance understanding about how society works.

Defining sociology

The British Sociological Association (BSA) defines sociology as the study of how society is organised and how we experience life (British Sociological Association,

2007). This definition highlights both how broad the subject of sociology is and the central concerns that unite all sociologists. Sociologists may investigate virtually any aspect of social life. Within sociology there are many branches and sub-fields. Perhaps most relevant to midwives are the sociology of health and illness (or medical sociology as it is also known), the sociology of human reproduction (which includes contemporary feminist approaches to pregnancy and childbirth), and the sociology of the body. All of the chapters in this book draw on sociological work from these fields, but for the purposes of this chapter I focus principally on issues that unite the discipline of sociology as a whole.

All sociologists share a common concern with the structure of societies, organisations and groups, and how people interact within these contexts. For sociologists the two main determinants of social outcomes (or in other words, how society works) are **structure** and/or **agency**. The exact definitions of structure and agency employed by individual sociologists vary according to their underlying theoretical perspective. Nevertheless, the term 'structure' is typically used to describe any relatively enduring pattern or interrelationship of social elements (Jary and Jary, 1991). For example, in British society the judicial, educational and occupational structures are surface social structures, whilst the rules that reproduce social systems, such as language, provide examples of deeper social structures. The actions of all of us are influenced by the structural characteristics of the societies in which we are brought up and live. However, at the same time we create (and also to some extent alter) those structural characteristics in our actions. The concept of 'agency' relates to the power of individuals or groups to operate independently of the determining constraints of social structure (Jary and Jary, 1991). For example, the provision of a state healthcare system is a social structure that can be challenged and changed by individual agency (i.e. individuals who pay for private healthcare). There are many competing theoretical perspectives within sociology, however all are to a greater or lesser extent concerned with the relationship between structure and agency.

Sociologists make important distinctions between the concepts of **society** and **culture**. A society is a system of interrelationships that connects individuals together, whereas culture refers to the ways of life of members of a society, or groups within a society. The role of a midwife represents an established occupational structure within British society, whilst an illustrative example of midwifery culture is the shared use of phrases, expressions, abbreviations or acronyms typically used. For example, all qualified midwives should be familiar with the phrase '*the FH is dipping*' (meaning a reduction in the fetal heart rate). Moreover, student midwives adopt such phrases quickly in order to become accepted members of the dominant culture. Thus at one level language provides an example of an underlying societal structure, whilst at another level it is illustrative of the meaning shared by individuals in a particular culture.

Fundamental to culture are **norms**, the rules of behaviour that reflect or embody a culture's values. For example, in white British culture women were traditionally responsible for childbearing and childrearing. However today family values have changed, with both parents now expected to have a 'hands-on' role in their child's upbringing. It has therefore become the norm for fathers to accompany their partners during antenatal clinic visits, be present at birth and take paternity leave in the first weeks of their child's life. Consequently, many midwives may think it is common sense that fathers want to share their partner's experience of pregnancy, birth and childrearing. However, examination of indigenous British culture across time, or other cultures with different values and role expectations, should lead you to challenge this assumption.

The processes by which children, or other new members of society, learn the way of life of their society are known as **socialization** (Giddens, 2001). Primary socialization occurs in infancy when children learn language and basic behavioural patterns, usually from their families. Secondary socialization takes place in later childhood and into maturity. Interactions with schools, peer-groups, organizations, the media, and the workplace mean individuals learn the values, norms and beliefs that make up their particular culture. Moreover, it is through the processes of socialization that individuals learn about social roles. In sociology the term **role** specifically refers to the ways in which society expects a person who occupies a given position to behave. Roles carry duties and obligations and they may also confer rights, privileges and status (Cox, 1989). The social role of a midwife, for example, encompasses a set of behaviours that should be enacted by all in the profession, irrespective of the specific individuals who occupy this position.

In this chapter so far I have provided a simple definition of sociology and introduced some key terms and concepts. In order to understand more about sociology today, there is a need for midwives to appreciate the chronology and key sociological perspectives that originate from **classical sociology**. The next section introduces some of the key figures from classical sociology.

Classical sociological perspectives

It is possible to trace a sociological tradition of thought to the ancient Greeks Aristotle and Plato. However, sociology as an academic discipline has its origins in eighteenth century philosophy (Swingewood, 1991). The legacy of the **Enlightenment**, a movement based on notions of progress through the application of reason and rationality, was one of the main influences on the work of the first sociologists (Annandale, 1998). Other key influences on the development of sociology as a distinct field of study include the Industrial Revolution of England (c.1780-1840) and the democratic revolutions of the United States of America (1776) and France (1789). Lee and Newby (1989) assert that it is no coincidence that mainstream sociological thought emerged around the same time as these events precipitated unprecedented changes in the organisation of society.

The Frenchman Auguste **Comte** coined the term '*sociology*' at the beginning of the nineteenth century. Comte's vision for sociology was that of a **positivist** science, which could explain the laws of the social world just as natural science explained the functioning of the physical world (Giddens, 2001). Harriet **Martineau** translated Comte's founding work and first introduced sociology to Britain. However, the most famous sociological theorists of the nineteenth century were Emile **Durkheim**, Karl **Marx** and Max **Weber** who are widely regarded as the 'founding fathers' of sociology. This trinity did not create sociology, but their enduring influence means that an introduction to their perspectives is essential to understanding sociology today (Hughes et al, 2003).

Durkheim and Marx were both **structural** theorists. Structural sociological perspectives (or **macro** as they are also known) focus on how surface structures and underlying rules make society as a whole work. Structural perspectives view society as a system of interconnected parts which influence each other in a variety of complex ways. The focus is less on the specific actions of individuals than on the roles that they occupy and the ways in which these roles relate to each other in society as a whole (Sharp, 2006). However, whilst Durkheim and Marx shared a structural perspective, their resultant sociological theories were very different. Durkheim's theory of how society works has been described as based on consensus, whilst Marx's theory was based on conflict. The summary in *Box 1.1* uses a famous quotation from Durkheim to illustrate the application of the structuralist view of society.

Emile Durkheim

Durkheim was French. He became the world's first professor of sociology in 1896 (Cox, 1989). Durkheim published four major sociological works: *The Division of Labour in Society* (1893), *The Rules of the Sociological Method* (1895), *Suicide* (1897) and *The Elementary Forms of Religious Life* (1912).

In *The Rules of the Sociological Method* (1938 translation) he outlined the subject matter of sociology, the key steps involved in sociological investigation, and developed the concept of **social facts**. Durkheim used the term social facts '...*to describe elements of society which can be studied independently of individual disposition*' (Morrison, 2004: 394).

Suicide (1951 translation) was an empirical study which enabled Durkheim to demonstrate how suicide rates can be explained within the framework of society, rather than the psychological state of the individual. This study is discussed in more detail in chapter eight.

Durkheim's most enduring contribution to sociology was his contribution to the establishment of the principles of the sociological perspective known as **functionalism**. Durkheim's work in *The Division of Labour in Society* (1933 translation) and *The Elementary Forms of Religious Life* (1976 translation), and the work of the English social evolutionist Herbert **Spencer,** laid the foundations for this perspective, which was particularly influential in sociology up until the 1960s (Lee and Newby, 1989).

The central tenant of **functionalist theory** is that society is a system and its

Box 1.1: The structural approach to understanding society

'When I perform my duties as a brother, a husband or a citizen and carry out the commitments I have entered into, I fulfil obligations which are defined in law and custom and which are external to myself and my actions. Similarly the believer has discovered from birth, ready fashioned, the beliefs and practices of religious life; if they existed before he did, it follows that they exist outside of him. The system of signs that I employ to express my thoughts, the monetary system I use to pay my debts, the credit instruments I utilise in my commercial relationships, the practices I follow in my profession, etc. — all function independently of the use I make of them. Considering in turn each member of society, the following remarks could be made for each single one of them'.

Emile Durkheim (1892, cited in Giddens 2001: 667)

component parts cannot be viewed in isolation from each other. A common analogy is made between the functionalist view of society and a living organism. Just as all the separate organs in a living body are linked and dependent on each other for the wellbeing of the whole, social institutions such as religion, the judicial system and education must all function properly for the wellbeing of society. Social change occurs gradually through the processes of adaptation or integration. All versions of functionalist theory are based on:

> '...the expectation that whatever adjustments occur in social behaviour and organisation, there are a set of underlying pressures which work towards the maintenance of stability, the co-ordination of activities and even the conformity of individuals'.
>
> *Lee and Newby (1989: 262)*

The main criticisms of functionalist theory are: firstly, its overt focus on the positive social functions of institutions, roles and norms, with little attention drawn to their negative consequences and the conflict they may generate. Secondly, like other structural theories, functionalism assumes that individuals are unable to alter social institutions or roles as a result of their own independent actions (Sharp, 2006).

The prominence of concerns with society as a whole meant that individuals' experiences of health were something of a sociological non-issue for Durkheim (Gerhardt, 1989). He never wrote about either the role of the midwife or women's experiences of pregnancy, childbirth or motherhood. Nevertheless, his inclusion in this chapter is important because of the continued relevance of his work, not only in sociology (see *Box 1.2*), but also to understanding how social influences may impact on midwifery practice. For example, consideration of the extent to which rates of Caesarean section may be considered social facts could reveal important social influences on the incidence of this procedure. Furthermore although Durkheim did not write about health, pregnancy or childbirth himself, his functionalist perspective gave rise to the work of many sociologists who have done so, and the work of who will be discussed in subsequent chapters of this book.

Box 1.2: Emile Durkheim's legacy to sociology

- He made a substantial contribution to the development of the sociological perspective known as functionalism.

- He showed how even such an intimate and individual act as suicide may be subject to social influences, and therefore, not all human behaviour can be explained by psychology or the natural sciences.

- He pioneered quantitative analysis (using statistical methods) in the investigation of society.

- He established sociology as an academic discipline.

- Twentieth century sociologists who developed Durkheim's approach include Talcott Parsons and those associated with some variants of structuralism.

Karl Marx

Karl Marx never held an academic post in sociology. He was more than a sociologist. He developed a body of ideas and theory that encompasses the whole of the social sciences and the humanities, and was the inspiration for the communist societies of the twentieth century (Lee and Newby, 1989). Marx was German. However, he lived in London for most of his productive life, where he principally sought to explain the changes that were taking place in society at the time of the industrial revolution. Marx's most famous work was *Capital: A Critique of the Political Economy*, with the first of three volumes published in 1867. His other key works included *The Communist Manifesto* published in 1848 with Friedrich Engels.

Marx's specific approach to analysing how society works drew on the notion of historical materialism. Historical materialism is the term used to conceptualise how the way in which economic production is socially organised can account for all other facets of society. Marx divides history into five separate epochs according to the dominant **mode of production**. These are, in chronological order: primitive communism; ancient society; feudalism; capitalism, and eventually socialism (Lee and Newby, 1989). In each epoch he made a crucial distinction between those human beings who are owners of the **means of production** (such as land in feudal society or factories in industrial capitalist society), and those who are not (Cox, 1989).

'Marx links the existence of social class to the development of property relations in society, and defines a class in terms of its relationship to the means of production'.

Morrison (2004: 310)

Under capitalism, Marx identifies two social classes — the owners of the means of production, the **bourgeoisie** and the other, which does not own the means of production, the **proletariat**. In a sense Marx offers a theory of social development where it is through class struggle that he asserts society principally transforms itself from primitive communism to socialism.

In addition to **social class**, other key concepts in Marx's work include the base/ superstructure distinction and his use of the term **ideology**. Marx asserts the base is the mode of production (sphere of economic activity) and the superstructure is the ideological aspects of society, such as religion and education, which are determined by the base. He defines ideology as the system of ideas that represents the dominant material relationships and class interests in society. Ideology serves to legitimise the existing class system, makes the subordinate classes politically quiescent, and conceals contradictions between the classes and the ultimate coercive nature of society (Morrison, 2004). The major criticisms of Marx's work are its emphasis on conflict, its degree of **economic determinism** (whereby the nature of the economy is seen as ultimately determining social relations and social change), and lack of recognition of the capacity for humans to act independently of social forces.

Like Durkheim, Marx did not personally write about pregnancy, childbirth or midwifery. However, his inclusion in this chapter is warranted not only because of his contribution to sociology (see *Box 1.3*), but also because of the enduring relevance of his key concepts to contemporary midwifery practice. For example, in chapter four — which focuses on inequalities in health — we will see the continued relevance of social class as a key determinant of health outcomes during pregnancy, birth and infancy. Moreover, like Durkheim, Marx has exerted an important influence on the work of later sociologists in the field of health and illness more generally.

Box 1.3: Karl Marx's legacy to sociology

- He made an unprecedented contribution to the analysis of capitalist society in Britain and the development of communist societies around the world.

- His work gave rise to Marxism, the sociological perspective that bears his name and its derivatives including variants of neo-Marxism, feminism, critical theory, structuralism and contemporary political economy perspectives.

- His influence in the field of stratification has been considerable, where non-Marxist's have adapted his use of concepts such as social class.

Max Weber

Weber's distinct approach to understanding society combines a macro-sociological conflict approach (where parallels may be drawn with Marx's structural approach) with a **micro-sociological approach**. In other words, his perspective recognises the contribution of individual action to society.

Weber was German and a professor of sociology from the age of 32 years (Morrison, 2004). Weber's key works included *The Protestant Ethic and the Spirit of Capitalism* (part 1 published in 1904 and part 2 in 1905) and *Economy and Society* published posthumously in 1922.

Weber is most famous for establishing the sociological perspective known as **social action theory**, which takes human individuals, their ideas, and their actions as a starting point for sociological analysis (Morrison, 2004). According to Weber all human action is social, with mere behaviour becoming action when it derives from dealings with others and when it is meaningful (or in other words orientated in its course). However, the meaning of action is never self-evident, it always requires interpretation and '...*this is the fundamental axiom of Weber's interpretive sociology: actions never speak for themselves — they always require the placing of meanings*' (Lee and Newby, 1989: 174). Central to this perspective is the notion of verstehen, which may be loosely translated to mean 'empathetic understanding':

> *'This means, in essence, that to gain a full understanding of an individual's action, we must look at the world from their point of view and, as it where, step into their shoes'.*
>
> Sharpe (2006: 18)

In many ways Weber was ahead of his time, particularly in his writings about the development of modern science, technology and bureaucracy; a process he described collectively as rationalization (Giddens, 2001). The related concept of rationality is a term that Weber used to refer to the capacity of social action to be subject to calculation in the means and ends of action. In other words, rationality may be defined as a standard of action whose substance lies in its weighing up of means and ends prior to action (Morrison, 2004).

Another important notion in Weber's work is the **ideal type**. Ideal types are conceptual models that can be used to understand the world. In the real world ideal types rarely — if ever — exist, with only some of the attributes present (Giddens, 2001). However, the concept of an ideal type is useful because a situation in the real world can be understood by comparing it to its ideal type, or in other words, it serves as a useful point of reference. Bogdan et al (1982) provide an illustrative example of an ideal type in their work on communication between staff and parents in a neonatal unit. They propose a conceptual scheme (or in other words a model) where on admission, staff categorise patients as either 'non-viable' or 'baby':

'Patients may remain an undifferentiated baby for a few minutes or a few days but eventually move into one of three categories: "very sick babies", "good babies" and "babies with special problems"'.

Bogdan et al (1982: 8)

In addition, a few patients will move from being 'non-viable' into the 'very sick baby' category. However, the point to make is that Bogdan's model is an 'ideal type' in the Weberian sense because it neither captures perfectly nor seriously distorts any of the units' actual schemes that effect everyday communication between staff and parents (Bogdan et al, 1982).

Weber's approach to understanding capitalism has been described as a 'debate with the ghost of Marx'. He disagreed with Marx on the purpose of sociology, viewing it as a discipline that should not aim to change society but search for valid historical truths and gather facts about society. Weber also disagreed that human destiny is shaped primarily by economic forces; instead he advocated that humans can shape their own destiny by their beliefs and ideas. Weber also extended Marx's theory of class to take into account other important social divisions, those of status and power, as well as relationship to the economic means of production. Thus, the contribution of Weber to sociology represents a bridge between the structural theories of the nineteenth century and the social action theories of the twentieth century. Moreover, according to Lee and Newby (1989), of all the major founding fathers,

---

Box 1.4 Max Weber's legacy to sociology

- He developed the sociological perspective known as social action theory.

- His so-called debate with the 'ghost of Marx' led to refining of key sociological concepts such as social class, and development of notions such as rationality.

- He was ahead of his time in recognizing the growing importance of the state in the modern world; his belief that capitalism was capable of enduring indefinitely as an economic system and his emphasis on the importance of technological change.

- He is credited with founding interpretive sociological approaches, and was a major influence on the second Chicago School. Interpretive approaches include symbolic interactionism, phenomenology, and ethnomethodology.

- Along with Marx, he was the key influence on the Frankfurt School of sociological analysis, which includes theorists Adorno, Marcuse and more recently Habermas.

Weber's contribution to modern sociology is arguably the most influential (see *Box 1.4*). Perhaps most significantly, Weber was responsible for sensitising sociologists to the need to account for social action from the point of view of human actors and is therefore credited with founding the **interpretive** branch of sociology that was to rise to prominence in the twentieth century (*Box 1.5*).

Box 1.5: The interpretive approach to understanding society

'Action is "social" in so far as its subjective meaning takes account of the behaviour of others and is thereby orientated in its course.'

Max Weber (1968 translation, cited in Lee and Newby 1989: 174)

This section has highlighted that Durkheim, Marx and Weber shared a desire to make sense of the changing societies in which they lived. However, most importantly, they sought to develop ways of studying the social world that could explain how societies work and what brings about social change (Giddens, 2001). I have purposively highlighted each of their legacies to sociology. During the 20th century, up until the 1970s at least, the dominant theoretical perspectives were functionalism (which owes a debt to Durkheim), conflict/critical (which owe a debt to Marx and Weber) and symbolic interactionism (which owes a debt to Weber). The next section will introduce each of these briefly before moving on to contemporary perspectives and debates, the key sociological perspectives discussed in this and subsequent sections and the relationship between them.

Twentieth century sociological perspectives

As previously stated, functionalism was a key sociological perspective up until the mid 1960s. In particular, a variant known as 'Parsonian structural-functionalism', after the work of Talcott Parsons, dominated. Talcott Parsons was an American sociologist whose key works include *The Social System* (1951), which we will return to in later chapters. He is credited with developing the notion of 'functional prerequisites in society' and a conception of social order that presents societies as internally interrelated and self-sustaining (Jary and Jary, 1991), as well as key concepts such as the sick role (discussed in chapter four).

Critical or conflict approaches are terms that are most commonly used to refer to the theories that emerged during the 1960s, which collectively contested the dominance of Parsonian structural-functionalism by highlighting the role of conflict (rather than consensus) in human societies. Some variants of conflict theory were derived directly from Marxist thought (with an emphasis on class conflict); others drew from Marx and Weber (i.e. Lockwood, 1964), whilst others still sought to highlight hitherto undocumented sources of conflict such as that between the sexes (which was to give rise to second-wave feminism discussed in the next section). One important branch of critical theory is associated with the **Frankfurt School**, a group of sociologists and philosophers who revisited the writings of Marx with the aim of bringing them up to date. In particular, their work emphasises the increasing importance of culture in late capitalist societies. Their perspective is principally associated with a variant of neo-Marxism but they were also influenced by the work of Weber. Key thinkers associated with the Frankfurt School include Theodor Adorno, Herbert Marcuse and Jürgen Habermas (discussed in chapter seven).

Around the same time as critical theory was contesting the ascendancy of structural-functionalism, the merits of interpretative sociology were also coming to the fore. Building on the work of Weber, a group of sociologists from the University of Chicago had developed a major theory of interpretive social action — **symbolic interactionism** (a body of work collectively referred to as the second **Chicago School**). In particular, the work of George Herbert **Mead** established the interactionist perspective around:

> '...*the proposition that, even though there is a biological base which underlies experience, selves are essentially social products which develop out of interaction with others*'.
>
> *Mead (1972 [1934] cited in Annandale, 1998:21)*

In other words the concept of '**the self**' is socially constructed; how we see ourselves is formed through interaction with others in society. Herbert **Blumer**, a contemporary of Mead, stresses three key principals central to this perspective: '...*human beings act toward each other on the basis of meanings; meanings arise out of interaction; meaning are mediated through an interpretive process*' (Sharrock et al, 2003: 196). Charles Cooley famously uses the term 'looking glass self' to capture key concepts inherent in interactionist perspectives, which are concerned with the negotiation of the self, impression management, and meaning creation (Coser, 1971). The empirical utility of this perspective was demonstrated in the late 1950s and early 1960s in a number of seminal studies including those by Erving **Goffman**. In her introduction to the *Sociology of Health and Illness*, Ellen Annandale (1998: 21) states:

> '...*the ways in which individuals give meaning to social events (such as childbirth, surgery, death); the ways in which they manage changed identities in ill-health; and the 'negotiation' that takes place in formal and informal healthcare settings – are the subject of interactionism*'.
>
> *Annandale (1998: 21)*

Other branches of interpretive sociology that have been employed in the sociology of health and illness include **phenomenology** and the even more elaborately named **ethnomethodology**. Phenomenology is a branch of philosophy which Edmund Husserl is credited with first developing. One of his students, Martin Heidegger, is also widely credited with developing a particularly influential later variant of phenomenology. However it was Alfred **Schutz** (1932), also a pupil of Husserl, who developed phenomenology into a distinct sociological perspective. In contrast to social action perspectives, phenomenology as a sociological perspective emphasizes the internal working of the human mind and tries to understand the meaning of phenomena, rather than explaining how they came into existence (Haralambos and Holborn, 2008).

Ethnomethodology is an approach first developed by Harold Garfinkel (1984) in an attempt to capture how individuals create social reality. In other words, it involves the study of the methods and social competence individual employ when constructing our sense of reality.

To a greater or lesser extent all of the approaches discussed so far, from functionalism to ethnomethodology, are still used by sociologists today. Whilst it is worth pointing out that Marxism and its derivatives have come under a new wave of criticism since the fall of the former Soviet Union, arguably the greatest challenges to the continued relevance of classical and twentieth century sociological perspectives comes from within the discipline itself, and wider changes in society associated with the rise of feminism and what has been termed a period of late, high or **post-modernity**.

Contemporary sociological perspectives and debates

It is fundamentally important to highlight that in recent years the dichotomy between structural and interpretative 'sociology(ies)' illustrated in *Figure 1.1* has been somewhat eroded. At one level, the work of the British sociologist Anthony Giddens, who has called for a bridging of the gap between structure and action approaches by recognising how humans actively make and remake social structure during the course of our everyday activities, is important. **Structuration** is the term Giddens (1984) uses to conceptualise the process of the active making and remaking of social structure in a theory that recognises how structure and action are necessarily related. In other words, the duality of both structure and action is recognised as important, rather than one being more important than the other. At another level, and arguably more significant, the impact of feminism and post-modernism has made this dichotomy superfluous.

During the late 1960s, throughout the 1970s and early 1980s there was what has been described as:

> '...*a broad based feminist assault on the perceived male bias both in sociological theory and methodology, and in the very subject matter of sociology*'.
>
> *Giddens (2002: 671).*

Figure 1.1   Key sociological perspectives

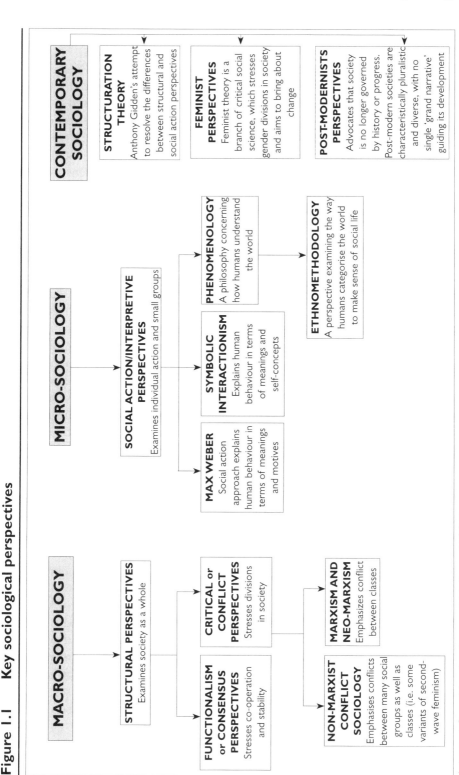

Adapted from Haralambos and Holborn (1991)

Consequently, sociology was to change in a number of ways. Feminism is not a unified perspective — it is more accurate to write of **feminism(s)**. For example, there are chronological distinctions between first-wave feminism (i.e. eighteenth century to early twentieth century), second-wave feminism (i.e. 1960s, 1970s and 1980s), and debates concerning whether or not we have entered into a third-wave (post-1990s to present day). There are also important distinctions made between different branches of feminist theory and methodology (see chapter eight). Moreover, there are bodies of feminist work across all disciplines, not just sociology. Arguably the only things all feminisms share is a central concern with **gender** and a commitment to improving the lives of those disadvantaged by gender inequality. One consequence of this rich, but varied, body of work is that it somewhat inevitably crosses the structure/agency or structuralist/interpretive sociology divide. Moreover, some variants look towards post-modernism. At this point it is perhaps important to highlight that what the linear schema presented in *Figure 1.1* does not convey well is that contemporary approaches co-exist with earlier variants of sociology. Moreover, they are not mutually exclusive. For example, there are present-day sociologists who would employ an interpretative approach whilst drawing on a distinct branch of feminist theory, whilst others may identify themselves as 'Marxist feminists' or 'post-modern feminists'.

Post-modernism is one of those scary words that turn many midwives off. In sociology what the term post-modernism typically refers to is the writings of those who think that the sorts of theories Durkheim, Marx and Weber sought to develop (that is overall theories of society and social change) are no longer achievable. Akin with feminism(s), post-modernism is not a unified body of thought (Annandale, 1998). Nevertheless, it is possible to say that almost all thinkers whose work has been associated with this perspective reject 'grand narratives' or meta-narratives such as those associated with Durkheim, Marx and Weber (Lyotard, 1985). Post-modern thinkers also tend to reject an overall notion of progress and highlight instead how the post-modern world is in a constant state of flux. In other words what we have is a complex 'mess' (my choice of word not theirs) that is constitutive of **post-modernity** (the term for the kind of society post-modernists suggest we currently inhabit). The relative merits of this approach should become clearer during the course of the book.

As we shall also see in subsequent chapters there are a number of key issues that constitute fundamental areas of debate in contemporary sociology. One such issue (and particularly pertinent in the field of health) is the rise of what Beck (1992) terms 'a global risk society'. Beck (1992) rejects post-modernism, instead he suggests that we are living in a world 'beyond the modern' that is entering a phase he terms 'the second modernity'. What postmodernists see as chaos or lack of pattern, Beck (1992) sees as risk or uncertainty and asserts that the management of risk is the prime feature of a new global order.

The term **globalization** refers to the process that is intensifying worldwide social relations and interdependence for societies and individuals. It is a concept that is closely related to the period of profound social change all contemporary sociologists believe we may currently be living in — however they may choose to theorize it.

Other key issues that we will explore include the rise of individualism/ **consumerism** as applied to health (particularly in chapters three, four and six) and the new **medicalization** debates, within which the media plays a significant role (see chapters three and seven).

In this chapter so far I have introduced the centrality of a number of key concepts in sociology, key perspectives in the development of classical sociological theory and some important influences on contemporary debates. A further thing that unites sociologists is what the American sociologist Charles Wright **Mills** famously termed 'the sociological imagination'.

Thinking sociologically

Writing in the late 1950s, Mills was reflecting on the impact that rapid social change has on people when he famously wrote:

> '...perhaps the most fruitful distinction with which the sociological imagination works is between "the personal troubles of milieu" and "the public issues of social structure".

> *Mills (1959: 8)*

Personal troubles of milieu are everyday occurrences; understanding more about how we interpret and deal with them requires us to connect our private troubles to public issues and in so doing to begin to think like a sociologist. More recently, Bauman asserts (1990) that thinking sociologically highlights:

> '...how the apparently familiar aspects of life can be interpreted in a novel way and seen in a different light'. [The aim is] '...not to "correct" your knowledge, but to expand it; not to replace an error with an unquestionable truth, but to encourage critical scrutiny of beliefs hitherto held; to promote a habit of self-analysis and of questioning the views that pretend to be certainties'.

> *Bauman asserts (1990: 18)*

For example, consider the antenatal 'booking' visit. This a routine interaction between midwives and women which takes place in antenatal clinics across Britain. For most women the booking visit in early pregnancy is the first contact they have with maternity services. Typically this interaction involves an ultrasound scan, the midwife taking a medical and social history, and blood tests. Now begin to think sociologically and look at this routine part of midwifery practice anew. Maybe first, consider the ultrasound scan:

- Why is it so important?

As a midwife you could argue that it is important to ascertain the viability and date the fetus. As a sociologist you would ask the following:

- What are the consequences of the application of this technology?
- It is a technology that was not designed for use on pregnant women but has been adapted for medical use — this could lead you to ask: How does the use of this technology serve medicine?
- Does it increase doctors, midwives and women's reliance on technology from this early stage in pregnancy onwards?
- In the resource-rich countries of the western world, which include North America, Europe and Australia, generally women are healthier than ever so why are they all routinely offered screening to identify a problem?
- Is it in medicine's interests the use of this technology or are there economic incentives for routine screening?
- Is the same scan machine used in hospitals in Australia as in the UK, whilst there is no scan machine available to a woman in suspected early pregnancy who is bleeding heavily in Mozambique?

In the UK, for many women the scan will confirm their fetus is viable, but for others it will not; yet for all of these women the scan will have particular cultural significance. This is because, as we shall see in chapter six, the use of technologies to visualise fetuses and ultrasound in particular has changed the way babies-before-birth are perceived in society.

- What are the consequences of not having the scan, and for whom?

If the fetus is viable then it will be born several months later (an ultrasound scan does not determine the actual date of delivery unless it is used to schedule an elective Caesarean section); and if it is not viable then the woman will miscarry at some point. Alternatively:

- What is the significance of identifying a fetal abnormality at 12 weeks and what does this say about attitudes towards caring for disabled children in our society?

Consider the medical and social history-taking next:

- What are the roles and rituals that govern this interaction?
- If a midwife was not a socially sanctioned role, would it be acceptable to ask a woman such personal details at a first meeting?
- What is the purpose of asking about her and her partner's occupation?

- How do midwives perceive women who do not attend antenatal booking visits in the first trimester?

Sociologists have long recognised that the effects of society begin not with the emergence of the child from the womb, but while the mother is still carrying it (Worsley, 1992).

Consider the second routine scan usually performed around 20 weeks. The obstetric rationale for the scan is to identify anomalies, and for prospective parents whose fetus is seen to be developing normally it may principally serve to inform them of their unborn child's sex. Whilst one's genes determine sex, once the sex of a fetus is known its gender role may be ascribed soon after:

- In your experience as midwives, what do women and their partners say when they know it's a boy or a girl?
- Do they discuss colours for clothes or the nursery, discuss whether or not they will be, for example, a footballer?

Thus, thinking sociologically requires critically thinking about how human behaviour cannot be adequately understood without reference to the ideas (the beliefs, norms, values, concepts and purposes) that inform it. Our social roles are guided by the norms of behaviour built into our culture, rather than our genes, and they have to be learned (Worsley, 1992). Moreover, what we may consider the most personal of experiences (i.e. the first visual image of our unborn child) is intimately linked to wider social structures. Thinking about these kind of issues is what makes sociology such a challenging, but rewarding subject — not only do you learn more about society, you learn about yourself too.

The distinctiveness of sociology

Sociology is about how society works, why people behave as they do, what factors in society affect their behaviour, how groups in society organize themselves and come to be as they are (Thompson, 1986). However, many of the social sciences could claim this focus. In particular, the boundaries between sociology and social **psychology**, and between sociology and social **anthropology** are often confusing for those unfamiliar with the disciplines. The purpose of this section is to clarify some important differences between sociology, psychology and anthropology.

Psychology has been defined as the scientific study of behaviour (Glassman, 2000). For psychologists, the term behaviour encompasses actions (observable behaviour), mental processes (unobservable behaviour) and the behaviour of animals (Paradice 2004). Social psychology is a branch of psychology that focuses on behaviour in social situations and examines how people are influenced by groups. Thus an overlap in focus between social psychology and some branches of sociology is somewhat obvious; however the theories and methods used by each discipline to understand how people behave in groups remain distinct. For example, social psychologists are most likely to study group behaviour using experimental methods, whereas interpretive sociologists would be more likely to use qualitative methods (see chapter eight for a detailed explanation of these terms). Similarly, whilst social psychologists would be more likely to theorize group behaviour using ideas from psychoanalytic, behavioural or cognitive psychology, sociologists are most likely to use ideas stemming from key sociological perspectives.

Social anthropology, or cultural anthropology, as it is also known, investigates the structures and cultures produced by human beings. Traditionally, social anthropologists have studied non-industrialised societies, a difference in focus that provided a clear line of demarcation between anthropology and sociology. Sociology is primarily the study of modern or post-modern societies. However in recent years, as anthropologists have increasingly turned their attention to their own cultures, the lines of demarcation between anthropology and sociology have become less clear. Nevertheless, the distinctiveness of anthropology and sociology remains in the methodological and theoretical orientations dominant to each discipline.

In this chapter I have introduced midwives to some of sociology's theoretical underpinnings. I also hope that I have shown sociology to be something other than common sense, and led midwives to begin to question their own assumptions about the world around them. I have tried to highlight the relevance of sociology to midwifery practice wherever possible. In the final section of this chapter I distinguish between a number of important ways in which I believe sociology can make important contributions to understanding midwifery.

Sociology in midwifery, sociology of midwifery and the sociology of human reproduction

Over 50 years ago, the American sociologist Robert Strauss first postulated a dichotomy between sociology *in* medicine and the sociology *of* medicine (Straus, 1957); a distinction which was based at the time on the sociology of medicine in the US (where sociologists had only fleeting contacts with physicians) and a sociology in medicine in the UK (where sociologists had a close proximity to medicine, health policy and practice).

More recently however, Jonathan Gabe, Mike Bury and Mary Ann Elston (2005) identify two (not dissimilar) strands of enquiry in contemporary 'medical sociology':

'On the one hand, a sociological perspective can be applied to the experience and social distribution of health and health disorders and to the institutions through which care and cure are provided. In this sense, medical sociology can have an applied orientation to understanding and improving health,

and can be seen as one of the many disciplines that might appropriately be studied by providers of healthcare. On the other hand, the sociological study of health, illness and institutions of healthcare can stand alongside analysis of other significant social experiences and institutions, as a means of understanding the society under study. Thus, medical sociology is also a theoretically orientated field, committed to explaining large-scale social transformations and their implications, as well as interactions n everyday settings, as these are expressed in health and illness.'

Gabe et al (2005: 4)

Moreover, Barbara Green (2005) extends the dichotomy between the sociology *of* medicine and sociology *in* medicine in a slightly different way when writing about the application of sociology to nursing:

'In general terms, when sociological analysis is applied to the essence of individual health care experience, whether it be that of patients or healthcare workers this is termed "sociology in *nursing". The 'sociology* of *nursing' usually refers to issues affecting the profession as a whole, such as it occupational status, or recruitment or attrition problems.'*

Green (2005: 30)

This book extends Green's (2005) distinction further by demonstrating both the application of 'sociology *in* midwifery' and 'sociology *of* midwifery'. The sociology of midwifery is the principal focus of chapter two, which introduces sociological insights into what it means to be a midwife across time and culture. In subsequent chapters the emphasis shifts more towards sociology in midwifery.

Finally, for the purposes of this chapter it is important to introduce the 'sociology of human reproduction'. The British Sociological Association's Human Reproduction Study Group was set up in 1975, from which emerged significant efforts to establish a 'sociology of childbirth' in the late 1970s and 1980s. Particularly noteworthy is Sally MacIntyre's (1977) review entitled *The Management of Childbirth: Sociological research issues.* It identified four types of sociological approach to childbirth that were available at the time:

1. Historical/professional approach (where historical context was studied using a sociology of science, social policy or professions framework)
2. Anthropological approach (where the focus was on prevailing belief systems in different cultures)
3. Patient-orientated approach (which aimed to articulate service users perspective)
4. Patient-services interaction approach (where the interplay between service users and service providers was the focus).

In 1980 Ann Oakley published *Women Confined: Towards a sociology of childbirth*, which was extremely critical of medicine's increasing control over pregnancy and childbirth. Although numerous other papers and books were published between 1980 and 1990 a distinct sociology of childbirth was never realised as interests broadened to encompass the emerging **new reproductive technologies** and women's health issues more generally. The edited collection *The Politics of Maternity Care: Services for childbearing women in twentieth-century Britain* (Garcia et al, 1990) represents perhaps the last significant text from this era. Having said that, as we shall see over the course of this book, a body of work that may yet become a new 'sociology of childbirth' is currently emerging.

Conclusion

This chapter has introduced midwives to sociology. It has offered both formal definitions and an introduction to thinking sociologically. This chapter has also introduced some key sociological concepts including society, agency, culture and socialization. Additionally, it has provided an introduction to classical sociology, key perspectives in the twentieth century and contemporary sociology, which includes feminism(s). It is hoped that this chapter has gone some way to challenge the views of some midwives that sociology is simply 'common sense'. It is also my intention that midwives do not find sociology overly difficult, on the contrary I hope this chapter has shown it can be accessible, interesting and most of all relevant to contemporary midwifery practice. This chapter has set the tone for the rest of the book; in the next chapter we will consider the role of the midwife.

References

Annandale E (1998) *The Sociology of Health and Medicine: A critical introduction.* Polity Press, Cambridge

Bauman Z (1990) *Thinking Sociologically. An Introduction for Everyone.* Basil Blackwell, Cambridge

Beck U (1992) *Risk Society: Towards a new modernity.* Sage, London

Bogdan R, Brown MA, Foster SB (1982) Be honest but not cruel: Staff/parent communication on a neonatal unit. *Human Organization* **41**(1): 6–16

British Sociological Association (2007) *https://www.britsc.co.uk*

Church S, Earle S (2006) Approaches to sociology within midwifery education. *British Journal of Midwifery* **14**(6): 342–45

Coser LA (1971) *Masters of Sociological Thought: Ideas in historical and social context.* Harcourt Brace Jovanovich, New York

Cox C (1989) *Sociology: An introduction for nurses, midwives and health visitors.* Butterworths, Sevenoaks

Durkheim E (1933 translation) T*he Division of Labour in Society.* The Free Press, New York

Durkheim E (1938 translation) *The Rules of the Sociological Method.* The Free Press, New York

Durkheim E (1951 translation) *Suicide.* The Free Press, New York

Durkheim E (1976 translation) *The Elementary Forms of Religious Life.* Allen and Unwin, London

Gabe J, Bury M, Elston M (2005) *Key Concepts in Sociology.* Sage, London

Garcia J (1990) *The Politics of Maternity Care: Services for childbearing women in twentieth century Britain.* Clarendon Press, London

Garfinket H (1989) *Studies in Ethnomethodology.* Blackwell, Oxford

Gerhardt U (1989) *Ideas About Illness; An intellectual and political history of medical sociology.* New York University Press, New York

Glassman WE (2000) *Approaches to Psychology.* 3rd edn. Open University Press, Milton Keynes

Giddens A (1984) *The Constitution of Society.* Polity Press, Cambridge

Giddens A (1989) *Sociology.* Blackwell, Oxford

Giddens A (1992) *The Transformation of Intimacy: Sexuality, love and eroticism in modern societies.* Polity press, Cambridge

Giddens A (2001) *Sociology.* 4th edition. Polity Press, Cambridge

Green B (2005) Why should nurses study sociology? In: Denny E, Earle S, eds. *Sociology for Nurses.* Polty Press, Cambridge: 29–46

Haralambos M, Holborn M (2008) *Sociology: Themes and perspectives.* HarperCollins, London

Hughes JA, Sharrock WW, Martin PA (2003) *Understanding Classical Sociology: Marx, Weber, Durkheim.* 2nd edn. Sage Publications, London

Jary D, Jary J (1991) *Dictionary of Sociology.* Harper Collins, Glasgow

Lee and Newby (1989) *The Problem of Sociology. An introduction to the discipline.* Unwin Hyman, London

Lyotard J (1985) *The Post-Modern Condition.* University of Minnesota Press, Minneapolis

Lockwood D (1964) Social integration and system integration. In: Zollschan G, Hirsch W, ed eds. *Explorations in Social Change.* Routledge, Kegan Paul, London: 244-56

MacIntyre S (1977) The Management of Childbirth: Sociological research issues.

Marx K (1867) *Capital: A critique of the political economy.* Volume I. Penguin, Middlesex

Marx K (1876) *Capital: A critique of the political economy.* Volume II. Penguin, Middlesex

Marx K (1894) *Capital: A critique of the political economy.* Volume III. Penguin, Middlesex

Marx K, Engels F (1848) *The Communist Manifesto.* Norton, New York

Mills CW (1959) *The Sociological Imagination.* Oxford University Press. New York

Morrison K (2004) *Marx, Durkheim, Weber: Formations of modern social thought.* Sage

Publications, London

Oakley A (1980) *Women Confined: Towards a sociology of childbirth*. Martin Robertson and Co, Oxford

Paradice R (2004) *Psychology for Midwives*. Quay books, London

Parsons T (1951) *The Social System*. The Free Press, New York

Schutz A (1932) *The Phenomenology of the Social World*. Heinemann, London

Sharpe K (2006) What is sociology? In: Denny E, Earle S, eds. *Sociology for Nurses*. Polity Press, Cambridge

Sharrock WW, Hughes JA, Martin PJ (2003) *Understanding Modern Sociology*. Sage, London

Straus R (1957) The nature and status of medical sociology. *American Sociological Review* **22**: 200–04

Swingewood A (1991) *A Short History of Sociological Thought*. 2nd edn. The Macmillan Press, Basingstoke

Thompson JL (1986) *Sociology*. Heinemann, London

Weber (1904) *The Protestant Ethic and the Spirit of Capitalism*. Scribner's, New York

Weber M (1922) *Economy and Society*. Volumes I and II. University of California Press, Berkeley

Worsley P, ed (1992) *The New Introducing Sociology*. Penguin Books, London

CHAPTER 2

Sociological perspectives and the role of the midwife

The previous chapter identified that a key aspect of sociology involves looking anew at the social influences that shape our lives and challenges our everyday assumptions. This chapter considers the social shaping of the role of the midwife in different societal and temporal contexts. It draws on illustrative examples to explore what being a midwife means. It introduces different types of societies and the roles of midwives within them. It also discusses the status of midwifery in Britain over time and key sociological approaches to the professions. The formal and informal social processes whereby students learn to become midwives are considered too.

The role of the midwife is of interest to sociologists, particularly feminist sociologists, for many reasons not least because the role of the midwife is fundamentally linked to the social meaning attached to childbirth within specific cultures. Childbirth is a profoundly gendered act. Whilst pregnancy and parturition are unique to the female sex, how women experience birth varies across societies, cultures and time. What is more, midwifery is a gendered occupation. In other words, it is an occupation principally associated with a feminine, caring role. It is also an occupation dominated by women. For example, in the UK in 2006/2007 there were 35,037 female midwives on the Nursing and Midwifery Council (NMC) register, compared with only 134 male midwives (NMC, 2008). Midwifery also has a particularly fascinating relationship with the obstetric branch of modern medicine, both in its history and today, which makes it an important focus for sociologists interested in the power of the medical profession.

Defining the role of the midwife

The International Confederation of Midwives (ICM) offers the following definition of a midwife (ICM, 2005):

> 'A midwife is a person who, having been regularly admitted to a midwifery educational programme, duly recognised in the country in which it is located, has successfully completed the prescribed course of studies in midwifery and has acquired the requisite qualifications to be registered and/or legally licensed to practise midwifery. The midwife is recognised as a responsible and accountable professional who works in partnership with women to give

the necessary support, care and advice during pregnancy, labour and the postpartum period, to conduct births on the midwife's own responsibility and to provide care for the newborn and the infant. This care includes preventative measures, the promotion of normal birth, the detection of complications in mother and child, the accessing of medical care or other appropriate assistance and the carrying out of emergency measures. The midwife has an important task in health counselling and education, not only for the woman, but also within the family and the community. This work should involve antenatal education and preparation for parenthood and may extend to women's health, sexual or reproductive health and child care. A midwife may practice in any setting including the home, community, hospitals, clinics or health units.'

ICM (2005)

This formal definition of a midwife's role paints a picture of a midwife that is constructed around a number of key assumptions. In accordance with this definition all midwives must have completed a midwifery educational programme recognised in the country in which it is located, acquired the requisite qualifications to be registered and/or legally licensed, be a responsible and accountable professional, work in partnership with women, conduct births on the midwife's own responsibility, provide care for the newborn and the infant, and they may practice in any setting including the home, community, hospitals, clinics or health units.

Whilst this definition of a midwife's role may resonate with most of the midwives reading this book it does not encompass all who would align themselves with the role of the midwife in societies and cultures less familiar to us. **Ethnocentrism** is the term used to describe the practice of judging other cultures by comparison with one's own. This is a practice that is particularly discouraged in sociology where comparison with other societies and cultures has shown that the world created by modern societies is not necessarily to be equated with progress.

As identified in chapter one, society is a system of interrelationships that connects individuals together, whilst culture refers to the ways of life of members of a society or groups within a society. Midwives need to know about different types of societies and the structures within them if they are to understand more about the role and status of the midwife in both their own and the cultures of others. Sociologists have identified a number of different types of society and their associated cultures. Most sociologists distinguish between pre-modern and modern societies, whilst others would add post-modern societies to this list. *Table 2.1* lists the main types of societies in the pre-modern and modern world, their periods of existence and their key characteristics.

Pre-modern societies include hunting and gathering societies, pastoral/ agrarian societies and traditional civilisations (also known as empires). Traditional civilizations (i.e. the ancient Egyptians, the Greek, Roman and Chinese empires) no longer exist. Moreover, whilst the entire human race is believed to have once

Table 2.1   Types of society

Types of premodern human society			Societies in the modern world		
Type	Period of existence	Characteristics	Type	Period of existence	Characteristics
Hunting and gathering species	50,000 BC to the present (now on the verge of disappearance)	Small numbers of people. Livelihood from hunting, fishing, and gathering edible plants. Few inequalities. Differences of rank limited by age and sex. Continue to exist only on the most and parts of Africa and the jungles of Brazil and New Guinea	First world societies	Eighteenth century to present	Based on industrial production and free enterprise, with a little rural agriculture. People live in towns and cities. Major class of inequalities but less pronounced than in traditional states. Distinct political communities or nation-states (e.g. the West, Japan, Australia and New Zealand)
Agrarian societies	12,000 BC to the present. Most are now part of larger political entities, and are losing their distinct identity	Based on small rural communities, without towns or cities. Livelihood from agriculture supplemented through hunting and gathering. Stronger inequalities than among hunters and gatherers. Ruled by chiefs	Second world societies	Early twentieth century (following Russian Revolution of 1917) to the early 1990s	Based on industry but economic system is centrally planned. Small proportion works in agriculture. Most live in towns and cities. Major class inequalities persist. Distinct political communities or nation-states. Until 1989 composed of Soviet Union and Eastern Europe
Pastoral societies	12,000 BC to present. Today mostly part of larger states; their traditional ways of life are becoming undetermined	From a few hundred people to thousands. Depend on domesticated animals for subsistence. Marked by distinct inequalities. Ruled by chiefs or warrior kings. Agrarian and pastoral societies continue to exist in areas of Africa, the Middle East and Central Asia	Developing societies ('Third world societies')	Eighteenth century (mostly colonized areas) to the present	Based on traditional agriculture. Some produce sold on world markets. Some have free enterprise systems, others are centrally planned. Distinct political communities or nation-states (e.g. China, India, most African and South American nations)
Non-industrial civilisations	6000 BC to the 19th century. All traditional civilisations have disappeared	Very large in size, some numbering millions of people. Based largely on agriculture. Cities exist with trade and manufacture. Government headed by king or emperor. Major inequalities exist among different classes	Newly industrialised countries	1970s to the present	Former developing societies now based on industry and free enterprise; some agriculture. Majority of people live in towns and cities. Major and pronounced class inequalities. Average per capita income considerably less than First World societies (e.g. Hong Kong, South Korea, Singapore, Taiwan, Brazil and Mexico)

Adapted from Giddens (2002)

lived in hunting and gathering societies, today they only continue to exist in the most arid parts of Africa and the jungles of Brazil and New Guinea. Thus agrarian and pastoral societies are the main types of pre-modern society that remains in existence today. In these societies livelihoods are gained through the tending of domestic animals (pastoral) or agriculture (agrarian). They can be found in areas of Africa, the Middle East and Central Asia.

Modern societies are typically known as industrialized or developed societies, and the timeframe in which this type of society dominates is known as **modernity**. Modern societies are synonymous with **industrialization**, a term that refers to the emergence of machine production based on the use of inanimate power resources (e.g. steam or electricity). The industrialized societies of the modern world originated in Europe at the end of the eighteenth century, however industrialization is a process that continues today. Examples of newly industrialized countries include the Latin America countries of Brazil and Mexico, South Korea, Singapore and Taiwan. As evident in *Table 2.1* in the modern world a distinction may also be made between first, second and third world societies, although as debates about globalisation intensify (the process whereby global trade, communication and immigration means barriers between nations and individuals are breaking down) these classifications are becoming superfluous.

As all midwives know, childbirth is a universal event that occurs across societal and temporal context. It is therefore not surprising that no single definition can capture the role of all midwives. In the sociological and anthropological literature on childbirth at least three distinct types of midwifery role are evident; traditional midwives, lay midwives and professional midwives. The 'traditional midwife' is a role that still exists in almost every village and in many urban neighbourhoods throughout Africa, Asia, Latin America and the Caribbean where childbearing women do not have access to medical health services. Typically these midwives are indigenous to the local community, and therefore familiar with local culture, tradition and birth practices.

The international health development literature favours the term traditional birth attendant (TBA) to refer to the indigenous healers and traditional midwives who assist women during childbirth. In the 1970s the World Health Organisation (WHO) estimated that between 60–80% of babies worldwide were delivered by TBAs (WHO, 1978). Consequently, successive health development programmes have targeted traditional midwives with training to prevent harmful practices. However, numerous anthropologists have observed such training to present only modern obstetric knowledge as authoritative (Jordan, 1993; Pigg, 1997). As a result the transfer of knowledge between developing and developed societies is rarely a two way process, and it is important to highlight some of the many anthropological studies of childbirth that document other ways in which midwives may approach the care of women during pregnancy and childbirth (Kitzinger, 1982; Sargent 1982, 1989, 1990; Konner and Shostak, 1987; Hillier, 2003).

The 'lay midwife' is a role that exists both in history and today. For example, in present day North America the term lay midwifery is frequently used to refer to independent, non-nurse midwives (also known as birth educators or birth attendants). Their training is through participation in home births, informal reading, and apprenticeships. Whilst certified nurse/midwives (CNMs) practice legally in every state across the US and Canada, direct-entry lay midwifery is legal in some states, illegal in other states, and not clearly defined in a few states (Foley and Faircloth, 2003). Thus, whilst these individuals self-identify themselves as midwives and undoubtedly undertake a midwifery role it is debatable as to whether not they meet the ICM definition of 'a midwife'. The lay midwife also exists in the history of midwifery in the UK, where before the seventeenth century attending women in childbirth was an exclusively female occupation (Stacey, 1990). Similar to present-day lay midwives, the knowledge and training these women received came from their own experience of having babies and from working with and listening to older midwives (Oakley, 1976). However, the rise of scientific medicine and the process of industrialisation during the eighteenth and nineteenth centuries meant these women's skills were increasingly discredited.

The 'professional midwife' is the role that most midwives reading this book will probably associate themselves with and is most closely aligned to the ICM definition. In the UK, for example, all practising midwives must have successfully completed a midwifery educational programme and be legally registered. With the notable exception of independent midwives, most are employees with a regular salary and most are instantly recognisable as healthcare professionals by their uniform. In the UK the Midwives Act of 1902 first constituted midwives as practitioners in their own right. In sociology, the term **professionalization** is used to refer to the process of achieving the status of a profession.

Sociological approaches to the professions

Is midwifery a profession? For most midwives the answer to this question may seem obvious. Certainly all of my friends and colleagues who are midwives consider midwifery to be a profession. Indeed, many claim midwifery to be the oldest of all professions, citing references to midwives in the Bible (Exodus 1:15-22; Genesis 35:17, 38:28). In the UK today midwives have a professional association (the Royal College of Midwives), a professional regulatory body with a code of conduct (the Nursing and Midwifery Council), and an annual requirement to declare their intention to practice on a professional register. Moreover, many midwives work as respected members of multi-disciplinary teams amidst other key healthcare professionals (i.e. obstetricians, neonatologists, general practitioners). Yet, the midwife Shelia Hunt and the sociologist Anthea Symonds state:

> '...midwifery occupies the classic terrain of the semi-professional or skilled worker but cannot be included in the definition of a profession'.
>
> Hunt and Symonds (1995: 21)

The concept of a **profession** as traditionally defined in sociology does not include midwifery. Elston (2005: 163) states:

'...within sociology the term profession is usually used to denote a type of occupation accorded high status and a high degree of autonomy over its work'.

Elston (2005: 163)

Whilst this definition does not necessarily preclude the occupation of midwifery in Britain today, law, medicine and the church are the occupations that have been traditionally used as examples of professions in sociology (MacDonald, 1999). Moreover, the branch of sociology commonly known as the sociology of the professions has been dominated by the study of medicine.

Elston (2005) identifies that sociological analyses of the professions centre around two complex and inter-related issues. The first is what, if anything, distinguishes those occupations that are generally accepted as being professions from those that are not? The second is to what extent can we trust these professionals' claims of trustworthiness and their connected demands for autonomy (freedom from external monitoring), and what are the consequences of accepting (or, indeed, of refusing to accept) professionals' claims?

Most introductions to the sociology of the professions begin with functionalist perspectives. Writing in the early twentieth century, Emile Durkheim (introduced in chapter one) asserted that the professions were an important integrative force in rapidly changing, industrializing societies. For Durkheim, the principal characteristic of the professions was occupations organised as cohesive communities based on shared ethical values (Durkheim, 1957). Durkheim's dual focus on professional ethics and the professions' functional contribution to society laid the foundations for functionalist approaches to the professions up until the 1970s. Of particular note is Talcott Parsons (1954) analysis of the medical profession's role as an agent of social control through its regulation of illness. Parson's (1954) work also identified a key characteristic of a profession (as evident in medicine at the time) to be the pursuit of community rather than self-orientated goals. Other key characteristics of the professions identified by functionalist approaches include the possession of a body of theoretical knowledge, self-regulating practice and authority over clients. The listing of the characteristics of an ideal type profession, against which actual examples of occupational groups could be assessed, is known as the trait approach. This approach provides a way of determining which occupations really are professions and therefore which ones were not but might be classified as semi-professions.

Nursing is one occupation often described in the 1950s and 1960s as a semi-profession because it lacked sufficient theoretical knowledge or powers of self-regulation to warrant designation as a profession. As stated earlier, in the UK the Midwives Act of 1902 first constituted midwives as practitioners in their own right. However, Jean Donnison (1977) points out that the Midwifery Act of 1902:

'...was like no other registration Act, before or since, and was to put midwives in a uniquely disadvantaged position among the professions'.

Donnison (1977: 174)

This is because not only was midwives' practice circumscribed to attend only 'normal' births, but the Board that was to regulate them had a medical majority and was not even required to include a midwife. Thus exemplifying what is known as the **logic of subordination** whereby medicine ensures its continued position at the top of the healthcare division of labour by demarcating other clinicians' sphere of practice (Larkin, 1981). If you accept this line of argument and use the trait approach then midwifery too (like nursing) may be classified as a semi-profession, rather than a profession.

However, an alternative argument is that over the course of the nineteenth and twentieth century UK midwifery provided the best example of a **professional project** and an attempt to achieve occupational closure (Witz, 1992). The term professional project is used in sociology to refer to the more or less conscious efforts of members of an occupation to work collectively to improve their status and their economic prospects (Elston, 2005). Medicine's professional project has been described as particularly effective because it used educational credentials to effect social closure (or in other words to restrict entry to the occupation to those able to obtain formal training) and a scientific basis to medical knowledge to espouse the credibility of its practice (Larson, 1977). However, from the 1860s onwards medicine's professionalization strategy existed alongside midwifery's own professional project, which was also based on legalistic and credentialist tactics in the pursuit of exclusionary aims (MacDonald, 1999). For example, the obstetrical Association of Midwives and the Female Medical Society sought legal independence from medical men and this was to some extent achieved in the Midwives Act of 1902. What is more, midwifery's professional project has continued throughout the twentieth century with the establishment of the Royal College of Midwives, the development of a university-based education and the formation of the Association of Radical Midwives to champion midwifery autonomy, normal birth and woman-centred care (Sandall et al, 2001). Thus Witz (1992) conceptualises midwifery's professional project as exemplifying a dual closure strategy. In other words, although midwives were excluded from practising obstetrics, they have nevertheless developed their own occupational closure strategy, which distinguishes them from obstetrics and has created its own exclusion practices.

During the 1960s the emergence of sociological concerns about what part professions play in the established order of society, and how do such occupations manage to persuade society to grant them a privileged position, marked the end of functionalist perspectives and the rise of conflict perspectives in the sociology of the professions (MacDonald, 1999). Whilst Marxist and political economy perspectives linked the socially powerful position of doctors to the role that medicine plays in capitalist accumulation (Johnson, 1972), it was

Eliot Freidson (1970a, 1970b), utilising a neo-Weberian perspective, who first turned attention towards the process of professionalization. It was Freidson who identified **legitimated authority** (or in other words, occupational self-control over the terms and conditions of work) as a characteristic crucial for professional status. Freidson argued that medicine, at least in the 1970s, had this to a very high degree (Elston, 2005). Freidson (1970b) also identifies that medicine's supremacy in the healthcare division of labour is attributable to both autonomy (the ability to control its own work activities) and dominance (control over the work of others in the healthcare division of labour).

However, another important line of argument in the sociology of the professions is that the medical profession achieved its dominant position in the healthcare **division of labour** not because of its inherently superior expertise, but because it managed to create and maintain control over certain technological procedures (Nettleton, 1995). Keith MacDonald (1999) asserts that midwifery provides the best example of the shift from **status knowledge** to technical, scientific knowledge that occurred in the course of the transition from agrarian to modern society. During the sixteenth and seventeenth centuries the power of the church, with which midwives had registered since 1512, was in decline, giving way to the Enlightenment (the social movement based on notions of progress through the application of reason and rationality or in other words scientific thought). This gave rise to a dispute between two kinds of knowledge about childbirth: traditional, experiential knowledge such as that possessed by the traditional midwives who were exclusively female, and the medical scientific knowledge that was the domain of men:

> *'By the seventeenth century the barrier which excluded men from midwifery had broken down'.*
>
> *Clark (1968: 265)*

However the new 'men-midwives' were predominantly interested in the problems of childbirth deriving from the new scientific approaches being applied to medicine, not childbirth *per se*. Thus the dispute between status knowledge and technical, scientific knowledge in the context of childbirth also became one centred on the material interests of two practitioners — midwives and men-midwives who were the predecessors to today's obstetricians. Whilst the Medical Acts of 1858 and 1886 consolidated the position of the man-midwife, it was the earlier development of forceps (which could only be used by male practitioners) that laid the foundations for doctors, and not midwives, to take professional responsibility for birth (Donnison, 1977; Oakley, 1976). Thus the shift from status knowledge to technical scientific knowledge fundamentally challenged the gender order, with childbirth no longer exclusively the domain of women.

The emergence of concerns about gender and the writing back in of women's involvement in professional projects signal the influence of feminism beginning to permeate into the sociology of the professions. The advent of feminism meant that the fact that professionalized medicine was overwhelmingly male and the semi-professions (i.e. nursing and midwifery) predominantly female, no longer went unquestioned. As we have seen, Witz (1992) developed a more general model of professional projects that included midwifery. Moreover, Witz (1992) draws particular attention to the relationship between male dominance, gender and the professions through her discussion of the concept of **patriarchy** — a concept we will return later in this and the following chapter. Davis (1995) also took issue with male sociologists for seeing the autonomous professional doctor through blinkers that obscure the incorporation of gender into the health division of labour, and the ways in which the possibility of being an autonomous professional is, in reality, sustained by the activities of other, mostly female workers. Using nursing (not midwifery) as a case study, Davis asserts that the notion of professional autonomy is a masculine one which is incompatible with many of the values nursing espouses. This is why, she argues, nursing has had such difficulties pursing the medical path to professional status and leads her to advocate a new model of professionalism in which partnership and reflective practice constitute the basis of expertise. Work by midwives has also highlighted that those who expect to 'get on in the profession' must approach their work in the same way male medics do (Sandall, 1995; Kirkham and Stapleton, 2000).

Recent sociological interest in the medical profession has begun to shift from accounting for its dominance to considering its possible decline. Annandale (1998) asserts that contemporary theoretical debates concerning the power of medicine are characterised by the increased questioning of the extent to which professional dominance is still evident. One controversial strand of these debates is known as **proletarianization theory**. McKinlay and Stoeckle (1988) define the proletarianization of physicians as:

'...*the process by which occupational category is divested of control over certain prerogatives relating to the location, content, and essentially of its task activities, thereby subordinating it to the broader requirements of production under advanced capitalism*'.

McKinlay and Stoeckle (1988: 200)

In other words, medicine is losing some of it power and control as doctors move from self-employed to employee status, as evident in the British National Health Service (NHS), for example.

Another controversial strand of contemporary debate is **deprofessionalization theory**. Deprofessionalization theory is defined as:

'...*a loss to professional occupations of their unique qualities, particularly their monopoly over knowledge, public belief in their service ethos and expectations of work autonomy and authority over clients*'.

Haugh (1973: 197)

In other words, medicine's authority is increasingly being undermined by members of the public who are increasing well-educated and informed, and therefore able to question both medical authority and medical practice. First advocated in 1973, deprofessionalization theory was ahead of its time predating the rise of consumerism in western healthcare systems (discussed later in chapter three). However, as identified by Freidson in his later work (1994), concepts such as professional dominance, proletarianization and deprofessionalization are loosing their utility in increasingly complex modern societies. Annandale (1998) too highlights that both inter- and intra-professional interactions are becoming enormously complex, asserting that the relative power of any one occupation in the healthcare division of labour today can only be fully understood through an examination of the intricate web of interactions with other occupations. For example, nurses and midwives play a vital yet unrecognised role in training and supporting junior doctors, particularly senior house officers (Hammond and Mosley, 1999). A study of decision-making in NHS delivery suites by Gloria Lankshear et al (2005) report that no one member of staff had total autonomy over decision-making, not even consultants. Moreover, whilst doctors could overrule midwives, midwives were seen to manipulate decision outcomes frequently.

Annandale and Clark (1996, 1997) have previously argued for greater recognition of how the discourse of midwifery and the discourse of obstetrics are relational and '*...elide and collide in response to local contexts*' (Annandale and Clark, 1996: 31). Further support for this position comes from Foley and Faircloth (2003) who draw on data from interviews conducted with 26 midwives in the US to show:

> '*...that while there is an inherent theoretical tension between medicine and midwifery, in practice, the medical model is not simply an oppositional framework used for the discrediting of a holistic approach*'.
>
> *Foley and Faircloth (2003: 166)*

They demonstrate three specific ways in which midwives use a discourse of medicine to construct a legitimising narrative of midwifery.

As midwives, you are perhaps best placed to observe how the occupational label of 'midwife' is dynamic and ever changing in practice. Whilst it remains debateable as to what extent midwifery may be regarded as 'a profession' in sociological terms, the sociologist Raymond De Vries (1993) usefully advocates that professional success for midwives can be measured in three dimensions:

- The interests of midwives as persons
- The interests of midwifery as an occupation
- The interests of midwifery as a service that promotes the health and well-being of women and babies.

The next section considers how individuals develop their professional identify.

Socialization of midwives

Do you remember how you felt the first time someone called you a midwife? If it was early in your training it may have felt strange and you may not have felt you knew enough to warrant the title. Do you remember how you felt the last time someone called you for a nurse, failing to appreciate the distinctiveness of a midwife's role? This innocent mistake may have given rise to feelings of indifference, or you may have felt aggrieved because your training emphasises important differences between the role and status of midwifery compared to nursing. As a midwife you are part of an organized occupational community with a strong sense of professional identify that more often than not disassociates itself with nursing.

Your identity as a midwife is acquired through the process known as **'professional socialization'**. Elston (2005) states:

> '...*in using the term socialization to describe the processes through which new entrants acquire their professional identities, sociologists are making an explicit analogy with primary socialization, the social processes through which children develop an awareness of general social values and norms from a distinct sense of self through interaction with others. Fundamental to the sociological approach here is that much more is involved in professional socialisation than book learning and gaining technical competence (although these are important aspects if the process)'.*

> *Elston (2005: 168)*

Elston (2005) emphasises the importance of informal modes of influence as well as formal teaching in professional socialization. For example, whilst there are aspects of the curriculum that all student midwives are taught, depending on where you train you will be informally socialized into a particular variant of midwifery specific to the local culture (for example in a consultant-led delivery suite).

Two studies of medical students, undertaken in the US during the 1950s and 1960s, were particularly important in shaping sociological thinking on professional socialization. Firstly, *The Student Physician* by Robert Merton et al (1957), which employed a functionalist perspective, showed how medical students learn to tolerate working with uncertainty arising from a personal lack of knowledge and the limits of scientific knowledge. Secondly, *Boys in White* by Howard Becker et al (1961), which employed a symbolic interactionist perspective, showed how medical students can be active participants in their learning. More recent studies of medical students have identified how they acquire a sense of medical mastery and the ability to conduct themselves with 'detached concern' (Hafferty, 2000).

There has been much less sociological research on the socialization of healthcare occupations other than medicine, with gender (and ethnicity) issues widely neglected. Having said that, one recurrent finding in the few studies of nursing socialization that have been undertaken is a disjuncture between what is taught in the classroom and what is actually done on the wards, which can be traced back to a seminal work by Olesen and Whittaker (1968). There is a dearth of sociological work reporting the socialization of midwives, although there are a number of discussion papers to be found in midwifery journals (Bosanquet, 2002; Parsons and Griffiths, 2007). Studies of the socialization of nurses (where technical skills are learnt alongside an emphasis on the feminine characteristics of caring and empathy) also highlight the importance of gender (Davies, 1995).

Gender and midwifery

Throughout this chapter, the relevance of gender has been omnipresent. Whilst the formal definition of a midwife presented at the beginning of this chapter failed to acknowledge that midwifery is a gendered occupation, this chapter has shown that it undoubtedly is. The gender dimension of midwifery is bound up in its changing status as a vocation, occupation or profession in different types of societies. Attending women in childbirth continues to be an exclusively female pursuit in pre-modern societies and in the developing (or third world) societies of the modern world. However, in the UK — one of the first of the modern world industrialized societies — there are clear associations between industrialization, Enlightenment, the rise of the medical profession and changes to the role and status of midwifery. The term 'patriarchy' refers to:

> '...a societal-wide system of gender relations of male dominance and female subordination, [and] the ways in which male power is institutionalised within different sites in society'.
>
> Witz (1992: 11)

Most feminists argue that patriarchy is more acute in industrialized societies, where the division of labour and the rise of science align men and women with different social spheres. The significance of this will be explored further in the next chapter.

Conclusion

This chapter has introduced midwives to the sociology of the professions. It has highlighted that descriptions of an occupation such as 'midwife' have no intrinsic meaning of their own, as to be a midwife is a cultural and historical experience, which differs from culture to culture and over time (Hunt and Symonds, 1995). Thus to understand what it means to be a midwife from a sociological perspective requires examination both of the development of midwifery in our particular society (i.e. its history) and consideration of midwifery practice in other societies (i.e. make cross-cultural comparisons).

References

Annandale E (1998) *The Sociology of Health and Medicine: A Critical Introduction.* Polity Press, Cambridge

Annandale E, Clark J (1996) What is gender? Feminist theory and the sociology of human reproduction. *Sociology of Health and Illness* **18**: 17-44

Annandale E, Clark J (1997) A reply to Rona Campbell and Sam Porter. *Sociology of Health and Illness* **19**: 521-32

Becker HS, Geer B, Hughes EC, et al (1961) *Boys in White: Student culture in medical school.* University of Chicago Press, Chicago

Bosanquet A (2002) Stones can amke people docile: Reflections of a student midwife on how hte hospital environment makes 'good girls'. *MIDIRS Midwifery Digest* **12**(3): 301–305

Clark A (1968) *Working Life of Women in the Seventeenth Century.* Frank Cass, London

Davies C (1995) *Gender and the Professional Predicament in Nursing.* Open University Press, Buckingham

DeVries R (1993) A cross national view of the status of midwives. In: Riska E, Wegar K, eds. *Gender, Work and Medicine: Women and the Medical Division of Labour.* Sage, London: 131–46

Donnison J (1977) *Midwives and Medical men: A history of inter-professional rivalries and women's rights.* Heinmann, London

Durkheim E (1957) *Professional Ethics and Civil Morals.* The Free Press, New York

Elston MA (2005) *Professions and professionalization.* In: Gabe J, Bury M, Elston MA, eds. *Key Concepts in Medical Sociology.* Sage, London: 163–168

Foley L, Faircloth CA (2003) Medicine as discursive resource: legitimation in the work narratives of midwives. *Sociology of Health & Illness* **25**(2): 165–84

Freidson E (1970a) *Medical Dominance.* Aldine-Atherton, Chicago

Freidson E (1970b) *The Profession of Medicine.* Dodd, Mead and Co, New York

Freidson E (1994) *Professionalism Reborn.* Polity Press, Cambridge

Giddens A (2002) *Sociology.* Polity Press, Oxford

Hafferty FW (2000) Reconfiguring the sociology of medical education: emerging topics and pressing issues. In: Bird CE, Conrad P, Fremont AM, eds. *Handbook of Medical Sociology.* 5th edn. Prentice Hall, New Jersey: 238-57

Hammond P, Mosley M (1999) *Trust me (I'm a doctor).* Metro, London

Haugh M (1973) Deprofessionalization: an alternative hypothesis for the future. *Sociological*

Review Monograph **2**: 195–211

Hillier D (2003) *Childbirth in the Global Village: Implications for midwifery education and practice*. Routledge, London

Hunt S, Symonds A (1995) *The Social Meaning of Midwifery*. Macmillan, Basingstoke

ICM (2005) Definition of the midwife. Website: *www.internationalmidwives.org*

Johnson T (1972) *Professions and Power*. Macmillan, London

Jordan B (1993) *Birth in Four Cultures: A cross-cultural investigation of childbirth in Yucatan, Holland, Sweden and the United States*. 4th edn, Waveland Press, Prospect Heights

Kirkham M, Stapleton H (2000) Midwives support needs as childbirth changes. *J Ad Nurs* **32**: 465–72

Kitzinger S (1982) The social context of birth: some comparisons between childbirth in Jamaica and Britain. In: McCormack CP, ed. *Ethnography of Fertility and Birth*. Academic Press, London: 181–203

Konner M, Shostak M (1987) Timing and management of birth among the Kung: biocultural interaction in reproductive adaptation. *Cultural Anthropology* **2**(1): 11–28

Lankshear G, et al (2005) Decision-making, uncertainty and risk: Exploring the complexity if work processes in NHS delivery suites. *Health, Risk & Society* **7**(4): 361–77

Larkin GV (1981) Professional autonomy and the ophthalmic optician. *Sociology of Health and Illness* **3**(1): 15–30

Larson MS (1977) *The Rise of Professionalism: A sociological analysis*. University of California Press, London

MacDonald KM (1999) *The Sociology of the Professions*. Sage, London

Merton RK, Reader G, Kendall PL, eds (1957) *The Student Physician: Introductory Studies in the Sociology of Medical Education*. Harvard University Press, Cambridge MA

McKinlay J, Stoeckle J (1988) Corporatisation and the social transformation of doctoring. *International Journal of Health Services* **18**: 191–205

Nettleton S (1995) *The Sociology of Health and Illness*. Polity Press, Oxford.

NMC (2008) The Nursing and Midwifery Council statistical analysis of the register 1 April 2006 to 31 March 2007. NMC, London. Available from: *www.nmc-org.uk*

Oakley A (1976) Wisewomen and medicine man: changes in the management of childbirth. In: Mitchell J, Oakley A, eds. *The Rights and Wrongs of Women*. Penguin, Harmondsworth

Olesen V, Whittaker E (1968) *The Silent Dialogue: A study of the social psychology of professional socialization*. Jossey-Bass, San Francisco

Parsons M, Griffiths R (2007) The effect of professional socialization on midwives' practice. *Women & Birth* **21**(1): 31–34

Parsons T (1954) The professions and social structure. In: Parsons T. *Essays in Sociological Theory*. Free Press, Glencoe

Pigg SL (1997) Authority in translation: finding, knowing, naming, and training traditional birth attendants in Nepal. In: Davis-Floyd RE, Sargent CF, eds. *Childbirth and Authoritative*

Knowledge: Cross-cultural perspectives. University of California Press, Berkeley: 233–62

Sandall J (1995) Choice, continuity and control. Changing midwifery towards a sociological perspective. *Midwifery* **11**: 201–9

Sandall J, Bourgeault IL, Meijer WJ, et al (2001) Deciding who cares: winners and losers in the late twentieth century. In: Devries R, Benoit C, van Teijlingen ER, Wrede, eds. *Birth by Design: Pregnancy, Maternity Care and Midwifery in North America and Europe.* Routledge, London: 139–65

Sargent C (1982) *The Cultural Context for Therapeutic Choice: Obstetrical care decisions among the Bariba of Benin.* Springer, Cambridge, Massachussetts

Sargent C (1989) *Maternity, Medicine and Power: Reproductive decisions in urban Benin.* University of California Press, Berkeley

Sargent C (1990) The politics of birth: cultural dimensions of pain, virtue and control among the Bariba of Benin. In: Penn Handwerker W, ed. *Births and Power: Social Change and the Politics of Reproduction.* Westview Press, Boulder: 69-80

Stacey M (1990) *The Sociology of Health and Healing: A textbook.* Routledge, London

Witz A (1992) *Professions and Patriarchy.* Routledge, London

WHO (1978) *The Promotion and Development of Traditional Medicine. Technical Report Series 622.* WHO, Geneva

CHAPTER 3

The social organisation of maternity care systems

Chapter two identified sociological perspectives relevant to the role of the midwife. It also highlighted aspects of the important, intertwined history between midwifery and medicine. This chapter builds on the previous one by exploring that relationship further, introducing key sociological concepts including medicalization, and discussing the current division of labour in British maternity care. The principal focus of this chapter is the social organisation of healthcare systems in general, and maternity care in particular. Healthcare systems are socially shaped in complex ways by the wider political and economic system of the society of which they are a part, as well as by societal norms, cultural values, government regulations, formal institutional policies, professional boundaries, informal practices, the actions of individual patients and their advocates (Benoit et al, 2005). As highlighted by Macintyre (1977):

> *'...in no society is the process of pregnancy and parturition treated as simply a physiological process. Where the birth is to take place, who is to be present, the position in which the woman labours and delivers, how she is to behave during childbirth — these matters are rarely left to the discretion of the parturient woman but are the subject of social controls and sanctions'.*
>
> *MacIntyre (1977: 18)*

Formal maternity care systems represent just one of the many ways (as we shall see over the course of this book) in which childbirth is socially marked.

Defining healthcare systems

Most midwives in the UK work as employees providing maternity care as part of a formal healthcare organisation. Consequently, the care they deliver is embedded within a complex network of organisational structures and inextricably linked to the roles of other workers (not just other healthcare professionals, but clerical workers, accountants and managers). Organisations may be defined as:

> *'...large groupings of people, usually structured on bureaucratic or impersonal lines, established to achieve specific objectives'.*
>
> *Elston (2005: 203)*

Today, most professional healthcare is provided through formal organisations, with both individual hospital units and entire national systems typically regarded as healthcare organisations.

Healthcare organisations are either public organisations (funded by statutory taxation) or private organisations (run by profit-making companies from which healthcare services are purchased in a free market). The NHS was the first publicly-funded, universal healthcare system in the world (see *Box 3.1*). Many other European countries also have such systems too.

The American healthcare system is an example of a private healthcare system where access to care is principally determined not by medical need but by the individual's ability to pay.

Box 3.1: The British National Health (NHS) Service

Many sociologists have studied the NHS because it is unique as a national healthcare system. It came into existence on the 5th July 1948, offering free medical care to the whole population 'from the cradle to the grave'. Since then the NHS has undergone many changes brought about by successive governments, economic pressures, technological change, professional interests, managerialism and consumerism.

During the 1990s, as part of the introduction of an internal market into the NHS (which formed a purchaser/provider split), individual hospital and community Trusts were created. Community Trusts have since been superseded by primary care Trusts (PCTs), and many acute Trusts are currently seeking NHS Foundation Hospital status. Other significant changes to the NHS in recent years at a macro level include the creation of the National Institute for Clinical Excellence (NICE), which produces National Service Frameworks (NSFs) and national guidelines (e.g. the antenatal care guideline, the intrapartum guideline). Individual Trusts' level of adherence to these documents are monitored regularly by the Healthcare Commission.

Other government polices and national reports that impact on current NHS service provision include *Changing Childbirth* (DH, 1993), *Making a Difference* (DH, 1999), *National Service Framework for Women and Children* (DH, 2004), *Maternity Matters* (DH, 2007a), *Safer childbirth: Minimum standards for the organisation and delivery of care in labour* (RCOG/RCM/RCPCH/RCA, 2007), *The Shribman Report: Making it better for mother and baby* (DH, 2007b) and Lord Darzi's recent review of the NHS *Our NHS, Our Future* (DH, 2008).

For further reading about sociological perspectives on the NHS, see Klein's (2006) *The New Politics of the NHS: From Creation to Reinvention*, and the edited collection *The Sociology of the Health Service* by Gabe et al (1991).

Sociological analyses of healthcare organisations may be divided into three categories according to the organisational level on which they focus:

First, **macro-level** approaches take healthcare at the level of society as their focus, or in other words, they investigate the broad features of national healthcare systems. The NHS is an example of a national healthcare system that has been widely studied at a macro level.

Second, **meso-level** approaches focus on the '...*intermediate layer where policy and organizational and managerial processes tend to be concentrated*' (Hunter, 1990: 215). Strong and Robinson's (1990) study of the implementation of management reforms in local NHS settings provides an example of a meso-level approach. They show how the official goals of central government are operationalised in practice via the process of local interpretation, negotiation and bargaining, a process that is influenced by local circumstances and history as much as government dictate.

Third, **micro-level** approaches focus on specific interactions between providers and users of care, or between different groups of professionals. Some studies link more than one level of analysis in the same study. One such study relevant to midwives is Murray and Elston's (2005) investigation of privately funded maternity care in Chile. They show how macro level political decisions, the meso-level through which government reforms are enacted, and the micro-level of clinical practice, individually and collectively contribute to Chile's exceptionally high Caesarean section rate.

Devries et al (2001) list four important ways in which the organization and provision of maternity care can be distinguished from other forms of medical care. First, what is at stake is not the survival of one patient but the reproduction of society. Second, latent in the care of women during pregnancy, parturition and early motherhood are ideas about sexuality, about women and about families. Third, while all other medical specialities (with the possible exception of paediatrics) begin with a focus on disease, the essential task in maternity care is the supervision of normal, healthy, physical growth. Fourth, the quality of maternity care (in both senses of the word, its character and its outcomes) is often used as a measure for the quality of an entire healthcare system (i.e. infant mortality rates have become shorthand for the adequacy of a society's health system and its overall quality of life).

Benoit et al (2005) takes midwifery as its starting point in a comparative analysis of the organisation of maternity care in the UK, Finland, the Netherlands and Canada. Benoit et al (2005) show that in all four systems midwifery is constantly redefined in relation to medicine, with the provision of care in the UK, Finland and Canada constantly changing in response to competing welfare state interests, professional boundary struggles and changing consumer interests. According to Benoit et al (2005) only in the Netherlands is there evidence of sustained commitment to midwifery as a woman-centred solution for the provision of maternity care. As midwives will know only too well, the maternity care system in the Netherlands is an exception to most and is widely recognised as offering a unique model of midwifery care where homebirth is routine.

Thus, whilst there are strong and important arguments for viewing maternity care as distinct from other forms of medical care, in practice it is predominantly medical frames of reference and knowledge that have been accepted and legitimated within most formal systems of modern maternity care. For example, in Britain the formation of the NHS consolidated the medical status of pregnancy and birth by subsuming it into a medical system responsible for treating everyone (Henley-Einion, 2003). Whilst the NHS gave all women access to free maternity care for the first time, which is to be applauded, it came at the price of strengthening consultant-based hospital services. The hospital as the centre for medical practice played a vital role in securing the medical profession's ascendancy as the dominant approach to healthcare provision.

The rise of hospital birth

The role of the hospital as a social organisation was a major topic of enquiry in medical sociology during the 1960s (Freidson, 1963). Initially, neo-Weberian perspectives were used to explore professional-bureaucratic relations within the hospital. Later, symbolic-interactionist perspectives came to the fore highlighting the need to appreciate organizational forms and structures as fluid (Bucher and Stelling, 1969). During the 1970s and 1980s there was considerable commentary on the impact of macro-level health service reforms and continued interest in the professions, whilst the 1990s saw studies highlighting the decline of the traditional hospital to reflect the changing nature of medical work (e.g. day-case surgery). However, it is feminist accounts, rather than mainstream sociology, which offer insights into the role the hospital played in facilitating childbirth coming under the jurisdiction of medicine.

The mass movement of people into towns and cities during the Industrial Revolution was key to the establishment and success of large hospitals (Doyal and Pennell, 1979). The burgeoning poor (with their associated ill-health) inevitably welcomed the provision of free medical care that hospitals provided. For poor women in particular, hospitals offered access to pain relief and medical care during childbirth, as well as the opportunity for respite from the exhaustion and squalor of their everyday lives (Lewis, 1990). However, less benevolently, Ehrenreich and English (1979) identify that nineteenth century medical schools principally attached themselves to charity hospitals to use the bodies of sick, poor women for training purposes and the pursuit of medical science. One well-documented consequence of the relationship between the hospital and the pursuit of medical knowledge in the eighteenth and nineteenth centuries was the spread of puerperal infection prior to knowledge of the importance of the aseptic technique. Nevertheless, by the end of the nineteenth century the hospital came to be viewed by many women (not just poor women) as an environment that offered improved safety and comfort during childbirth. During the twentieth century hospital replaced home birth almost completely.

Stacey (1988) highlights that within the space of 40 years there was an unprecedented shift from home to hospital as the principal place for women to give birth. In 1935, 35% of births were in an institution (a hospital, nursing or maternity home). By 1944 this figure had risen to 45%. But it was the 1960s and early 1970s which saw the greatest growth in the hospitalisation of birth following the publication of the *Peel* report (DHSS, 1970) which recommended hospitalisation for all births. The rationale behind a 100% hospital birth rate was statistical evidence which showed that as the rate of hospital births increased, rates of maternal and infant mortality decreased. However, some sociologists (amongst others Cochrane [1972]) offer an alternative explanation for the observed decline in maternal and infant mortality. The significance of social (i.e. improved housing standards, better nutrition), rather than medical determinants of health is a line of argument most notably associated with the sociologist McKeown (1979). The **McKeown thesis** is an argument based on a study of mortality rates in England and Wales from the eighteenth century onwards. Whilst it recognises the contribution of medicine to bringing relief from illness, it concludes that non-medical factors (including improvements in public health) are more significant in reducing mortality rates.

More recent work in sociology has also challenged the hospital's centrality to modern healthcare (Armstrong, 1998). This is an issue that we will return to towards the end of this chapter. First I consider the impact of industrialization and medicalization in shaping modern maternity care.

The industrialization of childbirth

As identified in chapter two, modern societies are synonymous with industrialization, the term that refers to the emergence of machine production based on the use of inanimate power resources (e.g. steam or electricity). Chapter two defined patriarchy as:

> '...a societal wide system of gender relations of male dominance and female subordination, [and] the ways in which male power is institutionalised within different sites in society'.
>
> *Witz (1992: 11)*

Many feminists assert that patriarchy is especially pronounced in industrialized societies where men are typically associated with the public sphere and women with the private sphere. Or in other words, as a consequence of industrialization gender roles became polarized as men became principally responsible for production outside the home and women for reproduction within the family (both human reproduction and societal reproduction through the process of primary socialization).

Obstetrics developed its power through claims of safer childbirth in hospitals under the supervision of men, a scientific base to male knowledge about childbirth, and the use of technology exclusively by men. According to Oakley (1993) the male role in the history of obstetrics reflects the male role in the history of industrialized societies where they have assumed control over women. Moreover, other feminist sociologists, anthropologists and midwives have drawn attention to an important analogy between the 'labour process' as the chief organising principle for both work and childbirth in industrial societies (Martin, 1987; Hunt and Symonds, 1995).

A seminal study by Martin (1987) shows how industrialization metaphors have permeated medical accounts of childbirth since the seventeenth century, around which time the body first came to be regarded as a machine. Martin (1987) identifies how in the development of obstetrics the metaphor of the uterus as machine combined with the use of actual mechanical devices (i.e. forceps) to replace female hands with male tools. According to Martin (1987) metaphors of efficient production continue to dominate obstetrics, both underlying and accounting for our willingness to apply technology to birth and to intervene in the process.

The use of technology is now integral to almost all women's experiences of pregnancy and childbirth. This has led Robbie Davis-Floyd to coin the term technocratic birth. Initially, she used the term the technological model of birth in order to draw attention to the influence of the technologically-orientated core value system of American society. Her later use of the word technocracy denotes a more precise term pertaining to '...*the ideology of modern industrial society, in which social policy and political debate presume scientific models of nature and society*' (Reynolds, 1991 cited in Davis-Floyd, 1994). During the course of multiple studies of birth in the USA during the 1980s it became apparent to Davis-Floyd '...*that contemporary obstetrics is a system that is co-created by obstetricians and women... [and] was forced to look again at the human-machine interaction that characterizes this reconstituted technobirth*' (Davis-Floyd, 1998: 259-260). Intertwined with the use of technology during birth are debates about the medicalization of childbirth.

Medicalization and childbirth

Broadly speaking, the term **medicalization** refers to the process whereby medicine's control in society is increased as non-medical problems become defined and treated as medical conditions. For Peter Conrad (1992) this process consists of:

'...defining a problem in medical terms, using medical language to describe the problem, adopting a medical framework to understand a problem, or using a medical intervention to treat it.'

Conrad (1992: 211)

The origins of medicalization as a sociological concept can be traced back to the 1960s and 1970s, when Freidson (1970) first highlighted how the high status of medicine and the medical profession had resulted in a redefining of problems such as gambling, drug use and crime not as social problems, but as medical problems warranting medical treatment, thus identifying medicine's power to create, as well as treat, illness. This was an argument that was further explored by Zola (1972), leading him to suggest that medicine was becoming a major apparatus of social control, 'nudging' aside the more traditional societal institutions of religion and law. Therefore, from the outset, the concept of medicalization was closely associated with the control of **deviance** (behaviour contrary to societal norms).

However, amongst early mainstream sociological conceptualizations of medicalization, it is Illich's (1976) that has been most widely applied in critiques of the medicalization of pregnancy and childbirth. Illich's (1976) conceptualization of medicalization is an overtly negative one. He asserts that medicalization, which for him is fundamentally linked to industrialization, is harmful to health. Moreover, he develops the associated notion of **iatrogenesis** to describe the increased levels of illness and social problems caused by what he perceives as unnecessary medical intervention resulting from medicalization.

Simultaneous to these analyses of medicalization, feminist critiques of the medicalization of reproduction in general (Boston Women's Health Collective, 1970; Ehrenreich and English, 1979) and pregnancy and childbirth in particular (Cartwright, 1979; Oakley, 1979, 1980) began to emerge. The medicalization of childbirth has been defined as a process that has led childbirth to become a medical event rather than a social one, in which human experience is redefined as a medical problem (Becker and Nachtignall, 1992). As identified by Alyson Henley-Einion (2003):

'...the issue is not that medicine has no place within maternity care, but that all pregnancies are medically managed, all of them are viewed as inherently pathological or risky, and normality is only ever defined in retrospect.'

Henley-Einion (2003: 177)

The feminist literature pertaining to childbirth is vast and it is important to highlight that it encompasses work both against and in support of the medicalization of childbirth (e.g. Firestone, 1970). Indeed it is one of the main criticisms of the medicalization thesis that there are some real clinical and symbolic benefits of medicalization, and a number of feminist authors have highlighted that some women actively participate in the medicalization process to meet their own needs (Davis-Floyd, 1992, 1994; Riessman 1989). Consequently, many variants of contemporary feminist approaches to childbirth (such as those cited earlier in this section) continuously grapple with the tension between not rejecting science, technology and medicine, but negotiating critical politics in its use and development (Cussins, 1998).

In the context of the medicalization debates more generally, there has also been a shift in emphasis from an overtly critical stance. For example, work has centred on the social construction of medical knowledge over time, and the move from hospital based medicine to new forms of medical **surveillance** (Foucault, 1973; Armstrong, 1983).

Conrad (2007) has also identified the changing drivers of medicalization over time. According to Conrad, in the past professional dominance and inter-professional rivalries were important; today biotechnology (pharmaceutical industry, genetics), managed care markets and the media are significant. There have been assertions that the term biomedicalization may be more appropriate to reflect the increasing role of biotechnology in extending the domain of medical science. The medicalization debate has also spawned the related term de-medicalization.

Sobal's (1995) sociological analysis of the medicalization and de-medicalization of obesity in the US is illustrative of the process this term refers to. For example, according to Sobal (1995), being fat was traditionally a moral conception (gluttony is bad). The medicalization of fatness meant 'obesity' became a sickness (diagnosed, managed and surgically treated by medicine). De-medicalization refers to the process whereby large body size has, arguably, become politically and socially acceptable.

The de-medicalization of childbirth would require an entirely different conceptualisation of childbirth to the one that currently exists.

Moving debates about midwifery and the organisation of NHS maternity care services forward

As identified in chapter one, within contemporary sociology there is a general consensus that the world is currently amidst a period of rapid social change. Some commentators refer to this process as **post-modernization** (Crook et al, 1992) whilst others prefer the term late modernism (Giddens, 1991). These wider social and cultural shifts are evident in contemporary healthcare systems. For example, globalization (the term referring to the process whereby individuals, groups and nations become more integrated through global trade, communication and immigration) is manifesting itself in the NHS (for example, product labels for drugs are in different languages, the ethnic diversity of midwives and pregnant women reflects recent patterns of migration, access to research evidence is global via online journals).

Both Nettleton (1995) and Annandale (1998) draw attention to the significance of broader social transformations from **modernism** to **post-** or **late-modernism** at one level, and Fordism to post-Fordism at another as impacting on the delivery of healthcare systems today. **Fordism** is the term for the form of work organization based around the notion that management needs to control the work force by specifying in some details what is to be done, how it is to be done, and in what quantity it is to be done (Harrison et al, 1992). **Post-Fordism** is centred around the premise that workers can be more productive if they are encouraged to use all their abilities in a relatively free rather than closely monitored way, and perhaps most significantly where responsibility is directed downwards to the point of contact with clients (Walby et al, 1994). According to Nettleton (1995) these changes in the structure of the economy translate into welfare reform that mark the shift from mass universal needs being met by a monolithic, paternalistic, professionally-led bureaucracy, to welfare pluralism, *quasi* markets and consumerism. In other words, and specifically in the context of the NHS, the principles of welfare pluralism have become evident in policies that encourage co-operation between state, voluntary and private sector healthcare providers, promote the role of the patient in healthcare decision-making, and reward certain types of management. So what does this all mean for midwives?

First, is the need to consider the extent to which professional autonomy is diminishing. Using Freidson's (1988) notion that the power of the medical profession rests on its autonomy (ability to control own work activities) and dominance (ability to control work of others in the healthcare division of labour), there is support for this line of argument. In an age of increased governance, doctors' (and indeed midwives') autonomy and self-regulation are under greater scrutiny than ever before.

Next, is the related concern that relationships between occupational groups are changing. According to Annandale (1998) professional boundaries are shifting in part because of nursing and midwifery's own professionalization strategies, but also in response to the statutory reduction in junior doctors hours and the realisation that non-physician providers can sometimes deliver a comparable service at a lower cost. This is particularly relevant to midwives, some of whom are now undertaking 'extended roles' that were previously the domain of doctors (i.e. amniocentesis, external cephalic conversion, forceps deliveries), whilst many others are having what they consider to be core aspects of their role devolved to maternity support workers. Support workers are increasingly being used in NHS maternity care in response to changes in the obstetric workforce deployment, revisions to medical training, the European Working Time Directive, obstetric staffing standards, and neonatal service reconfigurations. A study undertaken by Jane Sandall on behalf of the RCM (RCM, 2006) reports that managers are enthusiastic about the contribution that support workers are making to the work of the maternity team. In this report support workers were providing additional breastfeeding support in the community, providing continuity of care and one-to-one care in labour, having more time to support vulnerable women, attending home births, assisting in obstetric theatres and running antenatal and postnatal groups. Although substantial variations in title, range of activities, and required entry level of training were found, this study raises significant questions about future maternity care provision and the role of the midwife — not least who stands to benefit most from these evolved roles: women, professionals, or managers and the organisation? Intertwined into debates about professional autonomy and how relationships between occupational groups may be changing are concerns about the relative influence of professionals transferring to managers. For example, with whom should the midwife-manger identify her profession and 'ground floor' colleagues or the organisation?

There is also the need to consider to what extent the hospital remains central to healthcare provision. Whilst some sociologists suggest that the hospital is no longer the central locus for healthcare provision, arguably maternity care is one area of provision where it continues to dominate. On the one hand there is evidence of a shift from hospital to community care provision (e.g. satellite booking clinics), whilst on the other the organisation of maternity care is increasingly being led by large, centralised units. Moreover, in the UK all midwives are trained within hospitals and many work within hospitals or are attached to their organisational structure. This means they must be as conversant with the pathology of pregnancy and birth as they are with its natural processes and must also be skilled in the use of medical technology. The rise of new forms of service based on digital technologies is an issue for many areas of service provision, but in maternity care the arrival of 3D scanners and other forms of antenatal surveillance are, for now at least, associated with hospital care. Consequently, most women continue to associate antenatal care and birth principally with the hospital environment.

Finally, but perhaps most significantly, is the impact of consumerism on the organisation of maternity care services. Consumerism is both a term in common use and a sociological concept that is used to mean a variety of different things. Many sociologists have documented a general shift in NHS policy from paternalism to consumerism (Klein, 2006) where no longer does 'doctor know best' but where patients increasingly make demands and choices. This particular model of consumerism has been described as congruent with enterprise culture and the market, coupled with an emphasis on the rights of the individual (Nettleton, 1995). As part of this more general shift, and in response to the demands of consumer groups, choice has been an enduring theme in NHS maternity care policy since the 1990s (DH, 1993), most recently in *Maternity Matters* (DH, 2007a). Arguably, the rise of consumerism in maternity care may provide a new opportunity for the de-medicalization of childbirth if, for example, increasing numbers of women were to 'choose' home rather than hospital birth. However, hospital birth culture has been the norm for a generation of women, and the medicalization of childbirth has redefined what childbirth is. Consequently, not only will this process be hard to reverse, but some women may no longer even see it as desirable.

Conclusion

This chapter has introduced midwives to sociological perspectives concerned with the organisation and delivery of maternity care systems. Insights that enable us to understand the influence of social factors on current maternity care provision and how formal health care organisations (such as the NHS) shape both the experiences of pregnant women who access them and the experiences of the midwives who work within them.

References

Annandale E (1998) *The Sociology of Health & Medicine: A Critical Introduction*. Polity Press, Cambridge

Armstrong D (1983) *Political Anatomy of the Body. Medical knowledge in Britain in the twentieth century*. Cambridge University Press, Cambridge

Armstrong D (1998) Decline of the hospital: reconstituting institutional dangers. *Sociology of Health and Illness* **20**(4): 445–57

Becker G, Nachtignall RD (1992) Eager for medicalization: the social production of infertility as a disease. *Sociology of Health and Illness* **14**: 456–71

Benoit C, Wrede S, Bourgeault I, et al (2005) Understanding the social organisation of maternity care systems. *Sociology of Health and Illness* **27**(6): 722–37

Bucher R, Stelling J (1969) Characteristics of professional organizations. *Journal of Health and Social Behaviour* **10**: 2–13

Cartwright A (1979) *The Dignity of Labour? A study of childbearing and induction*. Tavistock, London

Conrad P (1992) Medicalization and social control. *Annual Review of Sociology* **18**: 209–32

Conrad P (2007) *The Medicalization of Society: On the transformation of human conditions into treatable disorders*. John Hopkins University, Princeton

Crook S, Pakulski J, Waters M (1992) *Postmodernization: Change in advanced society*. Sage, London

Cussins C (1998) Producing reproduction: Techniques of normalisation and naturalization in an infertility clinic. In: Franklin S, Ragoné H, eds. *Reproducing Reproduction*. Philadelphia, University of Pennsylvania Press: 66-101

Davis-Floyd R (1992) *Birth as an American Rite of Passage*. University of California Press, Berkeley

Davis-Floyd R (1994) The technocratic body: American childbirth as cultural expression. *Soc Sci Med* **38**(8): 1125–40

Davis-Floyd R (1998) From technobirth to cyborg babies: Reflections on the emergent discourse of a holistic anthropologist. In: Davis-Floyd R, Dumit J, eds. *Cyborg Babies: From techno-sex to techno-tots*. Routledge, London: 255–84

DHSS (1970) *Report of the Sub-committee on Domiciliary and Maternity Bed Needs* (Chairman, Sir John Peel). London, HMSO

DH (1993) *Changing Childbirth. Part 1: Report of the Expert Maternity Group*. The Stationary Office, London

DH (1999) *Making a Difference*. DH, London

DH (2004) *National Service Framework for Children, Young People and Maternity Services*. DH, London

DH (2007) *Maternity Matters*. DH, London

DH (2007) *The Shribman Report: Making it better for mother and baby*. DH, London

DH (2008) *Our NHS, Our Future*. DH, London

Devries R, Benoit C, van Teijlingen ER et al, eds (2001) *Birth by Design: Pregnancy, maternity care and midwifery in North America and Europe*. Routledge, London

Doyal L, Pennell I (1979) *The Political Economy of Health*. Pluto Press, London

Ehrenreich B, English D (1978) *For Her Own Good: 150 years of the experts' advice to women*. Doubleday, Anchor Press

Elston MA (2005) In: Gabe J, Bury M, Elston MA, eds. *Key Concepts in Medical Sociology*. Sage, London

Foucault M (1973) *The Birth of the Clinic. An Archaeology of Medical Perception*. Routledge, London

Firestone S (1970) *The Dialectic of Sex*. Jonathan Cape, London

Freidson E, ed (1963) *The Hospital in Modern Society*. Free Press, New York

Freidson E (1970b) *The Profession of Medicine*. Dodd, Mead and Co, New York

Gabe J, Calnan M, Bury M (1991) *The Sociology of the Health Service*. Routledge, London

Henley-Einion A (2003) The medicalization of childbirth. In Squires C, ed. *The Social Context of Birth*. Radcliffe Medical Press, Oxford: 173-186

Hunt S, Symonds A (1995) *The Social Meaning of Midwifery*. Macmillian, Basingstoke

Hunter D (1990) Organising and managing health care: a challenge for medical sociology. In: Cunningham-Burley S, McKeganey NP, eds. *Readings in Medical Sociology*. Routledge, London: 213–36

Illich I (1976) *Medical Nemesis*. Calder and Boyars, London

Klein R (2006) *New Politics of the NHS, The: From Creation to Reinvention*. Radcliffe Publishing Ltd. Oxford

Lewis J (1990) Mothers and maternity policies in the twentieth century. In: Garcia J, Kilpatric

R, Richards M, eds. *The Politics of Maternity Care, Services for Childbearing Women in Twentieth Century Britain.* Clarenden Press, Oxford

RCM (2006) *Re-focusing the Role of the Midwife. Guidance Paper 26.* RCM, London

Macintyre S (1977) The Management of Childbirth: Sociological research issues.

Martin E (1987) *The Woman in the Body: A cultural analysis of reproduction.* Beacon Press, Boston

Mckeown T (1979) *The Role of Medicine.* Blackwell, Oxford

Murray S, Elston MA (2005) The promotion of private health insurance and its implications for the social organisation of healthcare: a case study of private sector obstetric practice in Chile. *Sociology of Health and Illness* **27**(6): 701–21

Nettleton S (1995) *The Sociology of Health and Illness.* Polity Press, Oxford

Oakley A (1979) *From Here to Maternity: Becoming a Mother.* Penguin Books, Oxford

Oakley A (1980) *Women Confined: Towards a Sociology of Childbirth.* Martin Robertson & Co, Oxford

Oakley A (1993) *Essays on Women, Health and Medicine.* Edinburgh University Press, Edinburgh

Riessman CK (1989) Women and medicalization: a new perspective. In: Brown P, ed. *Perspectives in Medical Sociology.* Wadsworth, Belmont, California

RCOG/RCM/RCPCH/RCA (2007) *Safer Childbirth: Minimum standards for the organisation and delivery of care in labour.* RCOG, London

Sobal J (1995) The medicalization and de-medicalization of obesity. In: Maurer D, Sobal J, eds. *Eating Agendas: Food and nutrition as social problems.* Hawthorne, New York

Strong P, Robinson J (1990) *The NHS — Under New Management.* Open University Press, Buckingham

Stacey M (1988) *The Sociology of Health and Healing: A texbook.* Routledge, London

Witz A (1992) *Professions and Patriarchy.* Routledge, London

Zola I (1972) Medicine as an institution of social control. *Sociological Review* **20**: 487–54

CHAPTER 4

Health, illness, disease and social inequalities

This chapter focuses on sociological perspectives concerning health, illness and disease, with particular attention paid to social inequalities and health. As midwives will be only too aware, these interrelated concepts are central to everyday midwifery practice, the organisation of maternity services and individual women's experiences of pregnancy and birth. This chapter is different to many others that focus on health inequalities because it demonstrates how the social distribution of health, illness and disease vary across time, culture and social group, as do ideas about what constitutes health, illness and disease. It begins by highlighting a number of different ways in which sociologists have identified health, illness and disease and may be conceptualised in industrial societies, before considering the implications of the transformation from modernism to post- (or late) modernism on what health means.

As noted in chapter one, the sociology of health and illness (also known as medical sociology) is an important sub-field within sociology. This chapter draws from this field, but also identifies relevant work in public health and epidemiology. **Epidemiology** is the branch of medicine that involves the study of the prevalence and incidence of disease, and provides valuable research on which medical sociology relies (Gerhardt, 1989). **Public health** medicine shares concerns with medical sociology about the social determinants of disease, inequalities in health and structural barriers to improving health and health care (Green, 2005).

Defining health, illness and disease

'Health' is a concept used by numerous disciplines, as well as in society at large. According to the sociologist Bryan Turner (2003), in industrial societies the historical development of the concept of health (and the related concepts of illness and disease) is characterized by increasing secularization (where religious thinking, practice, and institutions lose significance), the rise of scientific theories, the separation of mental and physical illness, and the erosion of traditional therapies by scientific practices. This process is most evident in the biomedical model of health (also known as the medical model), which is principally concerned with diagnosing and combating disease (Ntau, 2004).

The (bio)**medical model** is the term used by sociologists to describe the dominant approach to disease in Western medicine, which was established during the nineteenth and early twentieth century. The medical model is based around the notion that specific aetiology underlies specific diseases (which alter anatomy and physiology, giving rise to specific symptoms). It is also commonly associated with the notion of science as objective (or in other words value-free), mechanical metaphors (as evident in chapter three), the mind-body dualism (discussed in chapter six) and a doctor-patient interaction based on individualism and intervention. The medical model of health taught in medical schools provides the basis for the organisation of modern healthcare systems, and is fundamental to the process of medicalization (as defined in chapter three). Consequently, it is a powerful **discourse** in modern society. In other words, the medical language and imagery associated with the medical model are constitutive of how we interpret the everyday world and how we act. Having said that, the biomedical model is not the only way of defining health.

In sociology, it is usual to differentiate between negative and positive definitions of health, as well as functional and experiential definitions (Calnan, 1987, cited in Nettleton, 1995). According to Calnan's (1987) categorization the medical model is characteristic of a negative definition of health because it is based on the absence of disease, rather the presence of health. Arguably, the best exemplar of a positive definition of health is that given by the World Health Organization (WHO), which advocates that:

'...health is a state of complete physical, mental and social well-being and not merely the absence of disease or infirmity'.

WHO (1948)

This positive conceptualisation of health has been associated with a **social model of health** (Townsend and Davidson, 1992) and its variants (i.e. the socio-economic model of health in Acheson [1998] discussed later in this chapter).

Midwives may already be familiar with the social model of health as it has been applied to childbirth. For example, Walsh and Newburn (2002) credit Marsden Wagner with developing a social model of childbirth (Wagner, 1994), which along with Rothman's (1982) medical and midwifery models of childbirth, and Davis-Floyd's (1992) technocratic and holistic models of childbirth, draw on dichotomized conceptions of medical and social models of health. However, according to Edwin van Teijlingen (2005) it is important to make distinctions between the different levels at which these models operate. First, Teijlingen (2005) offers the following definitions of the medical and social models of health as applied to pregnancy and childbirth:

'The school of thought adhering to the medical model is founded on the idea that "normal" childbirth requires medical control in order to guarantee

safety through monitoring which will enable intervention at the earliest sign of pathology, since risk prediction and selection is not really possible. The school adhering to the social model is founded on the idea that "normal" childbirth is "natural" childbirth, i.e. that the overwhelming majority of pregnant women have a normal and safe childbirth with little or no medical intervention, and that those women who are not expected to have a 'normal' childbirth can be predicted and selected out'.

Teijlingen (2005)

Teijlingen (2005) asserts that these respective models operate at three key levels:

- The analytical level (i.e. as sociological concepts at the level of theoretical abstraction and critique)
- The practical level (i.e. at the level of real people organising their work, pregnant women attending antenatal clinics)
- The ideological level (i.e. at the level of practitioners and supporters of a particular model seeking to justify their actions and claim control over certain aspects of childbirth).

Teijlingen (2005) concludes with the importance of disentangling these multiple applications if the conceptual utility of the medical model in sociology is to be retained. It is also important to recognise that at a practical level these two models of health are not exclusive (proponents of the social model can be found within medicine), and at an analytical level they are not exhaustive.

According to Nettleton (1995) an experiential definition of health takes an individual's sense of self into account, which may be contrasted with the functional definition of health that implies the ability to participate in normal social roles. The latter approach to defining health originates from the work of Parsons (1951), who first theorized ill-health (illness) as a social phenomenon, rather than at the level of a physical entity or an individual (Annandale, 1998). According to Parsons (1951) health is a valued social commodity, whilst illness is dysfunctional for society, preventing individuals from fulfilling valued social roles. This perspective led Parsons to conceptualise illness as deviance and to develop the concept of the **sick role** as a means of enabling individuals to be exempt from, recover and then return to their social roles.

Experiential definitions of health stem from the interactionist tradition where the notion that the self is a product of social experience that develops out of interaction with others is key. The interactionist tradition rose to prominence in the sociology of health and illness during the 1960s:

'The ways in which individuals give meaning to social events (such as childbirth, surgery, death); the ways in which they manage changed identities

in ill health; and the "negotiation" that takes place in formal and informal health-care settings - are the subject matter of interactionism'.

Annandale (1998: 22).

Classic examples of this approach centred on the patient's perspective and led to the development of enduring sociological concepts such as **stigma** (Goffman, 1963).

Another key perspective on health to emerge from sociology is the political economy tradition, which has its roots in Marxist thought. The **political economy perspective** is built around the notion that ill health is socially produced by capitalism either in general (McKinlay, 1977, 1984; Doyal, 1979; Navarro, 1986) or more specifically by the process of industrialization (Hart, 1982). Sociologists adopting this perspective explore how health objectives are rarely followed if they conflict with the pursuit of profit (Doyal, 1979), and the ways in which the search for profit in the field of health and health care is supported by the state and mediated by the medical profession. However, assertions of the changing nature of modernity, coupled with questions about the current status of Marxist thought (following the collapse of the former Soviet Union) mean this perspective is, according to Annandale (1998), currently undergoing a period of revitalization.

Contemporary sociological perspectives on health, illness and disease are complex. According to Beck (1992) modern society is in a period of reflexive modernity (rather than post-modernity) in which society has become a risk society. Beck uses the term reflexive modernity because, he argues, society has come to reflect upon modernity itself and the problems it creates. For example, Beck identifies that whilst developments in agriculture mean food is in plentiful supply, a plentiful supply of processed foods has led people to reflect on the risks of unhealthy diets and obesity. In essence, Beck is arguing that as Western industrialized societies have increasingly met people's essential material needs (food, adequate housing), conflict is based less on the distribution of wealth and more on the distribution of risk. What is more, at the heart of risk society is the phenomenon of health and an 'insatiable appetite for medicine' (Beck, 1992: 211).

Other strands of contemporary sociological theorising about health include work on health behaviour, lifestyle choices, and consumer culture in post-modernity. As we shall see in chapter six, the body itself has become a phenomenon of choices and options, some of which improve health (e.g. regular exercise) whilst others involve unnecessary risks (e.g. cosmetic surgery). Central to the literature on lifestyle and health is the idea that health can be promoted and disease can be prevented by the identification and control of risk factors. There are numerous examples of this in the field of maternity care, from media campaigns to reduce rates of smoking during pregnancy, to policy that promotes preconception care (DH, 2004a,b). Whilst sociologists accept the significance of biomedical research which shows that lifestyle modifications can increase the likelihood of a healthy pregnancy, they are principally concerned with the extent to which individuals are able to control their risk of disease and the consequences of this individualistic approach to health. One of the principal dangers of individualism is that it serves to mask burgeoning health inequalities between different sectors of society.

Studies show that in industrialized societies there are real health gains, not least in reduced infant mortality and increased longevity. However, whilst the absolute health of the population is known to increase, so is the gap between mortality and morbidity rates amongst the richest and the poorest sections of society, which equates to an increase in relative health inequalities. This process has been termed polarization and has been particularly pronounced in Britain since the 1980s (Acheson, 1998).

Inequalities and health

If health, illness and disease were entirely biological in origin then you would expect the incidence to be similar across geographical locations and social groupings. However this is not the case. The social patterns of health provides evidence that disease and illness do not affect all sectors of society equally. In particular, studies conducted in industrialized countries, especially Britain, suggest a clear social class gradient to health. Put simply, the higher the social class, the lower the rate of morbidity and mortality (Acheson, 1998). The infant mortality rate amongst babies born in lower class families, for example, is more than twice that of babies born into higher-class families (ONS, 2007). Class is a major preoccupation in sociology that, as noted in chapter one, has its conceptual roots in the works of Karl Marx and Max Weber. However, there is no single accepted way of defining social class. On the one hand social class may be defined as:

'...segments of the population sharing broadly similar types and levels of resources, with broadly similar styles of living and (for some sociologists) some shared perception of their collective condition'.

Townsend and Davidson (1992: 39)

To others though, social class may simply be defined in terms of an individual's occupation.

The discussion of social class and inequalities in health requires a distinction to be made between theoretical conceptualisations of class and the empirical utilisation of operational models of class (Annandale, 1998). Post-war, British sociology has analysed various expressions of class identify (Norman et al, 1969) and changes in the British class structure (Goldthorpe et al, 1969). In contemporary sociology, according to Annandale (1998) both strong (where class is collectively formed out of relations to other classes) and weaker (where a range of axes of inequality impact on health) theoretical conceptualisations of class are evident, whilst post-modern authors dispute its continued relevance altogether. These sociological approaches to class constitute one major tradition of socio-economic classification in Britain. The other major tradition — indeed the dominant one in terms of its use in the analysis of official data especially in relation to life, health and death — comes from successive generations of government statisticians (Rose and Pevalin, 2001).

Britain has a long tradition of analysing official statistics to uncover underlying linkages between death and social inequalities. This can be traced back to William Farr, the first Superintendent of Statistics when the General Register Office was set up in 1837. Rose and Pevalin (2001) acknowledge the enormous significance of the **Registrar General's Social Class** (RGSC) scheme to the study of health inequalities. The RGSC scheme was first used in 1913, substantially modified in 1921, renamed 'Social class based on Occupation' (SO) in 1990, and became the 'Revised Standard Occupational Classification' in 2000, before being replaced entirely by the National Statistics Socio-Economic Classification (NS-SEC) scheme in 2001. *Table 4.1* shows the RGSC, and *Table 4.2* shows the NS-SEC that has now superseded it. Many seminal works on inequalities in health use the RGSC, whilst more recent studies use the NS-SEC.

Over time the validity of the RGSC has been increasingly questioned. For example, changes in the structure of industry and occupations meant the manual/ non-manual divide became outdated. The RGSC has also been widely criticised

Table 4.1 Registrar General's Social Class (RGSC)

Class		Description of occupations
A	I	**Professional**: accountants, doctors, lawyers
B	II	**Managerial and technical/ intermediate**: managers, senior technicians, school teachers, police officers, nurses
C_1	IIIN	**Skilled non-manual**: clerk, secretary, waiter, shop assistant
C_2	IIIM	**Skilled manual**: HGV and PSV drivers, fitters, electricians
D	IV	**Partly skilled**: warehouse workers, machine tool operators
E	V	**Unskilled**: labourers (e.g. building), cleaners

Table 4.2 National Statistics Socio-Economic Classification (NS-SEC)

Operational categories	Analytical classes			
	Nine-class version	**Eight-class version**	**Five-class version**	**Three-class version**
1. Employees in large establishments	1.1 Large employers and higher managerial occupations (e.g. health service managers, company directors)	1. Higher managerial and professional occupations	1. Managerial and professional occupations	1. Managerial and professional occupations
2. Higher managerial occupations				
3. Higher professional occupations	1.2 Higher professional occupations (e.g. doctors, teachers, social workers)			
4. Lower professional and higher technical occupations	2. Lower managerial and professional occupations (e.g. midwives, police officers, laboratory technicians)	2. Lower managerial and professional occupations		
5. Lower managerial occupations				
6. Higher supervisory occupations				
7. Intermediate occupations	3. Intermediate occupations (e.g. dental nurses, secretaries)	3. Intermediate occupations	2. Intermediate occupations	2. Intermediate occupations
8. Employers in small establishments	4. Small employers and own-account workers (e.g. publicans, farmers, restauranteurs)	4. Small employers and own-account workers	3. Small employers and own account workers	
9. Own-account workers				
10. Lower supervisory occupations	5. Lower supervisory and technical occupations (e.g. train drivers, plumbers, electricians)	5. Lower supervisory and technical occupations	4. Lower supervisory and technical occupations	3. Routine and manual occupations
11. Lower technical occupations				
12. Semi-routine occupations	6. Semi-routine occupations (e.g. hairdressers, shop assistants)	6. Semi-routine occupations	5. Semi-routine and routine occupations	
13. Routine occupations	7. Routine occupations (e.g. waiters, cleaners, labourers)	7. Routine occupations		
14. Newer worked and long-term unemployed	8. Never worked and long-term unemployed	8. Never worked and long-term unemployed	Never worked and long-term unemployed	Never worked and long-term unemployed

as insensitive to the social positions of women and those not in paid employment (Bradley, 1996). The replacement of the RGSC was informed both by knowledge of its limitations and sociological research (in particular Goldthorpe, 1980; Erikson and Goldthorpe, 1992) on the relational aspects of class. Central to Goldthorpe's approach is the distinction between employers, self-employed and employees. This leads him to argue that any class schema based on employment relations must include these three basic class positions. The incorporation of the relational aspects of class into the NS-SEC (which is built not on skills but on employment conditions) unites the two British traditions of class research, the official and the sociological (Rose and Pevalin, 2001). As shown in *Table 4.2*, the NS-SEC is designed to facilitate a variety of analytical class breakdowns. For example, the three-class breakdown is the one currently used to define the Department of Health's target for infant mortality (DH, 2008).

To date, the ***Black* report** (Townsend and Davidson, 1992) arguably provides the most striking evidence of the extent of inequalities in health between the British social classes. The report, originally published in 1980, uses the RGSC to show that men and women in occupational class V have a two and a half time greater chance of dying before retirement age than those in occupational class I. Moreover, evidence of class inequalities in mortality were found at birth, during the first year of life, in childhood, adolescence and adult life. The *Black* report offers four possible ways of explaining such striking evidence of an association between social class and health inequalities. First, the relationship is an artefact of the data with little causal significance. An explanation that was dismissed after rigorous evaluation and subsequent studies added weight to the findings. Second, occupational class is a dependent variable with health carrying the greatest degree of causal significance. In other words, whilst physical weakness or poor health (natural selection) carries low social worth and economic reward (social selection), it is poor health that impacts most on mortality rates. This explanation was also dismissed as only a small amount of downward mobility (movement down the class hierarchy) is caused by illness. Third, materialist and structuralist explanations that emphasize the role of economic factors and associated structural factors were considered (i.e. low and insecure income, poor housing). It was these factors that were considered most important in explaining the association between social class and health inequalities. Fourth, the notion that poor health is attributable to individual behaviour (i.e. smoking, poor diet) was explored. These behaviours were evaluated as symptoms of socio-economic disadvantage that contribute to inequalities in health, not as the principal cause. The *Black* report concludes that tackling health inequalities means tackling social inequalities.

The importance of recognising the socio-economic determinants of health inequality was echoed in the findings of *The Health Divide* report, first published in 1987 (Whitehead, 1992) and the *Acheson* report (Acheson, 1998) from which the current UK governments approach to health inequalities stems. The *Acheson* report resulted from an independent inquiry into inequalities in health commissioned almost immediately after the Labour government took office in 1997. The inquiry adopted a socio-economic model of health and its inequalities; this is a model where the main determinants of health have layers of influence, one over another.

At the centre of the model are individuals with the age, sex and constitutional factors (i.e. genetics) that influence their health potential and are to a large extent fixed. Surrounding the individuals are layers of influence that could, in theory, be modified to improve health and reduce inequality. The innermost layer of influence is individual lifestyle factors (i.e. diet, smoking, exercise), however the model acknowledges that individual lifestyles do not exist in a vacuum, with the influence of friends, relatives and immediate community on health behaviours acknowledged in the next layer. The third layer recognises the variety of wider influences on a person's ability to maintain health, which include their living and working conditions, food supplies and access to essential services (i.e. utilities, healthcare, education). In the outermost layer are the economic, cultural and environmental conditions prevalent in society as a whole. The model emphasises interactions between these different layers, all of which impact on health (Acheson, 1998). The report advocates that socio-economic inequalities in health reflect differential exposure to risks associated with socio-economic position. In other words, the paths from social structure, represented by socio-economic status can be traced through to individual inequalities in health.

The Acheson report identified a number of inequalities that impact on the health of pregnant women, new mothers and infants (please note that the RGSC scale was used until the end of 2000):

• Women from households in social class V are four times more likely to smoke in pregnancy than those in social class I
• Smoking cessation rates are lower in mothers from lower socioeconomic groups
• Babies with fathers in social classes IV and V have a birthweight which is on average 130g lower than that of babies with fathers in social classes I and II
• Babies of fathers from social class I are more likely to be breastfed at birth than those from social class V
• Continued breastfeeding is much less common in the lower classes
• Obesity is more common in lower social classes.

The *Acheson* report recommended that high priority be given to policies aimed at improving health and reducing health inequalities in women of childbearing age, expectant mothers and young children (Acheson, 1998). Moreover, it advocated a joined-up networked approach with other health and social care policies. This set the tone for the first ever national health inequalities strategy *Tackling Health Inequalities: A programme for action* (DH, 2003). Exemplars of this 'top down' approach to tackling inequalities in health include services targeted as those with the most need such as *Sure Start* children's centres and the *Healthy Start* scheme for pregnant women and young families, which provides dietary advice and vouchers to exchange for milk, fresh fruit and vegetables.

Whilst the continued relevance of social class is up for debate in both sociology and society at large, arguably, it is a concept when considering health inequalities that we cannot do without. Having said that, it is also important to recognise the increasing significance of other axes of inequality that impact on health in late or post modernity. In sociology, **stratification** is the term used to describe the division of society into levels that form a hierarchy, with the most powerful at the top (O'Donnell, 2005). Social class is just one form of stratification. Other forms of stratification include religion, disability and sexuality. In addition to social class, the forms of stratification that have an established relationship to health are gender and ethnicity.

Gender

Gender is the term that refers to the culturally prescribed differences between men and women (Oakley, 1972). Whilst the adage 'women get sick and men die' has long dominated research findings in the area of gender inequalities in health, the male mortality disadvantage has slipped and is now relatively small in Western countries (Miers, 2000, cited in Letherby, 2005). Successive sociological studies show that women's own assessment of their physical and mental health is consistently worse than that of men (Blaxter, 1990; Rodin and Ickovics, 1990; Paykel, 1991; Whitehead, 1992). Moreover, women access healthcare services more often than men (Doyal, 1995). However, this is perhaps not surprising when you take female gender roles into account. As evident throughout this book, women bear most of the responsibility for biological and social reproduction within the family. Moreover, as discussed in the next chapter, women who work outside the home typically undertake 'multiple shifts' (the first in paid employment, the second in domestic labour and the third in emotional labour), all of which impact on their physical and mental health. However, it is also important to highlight that the category 'woman' is not homogeneous, with different women experiencing health and ill health in complex ways. For example, studies of working class women show they are more likely to hold functional conceptualisations of health linked to material disadvantage, which means they continue to fulfil their social roles as they '*can't afford to be ill*' when others would define them as ill (respondent quoted in Pill and Stott, 1982: 50).

Ethnicity

Ethnicity may be defined as the cultural values and norms that distinguish the members of a given group from others (Giddens, 2001). In other words, it is a socially constructed difference used to refer to people who see themselves as having common ancestry, often linked by geographical territory, and possibly sharing a language, religion or other social customs. In the context of healthcare, Culley (2006) asserts there is a need to think of ethnicity in terms of complexity and fluidity recognising differences within groups as well as between them. Moreover, whilst the concept of race is no longer tenable, healthcare professionals should not reject the importance of racialisation (whereby ideas about race are mapped onto particular groups or populations in specific contexts) and racism (with its various forms of racial discrimination). Until recently there has been little sociological research into the relationship between ethnicity and health in comparison to the wealth of epidemiological literature on the subject (Ahmad, 1992; 1993; Ahmad and Bradby, 2007). *Table 4.3* reproduces epidemiological

Table 4.3   Childbirth outcomes by ethnic group

	White	Black	Hispanic
Fertility rates (births per 1,000 women on childbearing ages)	57	72	102
Births to unmarried women	22%	69%	41%
Teen birth rates (per 1,000 teenagers)	36	91	97
Mothers who begin prenatal care in the first trimester	85%	72%	74%
Mothers with no or late prenatal care	3.2%	7%	6%
Caesarean section rate	21%	22%	20%
Low birthweight infants	1%	3%	1%
Infant mortality rates (per 1,000 births)	6	14	6

Adapted from Ventura et al (1999)

data on the marked differences in fertility and pregnancy outcomes of white, black and Hispanic women in the US.

In the UK, epidemiological research has also highlighted important ethnic differences in the patterns of morbidity and mortality (Culley and Dyson, 1993, 2005; Andrews and Jewson, 1993). Generally, health amongst ethnic minorities appears to be worse than amongst the majority white population (although there are counter trends to this in terms of some ethnic categories [Indians] and disease categories [cancers and respiratory disease]). According to Culley and Dyson (2005) these inequalities may be explained by the relative influence of genetic factors, migration, racism, access to services, materialist explanations, culture and social cohesion in different ethnic groups. However, a combination of social and economic factors is thought to be most significant. This is because:

> *'...people from minority ethnic groups, particularly black people, are more likely to be unemployed, or be in low paid jobs, living in poor housing and live in areas that lack adequate social and educational resources than white people. Black people share the disadvantages of white working class people and more (racism)'.*
>
> Blackburn (1991, quoted in Nettleton, 1995: 188).

We have seen that social class, gender and ethnicity are associated with particular health inequalities. Arguably what unites these forms of stratification in the contemporary world is living in below average conditions, or in other words, poverty.

Poverty, deprivation and social exclusion

Poverty may be defined exclusively in terms of health (i.e. malnutrition), or more widely in terms of an individual's general standard of living, their access to consumer durables, leisure activities and social participation (all of which undoubtedly have an impact on general health status). The concept of **absolute poverty** is based around ideas of basic subsistence requirements; whereas, the concept of relative poverty relates to the standards of a particular society at a particular time. In industrialized societies poverty is usually defined according to the normal or accepted standards of life. Moreover, Townsend (1979) asserts that poverty must be viewed in terms of relative deprivation. He asserts individuals, families and groups in the population can be said to be in poverty when they lack the resources to obtain the types of diet, participate in the activities and have the living conditions and amenities which are customary, or at least widely encouraged or approved in the societies to which they belong. Deprivation indices (see *Box 4.2*) are designed to measure the proportion of households in a defined small geographical unit with a combination of circumstances

Box 4.2: Measuring deprivation

There are a variety of deprivation indices in existence. This box details three such measures commonly used in the UK, but they are not the only ones; others include the Low Income Scheme Index, the ONS Area Classification, and the Breadline Britain Score. Deprivation indices are designed to measure the proportion of households in a defined small geographical unit with a combination of circumstances indicating low living standards and/or a high need for services (Bartley and Blane, 1994). Deprivation indices may be used to identify areas of relative concentration of disadvantage. However, not all individuals who live in such an area will necessarily be deprived, just as not living in a deprived area does exclude oneself from experiencing deprivation (Townsend et al, 1988; Sloggett and Joshi, 1994). When interpreting deprivation scores it is important to remember that they are relative measures, which means that the score for one area is standardised by reference to the mean for the total of all areas in the calculation. You cannot compare scores between indices, or for example, say Area A ranked 20 is twice as deprived as Area B ranked 40 in the same scale. However, it is possible to say Area B is more deprived than Area A.

The Jarman Underprivileged Area Score (UPA)
This scale, which has been widely used as a measure of deprivation, was originally constructed as a measure of general practice workload (Jarman, 1983). The variant of the score in common use is the UPA 8, which comprises eight weighted variables: unemployment, overcrowding, lone parents, under 5s, elderly living alone, ethnicity, low social class, residential mobility. The index has been criticised as better at defining inner city deprivation (Davies, 1998) and the nature of deprivation in London in particular at the expense of the different kind of deprivation found in the north of England.

The Townsend Material Deprivation Score
The Townsend score is based on just four variables that were selected to represent material deprivation: unemployment, overcrowding, lack of owner occupied accommodation, and lack of car ownership. The Townsend score was considered the best indicator of material deprivation available in England up until 2000, when the Indices of Deprivation were first released.

The Indices of Deprivation
These are the Government's official suite of deprivation indices, which includes the Index of Multiple Deprivation 2007. The 2007 release updates information provided in the Indices of Deprivation 2004 and Indices of Deprivation 2000. Further information about the Indices of deprivation can be found at:
http: //www.communities.gov.uk/communities/neighbourhoodrenewal/deprivation/ deprivation07/

indicating low living standards and/or a high need for health services (Bartley and Blane, 1994). However, official measurements of poverty rely on other statistical indicators, such as benefit provision. Having said that, sociological studies provide subjective understandings of poverty (Townsend, 1979). For example, the midwife Shelia Hunt's in-depth sociological study of 25 women's experiences of pregnancy and poverty is particularly insightful (Hunt, 2004), whilst Graham's (1990) investigation combines statistical data with insights into the health behaviours of women living in poverty.

Amidst the sociological literature on poverty and health inequalities is the controversial notion of an 'underclass'. Sociological explanations are divided as to whether this phenomenon is attributable to structural factors such as the restructuring of labour markets and social segregation (Walker, 1990), or personal and behavioural characteristics where individuals actively pursue a lifestyle characterized by unemployment, illegitimacy and crime (Murray, 1990). A much broader term developed by sociologists in the mid 1980s and favoured by politicians since the late 1990s is **social exclusion** (Alcock, 1997). Carol Thomas (2007) defines the 'socially excluded' as people who, through no inherent failing, do not have access to rights or resources taken for granted by the majority. However, Eve Bones (2007) identifies two traditions of theoretical analysis and political concern inherent in the inter-related concepts of social exclusion and inclusion. On the one hand there are those that focus on poverty, equality and material deprivation, while on the other hand there are those that propose that ideas of social cohesion, belongingness and integration are central. It is debatable as to which underpins the UK government's current approach to tackling health inequalities.

Addressing contemporary inequalities in maternal and infant health

In Britain, at the beginning of the twenty-first century, the field of health inequalities is characterised by a mix of government commitment to tackling inequality, the new public health, contemporary explanations as to why such inequalities exist, and continued evidence of persistent and widening inequality amidst the poorest sectors of society. Moreover, whilst the national strategy for tackling health inequalities (DH, 2003) emphasises a structural (top-down) approach to improving health, it co-exists with the government agenda around choice where policy initiatives — including '*Choosing Health*' (DH, 2004b) — emphasize individual (not governmental) responsibility for health.

Midwives need to be aware of three research-based explanations for contemporary health inequalities. First, the **psycho-social** explanation suggests that contemporary ways of life impact on the lower social classes disproportionately. According to this perspective high workload, job insecurity, poor promotion and low control combine to produce social stresses that affect mental wellbeing and physical health (Siegrist et al, 1990). In addition, these stresses induce coping behaviours that are harmful to health such as smoking, a poor diet and excessive alcohol consumption, whilst a lack of material resources (money and time) means social participation is limited, which is equally damaging to health (Kaplan et al, 1996). Second, the **life-course** explanation is based on research that suggests the consequences of socio-economic disadvantage accumulate from conception, through to childhood and adolescence to adulthood and in later life (O'Donnell, 2005; Bartley, 2004). This research includes the 'Barker hypothesis' that poor maternal nutrition during pregnancy and general poor health amongst disadvantaged mothers affect the developing baby during pregnancy and the concept of 'foetal programming' (Barker et al, 1989, 1992, 1994). This perspective also draws on research that shows low birth-weight babies are more likely to experience socio-economic disadvantage during childhood and adolescence (Bartley et al, 1994). According to Bartley et al (1997) there are 'critical periods' in the life course where human health and development are socially shaped. These include early pregnancy (when limited resources may restrict access to vitamins known to reduce risk of neural tube defects), the transition from school to work, the transition to parenthood, and the exit from the labour market. Third, there are **neo-materialist** explanations, which emphasise the importance of an unequal social structure on health inequalities. Adverse socio-economic and psycho-social environments and the experiences associated with them produce material circumstances. Or in other words, the unequal distribution of personal income and wealth shapes unequal access to food, transport, housing, healthcare, education, and lifestyle consumption, which all impact on health (O'Donnell, 2005). From this perspective the root of health inequality is seen as an unequal social structure, and thus tackling health inequality requires macro-level social change (Drever et al, 2000; Lynch et al, 2000).

The term **new public health** refers to the re-emergence of public health medicine since the late 1980s. According to Ashton and Seymour (1988) the new public health emerged from challenges to the dominance of therapeutic high technology medical interventions, which prompted a renewed focus on the social causes of illness and disease and community participation to improve health. This approach is evident in the previously discussed *Acheson* report and new health and social care community facilities. Other government initiatives aimed at reducing health inequalities include the Social Exclusion Unit, which amongst other things targets resources towards reducing teenage pregnancy. There is a strong association between teenage pregnancy and poverty, low educational achievement and social deprivation in the UK. Girls from social class V households are 10 times more likely to become teenage mothers compared to those in social class I (Botting et al, 1998). Moreover, babies of teenage mothers are 25% more likely to have birthweights below 2500g (Botting et al, 1998). The infant mortality rate for these babies is 60% higher than for infants of older women, and teenage mothers are 50% less likely to breastfeed. These young women are known to have additional problems because they book in late for antenatal care, and for many of them routine care is difficult because of their housing tenure (Social Exclusion Unit, 1999).

Despite current government initiatives, at the beginning of the twenty-first century (as in the nineteenth and twentieth centuries), the extent of maternal and infant inequalities continues to be illustrated most strikingly by differences in mortality. In 2005, in England and Wales the infant mortality rate among babies born inside marriage whose fathers were in semi-routine occupations was more than twice that of babies whose fathers were in large employers and higher managerial occupations (ONS, 2007). Moreover, during the same period, the most deprived women in society had a risk of dying that was seven times higher than that of the broad majority of pregnant women (Lewis, 2007).

For midwives, the most salient evidence of the heightened recognition of social influences on maternal outcomes is perhaps to be found in successive Confidential Enquires into Maternal Deaths. The most recent Enquiry, published in the report *Saving Mothers' Lives* highlights vulnerability and deprivation (see *Box 4.3*) as amongst the most important risk factors for maternal deaths (Lewis, 2007).

Consequently, two of the report's 'top ten' recommendations are concerned with facilitating better access to maternity services for vulnerable women, whilst a third targets additional support for migrant women. Research shows that the majority (98%) of pregnant women 'book' with NHS maternity services by 18 weeks gestation (Redshaw et al, 2007). However, around 20% of the women who died either booked for maternity care after 20 weeks gestation, missed more than four routine antenatal visits, did not seek care at all, or actively concealed their pregnancies (Lewis, 2007): '...*maternity service providers should ensure that antenatal services are accessible and welcoming so that all women, including those who currently find it difficult to access maternity care, can reach them easily and earlier in their pregnancy.*' According to the report, those who currently find it difficult to access maternity care and/or classified as vulnerable include:

- Teenagers
- Lone parents
- Women who are socially excluded (for example unemployed, living in deprived circumstances)
- Non-English speaking women
- Women seeking asylum and refugees
- Women with mental health problems
- Women who misuse drugs and/or alcohol
- Women subject to domestic abuse
- Women known to child protection services.

Despite policy initiatives which aim to target services and improve outcomes amongst vulnerable women, the disparity in maternal and infant outcomes remains stark. Differential access to services and the way vulnerable women are treated when they do engage with services are fundamental issues. Thus, the final parts of this section discuss the 'inverse care law', barriers to accessing services and the stereotyping of service users by midwives and other healthcare professionals.

The **inverse care law** is a phrase that was coined in the early 1970s by Hart (1971). His formulation of the inverse care law was based on his experience as a general practitioner (GP), where he had observed that those who have the most need of NHS health care services actually obtain them later, and in smaller amounts, whilst those who have less need use the health services more often. Hart (1971) concludes:

'In areas with most sickness and death, general practitioners have more work, larger lists, less hospital support, and inherit more clinically ineffective traditions of consultation, than in the healthiest areas; and hospital doctors shoulder heavier case-loads with less staff and equipment, more obsolete buildings, and suffer recurrent crises in the availability of beds and replacement staff. These trends can be summed up as the inverse care law: that the availability of good medical care tends to vary inversely with the need of the population served'.

Hart (1971: 11)

Subsequent research has confirmed this (Watt, 2002; Dixon et al, 2003). A number of studies have identified the inverse relationship between need and provision in antenatal care (Arnold, 1987; Brown and Lumley, 1995; Kirkham et al, 2002a) and antenatal education (Nolan, 1999).

The *National Service Framework (NSF) for Children, Young People and Maternity Services: Standard 11: Maternity Services* (DH, 2004a) sets out a vision for flexible, individualised, services designed to fit around the woman and her baby through pregnancy and motherhood, with emphasis on the needs of vulnerable and disadvantaged women. However, whilst it asserts the need for more inclusive services acknowledging that '*maternal and neonatal outcomes are poorer for women from disadvantaged, vulnerable or excluded groups*', there is an undertone blaming young women for not accessing such services when available. Sociological research highlights numerous barriers that may restrict access to services through no fault of these women. Inequalities with regard to service access or utilization may result from two sorts of disadvantage; first, those that make access to service difficult, such as lack of transport and available time away from work, and second, those that make consultations less productive, such as patients being less assertive about demanding information, participation in treatment decisions, and appropriate referrals for further treatment (Dixon et al, 2003). Midwives need to be aware that the lives of women in vulnerable groups do not fit easily into the trajectory prescribed for healthy pregnancy in the NSF and that accessing appropriate care is difficult (Lavender et al, 2007). Moreover, whilst policies address inequality at structural level, at individual level 'woman centred-care' means both listening to women and being their advocate irrespective of their social situation. However in practice research shows this does not always happen, particularly when midwives stereotype women.

A **stereotype** is, by definition, a set of simplistic generalizations about a group of individuals that enables others to categorize individuals who are members of that group and treat them according to pre-defined expectations

---

Box 4.3: Vulnerability and other risk factors for maternal deaths identified in *Saving Mother's Lives* (Lewis, 2007: 2)

• Vulnerable women with socially complex lives who died were far less likely to seek antenatal care early in pregnancy or to stay in regular contact with maternity services. Overall 17% of the women who died from direct or indirect causes booked for maternity care after 22 weeks of gestational age or had missed over four routine antenatal visits compared to 5% of women who were employed, or who had a partner in employment. Of the women who died from any cause, including those unrelated to pregnancy:

-14% self-declared that they were subject to domestic abuse
-11% had problems with substance abuse, 60% of whom were registered addicts
-10% lived in families known to the child protection services

• A third of all women who died were either single and unemployed or in a relationship where both partners were unemployed.

• Women with partners who were unemployed, many of whom had features of social exclusion, were up to seven times more likely to die than women with partners who were unemployed. In England, women who lived in the most deprived areas were five times more likely to die than women living in the least deprived areas.

• Black African women, including asylum seekers and newly arrived refugees, have a mortality rate nearly six times higher than White women. To a lesser extent, Black and Caribbean and Middle Eastern women also had a significantly higher mortality rate.

(Jary and Jary, 1991). Consequently, stereotyping a woman according to her class, race, or gender can lead to poor midwifery care based on unjustified preconceptions. Evidence of midwives using social class to stereotype women accessing maternity services can be found in a number of studies (Cartwright, 1979; MacIntyre, 1982; Kirkham, 1989: Hunt and Symonds, 1995; Hunt, 2004; KirKham et al, 2002b). The midwife Shelia Hunt and the sociologist Anthea Symonds (1995: 90) state that '...*the first thing they [the midwives] did when they obtained the notes of a woman expected to arrive in labour was to look at the occupation of her partner and herself*', leading them to communicate differently with 'the posh' women compared to 'the unemployed' women. Moreover, in Hunt's (2004) study of poverty she directly quotes a number of midwives to demonstrate their intolerance and poor understanding of the complexities of living in material deprivation.

An earlier study by the midwife Mavis Kirkham (1989:122) reports that women of a higher social class '...*gained more information from midwives both in answer to their questions and as information offered by midwives unasked*' based on (unfounded) assumptions about their intelligence. More recent work led by the same author (Kirham et al, 2002b) highlights the complexity of midwives' use of stereotyping reporting and how it serves as a defence mechanism in the face of limited resources. They highlight how stereotyping may be used to protect the midwife from what they consider to be inappropriate requests, to blame women who they perceive as unreceptive to the views of midwives and obstetricians, and to simultaneously protect and control women by withholding information. This behaviour leads such stereotypes to be self-fulfilling (i.e. lone teenage parents who are not offered information, who do not know what is available and become categorised as 'not wanting information'). Kirkham et al (2002b) conclude that whilst midwives may reap short-term benefits by stereotyping (i.e. not having to spend lengthy amounts of time explaining care to women who cannot read), its effects on women are corrosive particularly in relation to choice and decision-making.

Conclusion

This chapter has drawn together a myriad of work from the sociology of health and illness, epidemiology, medicine and midwifery to demonstrate the social context of health, illness and disease. From the outset it aimed to demonstrate what sociology can add to midwifery when considering health inequalities. It has highlighted the importance of structural inequalities that may help midwives to improve care by acknowledging the direct effects of poverty, working to limit the effects of variations in behaviour and by targeting specific groups to reduce differential access to services.

References

Acheson D (1998) *Independent Inquiry into Inequalities in Health Report.* Stationery office, London:

Ahmad WIU (1992) Is medical sociology an ostrich? Reflections on 'race' and the sociology of health. *Medical Sociology News* **17**(2): 16-21

Ahmad WIU (1993) *'Race' and Health in Contemporary Britain.* Open University Press, Buckingham

Ahmad WIU, Bradby H (2007) Locating ethnicity and health: exploring concepts and contexts. *Sociology of Health and Illness* **29**(6): 795-810

Alcock P (1997) *Understanding Poverty.* 2nd edn. Macmillan, Basingstoke

Andrews A, Jewson N (1993) Ethnicity and infant deaths — the implications of recent statistical evidence for materialist explanations. *Sociology of Health & Illness* **15**(2): 137–56

Annandale E (1998) *The Sociology of Health and Medicine: A critical introduction.* Polity Press, Cambridge

Arnold M (1987) The cycle of maternal deprivation. *Midwife Health visit Community Nurse* **23**(12): 539–42

Ashton J, Seymour H (1988) *The New Public Health.* Open University Press, Milton Keynes

Barker DJP, Martyn CN, Osmond C, Hales CN, Fall CHD (1989) Growth in utero, blood pressure in childhood and adult life, and mortality from cardiovascular disease. *British Medical Journal* **298**: 564–7

Barker DJP (1992) *Fetal and Infant Origins of Adult Disease.* BMJ Books, London

Barker DJP (1994) *Mothers, Babies, and Disease in Later Life.* BMJ Books, London

Bartley M, Blane D, Montgomery S (1997) Socioeconomic determinants of health: Health and the life course: why safety nets matter. *BMJ* **314**(1194): 19 April

Bartley M (2004) *Health Inequality: An introduction to theories, concepts and methods.* Polity, Cambridge

Bartley M, Blane D (1994) Appropriateness of deprivation indices must be ensured. *BMJ* **309**: 1479

Bartley M, Power C, Blane D, Smith GD, Shipley M (1994) Birth weight and later socio-economic disadvantage: evidence from the 1958 British cohort study. *BMJ* **309**: 1475-8

Beck U (1992) *Risk Society.* Sage, London

Blaxter M (1990) *Health and Lifestyles.* Tavistock Routledge, London

Bones E (2007) Women's health, social values and pregnant teenagers. *Midwifery Digest* **17**(4): 483–9

Botting B, Rosato M, Wood R (1998) Teenage mothers and the health of their children. *Population Trends* **93**

Bradley H (1996) *Fractured Identities: Changing patterns of inequality.* Polity, Cambridge

Brown S, Lumley J (1995) Antenatal care: a case of the inverse care law? *Aus J Pub Health* **17**(2): 95–103

Calnan M (1987) *Health and Illness: The lay perspective*. Tavistock, London

Cartwright A (1979) *The Dignity of Labour*. Tavistock, London

Cochrane AL (1972) Effectiveness and efficiency: Random reflections on health services. Nuffield Provincial Hospitals Trust, London

Culley L, Dyson S (1993) Race, inequality and health. *Sociology Review* **3**(1): 24–8

Culley L, Dyson S (2005) Race and ethnicity. In: Denny E, Earle S, eds. *Sociology for Nurses*. Polity Press, Cambridge: 161–80

Culley L (2006) Transcending transculturalism? Race, ethnicity and healthcare. *Nursing Inquiry* **13**(2): 144–53

Davies J (1998) Healthy living centres. *Health Services Journal* **5 November**: 1–5

Davis Floyd R (1992) *Birth as an American Right of Passage*. University of California Press, London

Dixon A, Le Grand J, Henderson J, Murray R, Poteliakhoff E (2003) 'Is the NHS equitable? A review of the evidence. *LSE Health and Social Care Discussion Paper 11*. London School of Economics, London

Doyal L (1979) *The Political Economy of Health*. South End Press, Boston

Doyal L (1995) *What Makes Women Sick: Gender and the political economy of health*. Macmillan, Basingstoke

DH (2003) *Tackling Health Inequalities. A programme for action*. DH, London

DH (2004a) *National Service Framework*. Department of Health, London. Website: *https://www.dh.gov.uk*

DH (2004b) *Choosing Health*. DH, London

DH (2008) *Tackling Health Inequalities: 2007 Status report on the programme for Action*. DH, London

Drever F, Fisher K, Brown J, Clark J (2000) *Social Inequalities*. Stationary Office, London

Erikson R, Goldthorpe JH (1992) *The Constant Flux*. Clarendon Press, Oxford

Gerhardt U (1989) *Ideas About Illness: An intellectual and political history of medical sociology*. New Your University Press, New York

Green J (2005) In: Gabe J, Bury M, Elston MA, eds: *Key Concepts in Medical Sociology*. Sage, London

Giddens A (2001) *Sociology*. 4th edition. Polity Press, Cambridge

Goffman E (1963) *Stigma: Notes on the management of spoiled identity*. Doubleday Anchor, New York

Goldthorpe J, Lockwood D, Bechhofer F, Plat J (1969) *The Affluent Worker in the Class Structure*. Cambridge University Press, Cambridge

Goldthorpe J (1980) *Social Mobility and Class Structure in Modern Britain*. Clarendon, Oxford

Graham H (1990) Behaving well: Women's health behaviours in context. In: Roberts H, ed: *Women's Health Counts*. Routledge, London: 195–219

Green JM, Kitzinger JV, Coupland VA (1990) Stereotypes of childbearing women: a look at some of the evidence. *Midwifery* **6**: 125–32

Hart JT (1971) The inverse care law. *The Lancet* **1**: 405–12

Hart N (1982) Is capitalism bad for your health? *British Journal of Sociology* **33**: 435–43

Hunt S, Symonds A (1995) *The Social Meaning of Midwifery*. Macmillian, Basingstoke

Hunt S (2004) *Poverty, Pregnancy and the Healthcare Professional*. Books for Midwives, Edinburgh

Jarman B (1983) Identification of underprivileged areas. *British Medical Journal* **286**: 1705–9

Jary D, Jary J (1991) *Dictionary of Sociology*. HarperCollins, Glasgow

Kaplan GA, Pamuk E, Lynch JW et al (1996) Income inequality and mortality in the United States: analysis of mortality and potential pathways. *BMJ* **312**: 999–1003

Kirkham M (1989) Midwives and information giving in labour. In: Thompson A, eds. *Research, Midwives and Childbirth. Volume 1*. Chapman and Hall, London: 117–38

Kirkham M, Stapleton H, Curtis P, Thomas G (2002a) The inverse care law in antenatal midwifery care. *British Journal of Midwifery* **10**(8): 509–13

Kirkham M, Stapleton H, Curtis P, Thomas G (2002b) Stereotyping as a professional defence mechanism. *British Journal of Midwifery* **10**(9): 549–52

Lavender T, Downe S, Finnlayson K, Walsh D (2007) *Access to Antenatal Care: A systematic review*. Confidential Enquiry into Maternal and Child Health. CEMACH, London

Letherby G (2005) Gendered concerns. In: Denny E, Earle S, eds. *Sociology for Nurses*. Polity Press, Cambridge: 87–103

Lewis G (2007) *The Confidential Enquiry into Maternal and Child Health (CEMACH). Saving Mothers' Lives: reviewing maternal deaths to make motherhood safer — 2003–2005*. CEMACH, London

Lynch JW, Smith GD, Kaplan GA, House JS (2000) Income inequality and mortality: importance to health of individual income, psychosocial environment, or material conditions. *BMJ* **320**: 1200-4

MacIntyre S (1977) The Management of Childbirth: Sociological research issues.

McKinlay J (1977) The business of good doctoring or doctoring as good business: reflections on Freidson's view of the medical game. *International Journal of Health Services* **7**: 459–83

McKinlay J (1984) *Issues in the Political Economy of Health Care*. Tavistock, London

Murray C (1990) *The Emerging British Underclass*. IEA Health and welfare Unit, London

Navarro V (1986) *Crisis, Health and Medicine*. Tavistock, London

Norman D, Henriques F, Slaughter C (1969) *Coal is our Life*. Tavistock, London

Nettleton S (1995) *The Sociology of Health and Illness*. Polity Press, Oxford

Nolan Ml (1990) *Empowerment and Antenatal Education*. Unpublished PhD thesis. University of

Birmingham, Birmingham

Ntau C (2004) Health and development. In: Gabe J, Bury M, Elston M, eds. *Key Concepts in Medical Sociology*. London, Sage

O'Donnell T (2005) Social class and health. In: Denny E, Earle S, eds. *Sociology for Nurses*. Polity Press, Cambridge: 141–60

Oakley A (1972) *Sex, Gender and Society*. Temple Smith, London

ONS (2007) *https://www.ons.gov.uk*

Parsons T (1951) *The Social System*. Free Press, New York

Paykel E (1991) Depression in Women. *British Journal of Psychiatry* **58**(10): 22-9

Pill R, Stott NCH (1982) Concepts of illness causation and responsibility: some preliminary data from a sample of working class mothers. *Social Science and Medicine* **16**: 43–52

Redshaw M, Rowe R, Hockley C, Brocklehurst P (2007) *Recorded Delivery: A national survey of women's experience of maternity care 2006*. National Perinatal Epidemiology Unit Oxford

Rodin J, Ickovics J (1990) Women's health: review and research agenda as we approach the 21st century. *American Psychologist* **45**(9): 1018–34

Robinson S, MacIntyre S (1982) Communications between pregnant women and their medical and midwifery attendants. *Midwives' Chronicle* **November**: 387–94

Rose D, Pevalin DJ (2001) *The National Statistics Socio-economic Classification. Unifying Official and Sociological Approaches to the Conceptualisation and Measurement of Social Class. ISER working papers 2001–4*. University of Essex, Colchester

Rothman BK (1982) In: *Labor: Women and power in the birthplace*. New York: WW Norton and Co, New York

Siegrist J, Peter R, Junge A, et al (1990) Low status control, high effort at wotrk and ischemic heart disease: prospective evidence from blue collar men. *Social Science and Medicine* **31**(10): 1127–34

Slogget A, Joshi H (1994) Higher mortality in deprived areas: community or personal disadvantage? *British Medical Journal* **309**: 1470–4

Social Exclusion Unit (1999) *Teenage Pregnancy*. The Stationery Office, London

Teijlingen E van, (2005) A critical analysis of the medical model as used in the study of pregnancy and childbirth. *Sociological Research Online*. **10**(2): June

Thomas C (2007) *Sociologies of Disability and Illness*. Palgrave Macmillan, Basingstoke

Townsend P (1979) *Poverty in the United Kingdom*. Penguin, Harmondsworth

Townsend P, Davidson N (1992) *Inequalities in Health: The Black Report*. Penguin, Harmondsworth

Turner BS (2003) The history of the changing concepts of health and illness: Outline of a general model of illness categories. In: Albrecht GL, Fitzpatrick R, Scrimshaw SC, eds. *The Handbook of Social Studies in Health and Medicine*. Sage, London

Wagner M (1994) *Pursuing the Birth Machine: The search for appropriate birth technology*. ACE Graphics, Camperdown

Walker A (1990) Blaming the victims. In: Murray, C. *The Emerging British Underclass.* IEA Health and welfare Unit, London: 49–65

Walsh D, Newburn M (2002) Towards a social model of childbirth: Part 1. *British Journal of Midwifery* **10**(8): 476–81

Watt G (2002) The inverse care law today. *The Lancet* **360**: 252–4

Whitehead M (1992) The Health Divide: Penguin, Harmondsworth

WHO (1948) *Preamble to the Constitution of the World Health Organization as adopted by the International Health Conference.* WHO, Geneva

CHAPTER 5

Motherhood and the family

The family is an important issue within sociology. It has been conceptualised as the most basic unit of social organisation, which can be found in most, if not all, societies. In most Western societies the family is also an important political issue, with successive governments asserting that the decline of 'traditional' family values is the root of many contemporary social problems. For midwives too, the family is of fundamental importance. Midwives play a pivotal role in the delivery of the next generation. Not only do midwives share the moment new families are made, but they rarely care for women in isolation, thus making consideration of existing familial structures an essential part of midwifery practice. Moreover, as midwives know only too well, particular childbirths can create or break families: they also:

> *'...establish the ownership of property and entitlements to poverty or privilege [and] they may alter the statuses, rights and responsibilities of persons, communities and nations'.*

> *Oakley (2005: 151)*

The purpose of this chapter is to challenge midwives to think about the role of 'the family' in society and to highlight the diversity of contemporary families. This chapter introduces midwives to the main sociological perspectives and some of the key studies that have shaped sociological understanding about the family, before focusing more specifically on the experiences of women within families. The majority of the discussion concerns women's roles; not because men's are not important, but because there has been comparatively less work on fatherhood than on female gender roles, mothering, motherhood and the family.

Defining the family

The family may be defined most simply as:

> *'...a group of persons directly linked by kin connections, the adult members of which assume responsibility for caring for the children. Kinship ties are connections between individuals, established either through marriage or through the lines of descent that connect blood relatives'.*

> *Giddens (2001: 173)*

A more detailed definition (if somewhat dated) is offered by George Murdock, a sociologist who famously studied 250 societies and claimed that some form of the family existed in every one. Murdock (1949) defines the family as:

'...a social group characterised by common residence, economic co-operation and reproduction. It includes adults of both sexes, at least two of whom maintain a socially approved relationship, and one or more children, own or adopted, of the sexually cohabiting adults'.

Murdoch (1949)

This definition assumes that the family lives together, shares its resources, cares for its offspring, and at least two adults maintain a sexual relationship according to the norms of their particular society (Haralambos and Holborn, 2008). It does not, however, presuppose that there are only two adults, or that a husband is the biological father of any offspring. The social norms regarding marriage, sexual relationships and reproduction vary from society to society.

During the twentieth century sociological perspectives on the family were principally concerned with the existence of two types of family structure: the **nuclear family** and the **extended family**. The nuclear family is defined as consisting of a husband, wife and their dependent children. Murdock (1949) and Talcott Parsons (1959) both used the term nuclear family, whilst later sociologists have referred it as the symmetrical family (Young and Wilmot, 1973), the conventional family (Oakley, 1982), the Western family (Laslett, 1983, 1984) or the traditional family (Nicolson, 1997). Any family structure that is larger than the nuclear family is generally known as an extended family. Extended families may include grandparents (i.e vertical extensions of the nuclear family) and/or additional wives (i.e. horizontal extensions of the nuclear family). In Western societies marriage and the family are associated with monogamy, and it is illegal for a man or woman to be married to more than one spouse at the same time. However, polygamy, which allows a man or woman to be married to more than one spouse, is normal in many developing and newly industrialised societies.

Towards the end of the twentieth century many sociologists began to highlight the diversity of family and household types in modern industrialised and post/late modernist societies. Across Europe, divorce rates have risen, cohabitation has increased and birth rates have declined (Boh, 1989), giving rise to alternative family structures. For example, in the UK in 2006 a total of 92,870 marriages were remarriages for one or both parties, which accounts for 39% of all marriages (ONS, 2008). In sociology, a **reconstituted family** is the term used to describe a family in which at least one of the adults has children from a previous marriage or relationship (stepfamilies in other words). Lone parent households or single parent families have also become increasingly common in Britain since the mid 1980s (Crow and Hardey, 1992). Thus, the stereotype of the nuclear family as comprising of a father, mother and at least two residing children has become misleading. Moreover, many more women now work outside the home as well as within it, resulting in what has been termed the British neo-conventional family (Chesler, 1985). '*There [is] now no single British family, but a rich variety of forms, states, traditions, norms and usages, a plurality that is important to underline*' (Laslett, 1984: xii). The diversity of families today is a theme that underpins the whole of this chapter, but before I explore this in more detail in relation to motherhood it is important to provide a brief overview of key sociological perspectives on the family.

Sociological perspectives and the family

Early sociological approaches to understanding the family include the work of Murdock (1949) and Parsons (1959) using a functionalist perspective. According to Parsons (1959; 1965) the family performs two basic and irreducible functions for individuals and society: the primary socialization of children, and the stabilization of adult personalities. For Parsons, primary socialization (which occurs during infancy and early childhood) involves the dual processes of internalizing a society's culture and structuring individual personality, whilst the stabilization of adult personalities refers to the emotional security that the family provides.

Early functionalist work on the family provides useful insights into its role as a principal source of social reproduction and social cohesion. However, it is somewhat idealized and very much of its time. It has been criticized for valorising the nuclear family and a domestic division of labour where men are 'breadwinners' and women are 'homemakers', failing to consider variations in family structure or the role of secondary socialization, in shaping individual personalities and action.

The second influential branch of sociological thought concerning the family is the conflict perspective, which includes work by Marxists and some feminists associated with the second wave. Conflict perspectives, in contrast to functionalist perspectives, emphasise a less harmonious, even detrimental, role of the family in society. Most acknowledge that women in particular are exploited in marriage and family life. The first writings on the family from a Marxist perspective are those of Karl Marx's friend and collaborator Friedrich Engels in *The Origins of the Family, Private Property and the State* (Engels, 1972, first published 1884). According to Engels the nuclear family serves to limit sexual relationships to those that best serve the interests of capitalism, which includes the production of legitimate heirs and greater control over women by men (patriarchy). Engels' account of the evolution of the family from the promiscuous horde of primitive communism to the monogamous nuclear family is not without criticism, but his central argument does have some historical and anthropological basis (Gough, 1972). Later, Marxist accounts of the family also expose the myth that the 'private life' of the family is separate from the economic system (Zaretsky, 1976). From a Marxist perspective the family serves the interests of the ruling class (the bourgeoisie) as both a unit of reproduction for capitalism (it produces a ready workforce) and a unit of **consumption** (purchasing the goods produced).

The feminist literature on the family is vast and has been particularly influential. What is more, as identified in chapter one, there are many variants of feminist theory, which include Marxist feminism, liberal feminism, radical feminism, and post-structuralist feminism. Therefore, whilst some feminist work may be encapsulated under the conflict perspectives heading, feminist approaches to the family invariably warrant discussion as a distinct body of work in their own right. It was feminist sociologists who first introduced the domestic division of labour as worthy of study (Gavron, 1966; Oakley, 1974), the unequal power relationships between men and women that give rise to abuse (Millett, 1971; Oakley, 1992), the destructive ideology of the family (Barret and McIntosh, 1982), and the caring activities predominantly undertaken by women. In particular, the institution of motherhood (Rich, 1976) and women's experiences of mothering (Oakley, 1979) became an important focus that continues to the present day (Hays, 1996; Gatrell, 2005). We will return to this literature throughout the rest of this chapter, but first it is important to highlight more recent sociological perspectives on the family.

Contemporary sociological perspectives on the family are characterised by an emphasis on the diversity of family structures and the increased freedoms individuals now have to 'choose' how they live. Robert and Rhona Rapoport (1982, 1989) were amongst the first sociologists to argue that family diversity is a growing, global trend, identifying that whilst the nuclear family is upheld as the norm, families consisting of married couples with children in which the husband is the sole breadwinner are a small minority. Moreover, Rapoport (1989) was the first to identify a number of distinct elements of family diversity in Britain. These include organizational diversity (e.g. variations in family structure that include nuclear families, one-parent families, dual worker families, etc), cultural diversity (e.g. differences between ethnic groups and religious beliefs), class diversity (e.g. differences in the socialization of working class and middle class families), life-cycle diversity (e.g. family life is different for a couple with young, dependent children compared to a couple without children), and cohort diversity (e.g. differences in how the period in which one lives affect family life such as periods of high unemployment). In the early 1990s, O'Brien and Jones (1996) replicated Wilmott's (1963) classic study of familial networks (undertaken in north London in the 1950s), adding weight to arguments about the diversification of family life. O'Brien and Jones (1996) report that whilst family networks remained evident (i.e. grandparents living nearby) there was a greater plurality of family types (i.e. step-families, lone parents), an increase in marital breakdowns, and a big rise in dual earner households.

Allan and Crow (2001) suggest that the trend towards increased family diversification has intensified in recent years. According to Allan and Crow (2001) there now exists so much diversity in people's domestic arrangements that we can no longer talk of a clear **family cycle** (whereby most individuals leave home, get married, move in with their spouse, have children, children leave home and the cycle starts again). They argue that rising divorce rates, an increase in the number of lone parent households, cohabitation outside of marriage, declining rates of marriage and a large increase in the number of stepfamilies means individuals now follow an unpredictable family course. However, Silva and Smart (1999) turn these statistics around to suggest that fairly traditional family forms do remain important. For example, in 1996, 73% of households were composed of heterosexual couples (with just under 90% of these being married). Nonetheless, they concede that personal choices regarding family life appear increasingly autonomous and fluid.

The notion of **chosen families** is increasingly being used in sociology to refer to the diverse kinds of families evident today. Weeks et al (1999) use this term when discussing homosexual households and their wider social networks. Roseneil (2005) develops the concept further, suggesting that the heternorm on which the nuclear family rests is breaking down. She asserts:

> *'...the heterosexual couple, and particularly the married co-resident heterosexual couple with children, no longer occupies the centre-ground of Western societies and cannot be taken for granted as the basic unit of society'.*

> *Roseneil (2005: 247)*

Other factors contributing to family diversity studied by sociologists include the impact of techniques for assisted conception, which are fundamentally changing kinship relationships (MacIonis and Plummer, 1997; Franklin and Ragoné, 1998). This is an issue we will return to later in the chapter.

A number of other authors have also drawn attention to how societal change impacts on the family. For example, Giddens (1992) asserts that in high modernity major changes have taken place in intimate relationships between people; we have a greater degree of choice over our sexuality, relationships are actively worked at, and we are increasingly reflective about how we want to live. Similarly, Ulrich Beck (introduced in chapter four) and his wife Elisabeth Beck-Gernsheim assert that against a backdrop of a rapidly changing world personal relationships are changing too. According to Beck and Beck-Gernsheim (1995) the concept of love has become central to contemporary relationships over which we increasingly have choices, but also increasing conflict. Both of these perspectives show how contemporary relationships and family structures are negotiated, which goes some way to explain current trends in family life (increasing divorce rates, step-families, lone parents).

Stacey (1996), drawing on empirical research from the US, goes further and asserts that there has been a fundamental shift to what she terms the **post-modern family**, in which family culture is contested, ambivalent and undecided and family relationships are diverse, dynamic and unresolved. According to Stacey

(1996) homosexual families have played a pioneering role in the development of the post-modern family, as has the women's rights movement. Since the late 1980s a growing number of same-sex partners have been able to openly live together. In the UK, civil partnerships (introduced in December 2005) mean homosexual couples can now access many of the same rights as heterosexual married couples. An increasing number of children are being brought up by homosexual couples, giving rise to both new models of parenting and new kinds of families which research suggests are more tolerant, egalitarian and less aggressive (Stacey, 1996).

Thus, contemporary sociological perspectives on the family seek to capture how individual agency and wider structural changes are creating increasingly diverse social units. Moreover, the focus is less about what the family is and more about what being in a family means.

Mothering, motherhood, identity and the family

In most societies there is a culturally-held assumption that the family is defined by the presence of children. Society and culture exert powerful influences over when, where and how women become mothers, what motherhood means, and the experience of mothering. In Western industrialised societies studies show that girls are socialized to become mothers from an early age (Sharpe, 1976; Walkerdine et al, 2001). Moreover, motherhood is intimately linked to notions of womanhood and femininity throughout the life-course (Oakley, 1979). Feminist research on the family challenges these processes, exposing motherhood as a social and historical construction (Bassin et al, 1994; Glen, 1994; Risman, 1998). In other words, they identify how the family, and the role of women within the family in particular, could be otherwise.

For many feminists the issue is not that women should be freed from their biological role in reproduction, but that this should not dictate their place in society. The notion that the female sex's role in reproduction determines a woman role in society is known as **biological determinism**. Numerous variants of feminism have questioned the taken-for-granted assumptions of what is 'natural' or 'innate' about pregnancy, childbirth and mothering, asserting that it is gender, not sex, which determines women's role as the principal carer for children and families (Bobel, 1992; Duden, 1993; Hayes, 1996).

Moreover, many feminists argue that the family is a key institution for the reproduction of patriarchy. Since the Second World War many more women have worked outside the home. Nevertheless, female gender roles continue to principally associate women, not men, with unpaid domestic work. Recently, sociologists have also identified **emotion work** as an important component of the feminine role women undertake for the family. The concept of emotion work was first used by Hochschild (1983) to capture the kind of work done by airline cabin crew trying to keep airline passengers happy. In the context of the family, it is argued that women work a first shift in paid employment, a second shift in unpaid domestic work and a third shift in emotion work, which involves trying to keep other family members (husband, children) happy (Duncombe and Marsden, 1995).

A number of feminists have drawn attention to the romanticized ideal to which all mothers are supposed to aspire in modern, westernised cultures, which is known as the **ideology of motherhood**. Ideology is the term used to refer to a system of ideas that justifies or legitimates the subordination of one group over another. According to Rothman (1994), the ideology of motherhood serves to uphold patriarchal relationships in the family and men's position over women in society. The conventional ideology of motherhood posits a white, middle class, stay-at-home, heterosexual, biological mother who delivers constant care and attention to her children as the feminine ideal (Boris, 1994). It is a conception that reinforces women's primary role in the domestic (private) sphere and men's in the public (as breadwinner). This conventional ideology of motherhood has been widely criticised, not least because it is based on a model of the family with a relative degree of economic security and racial privilege (Collins, 1994). It also fails to recognise the variety of family types that exist today.

In developed societies motherhood is a legal institution and the ideology of motherhood has become normalized: this has brought with it notions of 'good' and 'bad' mothering. It is culture that defines and rewards good mothers (i.e. women who conform to the ideology of motherhood), whilst sanctioning bad mothers. So-called 'bad mothers' encompass working class mothers, ethnic mothers, homosexual mothers, drug abusing mothers, teenage mothers and others whose experience of mothering is outside the ideology of motherhood (i.e. mothers of children with a disability). In-depth studies involving women labelled 'bad' mothers (also known as 'other' mothers) show that on the one hand they talk about exhibiting behaviours associated with socially acceptable parenting, whilst on the other hand as mothers they create for themselves more inclusive boundaries for acceptable mothering (Phoenix, 1991; Berryman, 1991; Bailey et al, 2002; Lewin, 1994; Baker and Carson, 1999). In other words, these women sought to conform both to the conventional ideology of motherhood and an alternative conception of 'good mothering' derivative of the circumstances in which they lived.

Recent feminist research has identified competing ideologies of motherhood (i.e. stay at home mum versus working mothers), coupled with an emergent discourse that dictates that all mothers follow the principles of **intensive mothering** (Buxton, 1998). Intensive mothering may be defined as a process that is '*child centred, expert guided, emotionally absorbing, labour intensive and financially expensive*' (Hays, 1996: 8). According to Hays (1996) and Benn (1998) there has been a conflation of good mothering discourse with intensive mothering discourse, whereby individual mothers are increasingly expected to invest heavily (time, energy, money and emotion), to enhance their child's intellectual, physical, social and emotional development. Hays (1996) suggests that it is middle class mothers who go about this process most intensely. This is a suggestion supported by a study of middle class working mothers from the UK, which reports women practising a form of 'professional' intensive mothering (Vincent et al, 2004). Thus, contemporary feminist research on mothering demonstrates, as suggested by Beck (1992), that in late modernity '...*the lives of women are pulled back and forth by the contradiction between liberation from and reconnection to the old ascribed role*' (Beck, 1992, quoted in Vincent et al, 2004: 585).

Feminist research on the source of ideologies and discourse surrounding motherhood includes exploration of gender roles (Chodorow, 1978) and cultural expectations on the construction of motherhood (Rich, 1976), the role of the media (Keller, 1994; Johnston and Swanson, 2003), historical analysis of the self-help literature (Zimmerman et al, 2001), parenting books (Dally, 1982; Eyer, 1996) and expert advice (Ehrenreich and English, 1978). It is hoped that this chapter will encourage midwives to think about how notions of what constitutes 'good' and 'bad' mothers are currently imposed on all women who access maternity services through appointment schedules, expert advice and in wider society.

It is particularly important that midwives are aware of the power of such discourse because it is this that creates such a disjuncture between women's expectations of motherhood and their actual experiences. In practice, midwives are ideally placed to support women as they negotiate this disjuncture. Oakley's (1979) *Becoming a Mother* is a seminal study that vividly demonstrates this disjuncture using the accounts of 66 women who had their first babies in London between 1975 and 1976. Over 30 years later another UK study demonstrates the persistence of this disjunction (Miller, 2007). However, interestingly for midwives, Miller identifies how birth experiences can act as a 'discursive turning point' that leads women, eight to nine months after birth, to challenge once accepted knowledge about how childbirth and motherhood should be (i.e. medical discourse, natural childbirth discourse and intensive mothering discourse) with how it is for them. Nevertheless, Miller (2007) concludes that any further fragmentation of 'good' mother discourse will require more women's voices to be heard and a collective challenge of dominant social constructions of motherhood in our society.

This section has introduced the ideology of motherhood and other discourses that shape contemporary experiences of mothering in western culture. It has also highlighted that for many modern mothers 'having it all' (career, husband, children) means 'doing it all' (paid work, domestic work including childcare/ development, emotion work). Drawing both from this section and the previous (which identified increased family diversity), the next section explores what these sociological insights offer to midwives seeking to understand more about the social shaping of the contemporary birthing population.

Conceiving time: becoming a mother in the 21st century

Patterns of fertility in the UK are changing significantly. Since the late 1960s fertility patterns have been characterised by falling fertility rates (as illustrated in *Table 5.1*), a rising mean age at first birth, and increased levels of childlessness (Self and Zealey, 2007). According to some sociologists this trend reflects a general decline in family life (Morgan, 2003), whilst others argue that the trend towards smaller families means they have become more, not less, child-centred.

Explanations for the decline in fertility rates that is evident in all developed societies and include:

- Access to contraception, sterilization and abortion (which make family planning easier)
- Increased desire for material goods coupled with the escalating costs of raising children (which act as disincentives for large families)

Table 5.1   Fertility rates by age of mother 1971–2005

	1971	1981	1991	2001	2005
Under 20[1]	50.0	28.4	32.9	27.9	26.2
20–24	154.4	106.6	88.9	68.0	70.5
25–29	154.6	130.9	119.9	91.5	98.3
30–34	79.4	69.4	86.5	88.0	100.7
35–39	34.3	22.4	32.0	41.3	50.0
40 and over	9.2	4.7	5.3	8.6	10.6
Total fertility rate[2]	2.41	1.82	1.82	1.63	1.79
Total births (thousands)[3]	901.6	730.7	792.3	669.1	722.5

[1] Live births per 1,000 women aged 15–19
[2] Number of children that would be born to a woman if current patterns of fertility persisted through her childbearing life. For 1981 onwards, this is based on fertility rates for each five-year age group
[3] Total live births per 1,000 women aged 15–44

Adapted from Self and Zealey (2007)

- The greater participation of women in paid work (which leads women to delay childbearing until careers are established)
- A decline in the infant mortality rate (which means there is less pressure to have lots of children in case one or more dies before reaching adulthood [Waugh, 2000, cited in Haralambos, and Holborn, 2008]).

All these are explanations that add weight to the arguments of Giddens (1992), Beck and Beck-Gernsheim (1995) and Stacey (1996) that families (and family size in particular) has become a lifestyle 'choice'.

However, Porter et al (2006) report that women account for circumstances beyond their control (i.e. experience of the first birth, health, lifestyle, influence of partner, age, fertility problems) rather than free-choice as influencing the decision to limit their fertility. Porter et al (2006) acknowledge that the women in their study may have presented their choices in this way to make their actions appear more socially acceptable and their motivation as blameless. Yet other research also suggests a discrepancy between the numbers of children Britons want and the number they actually have. According to Dixon and Margo (2006) there exists a 'baby gap' of more than 90,000 babies a year, one major reason for which is that people are not able to reconcile work and family life.

Having highlighted the significant trend towards declining fertility observed in recent years, you will notice in *Table 5.1* that in 2005 the fertility rate in the UK had actually increased. This is attributable to changing patterns of immigration. Although less significant to the overall fertility rate you will also notice the increasing numbers of women who are having children over the age of 30. The fertility rate amongst women aged 30–34 is increasing (exceeding that of 25–29 year old's for the first time in 2004). Moreover, rates of conception amongst women aged 40 and over are increasing.

Studies suggest that pregnancies in women older than 35 years are increasing markedly in many Western countries (Botting and Dunnell, 2003). In the UK in 2005/6 there were 11.4 live births per thousand women aged between 40–44, a figure that has more than doubled since 1986 (ONS, 2007). There have always been women who have delivered healthy children in their forties, however, what is changing is the number of women delivering their first baby in their forties. In addition to the previously listed explanations for the decline in fertility rates, suggested reasons for women 'delaying' childbearing include idealized notions of establishing a career, achieving financial security and finding 'the right' partner. The medical disadvantages of childbearing after the age of 35 are well documented; not only is it harder for older women to become and stay pregnant, but outcomes for the mother and child are poorer (Bewley et al, 2005). Moreover, the inevitable diminished fitness, illness and bereavement associated with late motherhood pose real social, as well as medical concerns. Evidence of the advantages of late motherhood is sparse but includes modest improvements in school attainment amongst the children of older mothers and the advantages of maturer parenting (Kalmijn and Kraykaamp, 2005).

The 'epidemic of pregnancy in middle age' is generating increased societal attention (Lavender and Bedwell, 2006). The culture of individualism blames women for delaying childbirth, holding them responsible for adverse outcomes and reduced family size. However, as evident in Margo and Dixon (2006) society does little to support families and it is women who still bear full domestic burdens, as well as work and financial responsibilities (Benn, 1998; Vincent et al, 2004; Gatrell, 2005). In late modernity a woman may reflexively ask: 'When is the best time to have children?'.

For most young women the onset of regular menstruation (menarche) marks the time when they can biologically reproduce. However, it is the norms of individual societies that dictate when it is socially acceptable to do so. Norms concerning fertility and the timing of parenthood vary both historically and culturally. In many Western societies teenage pregnancy (in particular pregnancies occurring in a woman under 18 years of age) is constructed as a social problem. Murcott (1980) argues that whilst teenage pregnancy may entail an illegitimate pregnancy, questions of legitimacy have as much to do with the allowability of the conception in the first place, as to do with the marital status of the mother. This is because teenage pregnancy is located at the intersection of ideologies of reproduction on the one hand and ideologies of childhood on the other. Thus, it is social and moral, not medical concerns, which arguably make teenage pregnancy a national priority that receives attention out of proportion with its incidence (see *Table 5.1*). Whilst the government's *Teenage Pregnancy Strategy* (DH, 1999) aims to halve the under 18s conception rate by 2010, sociological studies with teenage parents suggest that the adverse consequences may be overstated (Phoenix, 1991) and shaped most powerfully by poverty, not the timing of motherhood (Emisch and Pevalin, 2003). Moreover, cross-generational research shows teenage pregnancy can be the start of a strong family unit which benefits from youthful health and energy (Hirst et al, 2006).

Therefore we return to the question of when is the best time to start a family? Is it really something women can choose? The demographic shift towards delaying parenting has given rise to the now ubiquitous discourse of the female biological clock. The biological clock is a powerful metaphor that serves to remind women of the finite period of clock time in which they may biologically reproduce (Martin, 1987). In Western societies the biological clock is stereotypically associated with Caucasian, educated, middle class women, with access to birth control and legal abortion, who have an established career, which has led them to delay first-time parenthood until their mid- to late- thirties (McKaughan, 1987). For women, the biological clock is a uniquely gendered deadline, which gives rise to feelings of guilt amongst those who experience difficulties conceiving or difficult pregnancies and births because 'of their age.' In recent years a number of sociologists have turned their attention to the relationship between time and reproduction (Ettorre, 2004; Friese et al, 2006; Earle and Letherby, 2007). Earle and Letherby (2007) assert that time is integral to the experiences of women who do or do not conceive, with the medicalization of reproductive time enforcing the idea that there are fixed bio-social stages in the life of an individual. Yet, as identified earlier in this chapter the existence of a clear family cycle is now up for debate (Allen and Crow, 2001). Understanding when women conceive (or not) requires consideration of individual and family circumstance as much as any predetermined biological cycle into which women's lives unequivocally fit. Moreover, the development of techniques for assisted conception offers entirely new opportunities for women to gestate and birth babies beyond the confines of the biological clock (Friese et al, 2006).

As identified earlier in the chapter, these techniques (known in sociology and the feminist literature as reproductive technologies) are also contributing to increased family diversity and fundamentally changing kinship relationships (MacIonis and Plummer, 1997). They have far-reaching implications for mothering, motherhood and what is considered natural or normal about contemporary human reproduction. Arguably, nowhere has the ideology of motherhood been used more effectively than in the medicalization of infertility. However, over the course of the last 30 years since the birth of Louise Brown (the first baby to be born as a result of *in vitro* fertilisation (IVF) various feminist perspectives have emerged, not all of which are critical. Thompson (2005) identifies three chronological phases in feminist theorising and research concerning assisted conceptive techniques:

- Phase 1 (between 1984 to 1991) when feminists first began to engage with the new reproductive technologies and many lines of argument were overtly critical. For example, some writers developed themes inherent in second-wave critiques of the medicalization of childbirth, others focused on the (in)equity of infertility treatment (along the lines of gender, class, race, age, able-bodiedness), whilst others concentrated on the ethical issues raised by these technologies.

- The transition phase (between 1992 and 2000) when feminists began to move away from a 'just say no' approach to address the 'paradox of infertility'. For example, feminists began to undertake research addressing how these technologies raised issues for women at a structural level, whilst simultaneously offering real solutions for infertile women at the level of individual agency. It was also during this phase that a resurgence of interest in kinship emerged.

- Phase 2 (between 2000 to present day) which is characterised by a change both in tone and focus. Current feminist writing on assisted conceptive techniques caution against simplistic readings of physicians and scientists (and women), are often undertaken in clinical settings in collaboration with clinicians, and focus on the active role of technology in shaping new and emerging relations of reproduction.

New reproductive technologies now offer exceptional ways of constructing parenthood and families, for example through gamete donation, donor insemination and gestational surrogacy (Hargreaves, 2006). Nevertheless, a study of families with children conceived by donor insemination in New Zealand found that despite the apparent diversity of family forms evident in modern societies today, Western culture *'continues to privilege biological ties, to uphold the "ideal" of the biological nuclear family and conceptualise biological parents as the "real" parents, [thus] the role of the donor in the child's make-up cannot be ignored'* (Hargreaves, 2006: 280). In addition, a study involving women who used assisted conceptive techniques beyond the menopause reports that they worried about the message their success sends to other women for whom delaying childbirth may lead to involuntary childlessness (Friese et al, 2006).

There is an increasing body of feminist writing on women's experiences of maternity and motherhood that fall outside conventional representations of mothering and motherhood. The terminology used to capture these women's experiences is problematic (Letherby, 1994). Nevertheless Throsby (2004) usefully includes in this field studies of those who have chosen to live without children, experience involuntary childlessness, surrogacy, adoption, parenting children with disabilities, pregnancy loss and/or 'bad' mothering.

Midwives encounter these aspects of 'other' and 'non-motherhood' in a variety of forms. For example, midwives who care for women who experience miscarriage or stillbirth, or women whose infants are legally removed from them immediately after birth. Moreover, in an occupation dominated by women, it is to be expected that some midwives will have personal experience of 'other' mothering or non-motherhood. The Office of Population Census and Surveys predicts that 22% of women born between around 1980 will remain childless (ONS, 2003). However, as identified by Porter et al (2006), fewer babies are being born across Europe but more are being born by Caesarean section. This fundamental change in how many babies are born arguably necessitates a reduction in family size. Midwives may wish to consider to what extent smaller families and increased childlessness reflects changes in the nature (and women's perceptions) of birth or what sociologists have identified as a trend towards more 'chosen families'.

Conclusion

This chapter has introduced midwives to sociological perspectives on the family and feminist perspectives on mothering and motherhood. It has highlighted the increasing diversity of family structures in contemporary society and women's greater involvement in paid employment. This chapter has challenged what it means to be a 'mother.' Most midwives see expectant or new mothers every day of their working lives. Moreover, many midwives are privileged to share the actual moment of birth with women regularly. However, it is naïve to view giving birth to a baby as the defining characteristic of what it means to be a mother. This chapter has also identified that science and medicine perhaps present the greatest opportunities and the greatest challenge to what it means to be a mother today.

References

Allan G, Crow G (2001) *Families, Households and Society*. Palgrave, Basingstoke

Baker PL, Carson A (1999) 'I take care of my kids': Mothering practices of substance-abusing women. *Gender & Society* **13**: 347–63

Bailey N, Brown G, Wilson C (2002) 'The baby brigade': Teenage mothers and sexuality. *Journal of the Association for Research on Mothering* **4**(1): 101–10

Barrett M, McIntosh M (1982) *The Anti-social Family*. Verso, London

Bassin D, Honey M, Kaplan M (1994) *Representations of Motherhood*. Yale University press, New Haven, Connecticut

Beck U (1992) *Risk Society: Towards a New Modernity*. Sage, London

Beck U, Beck-Gernsheim E (1995) *The Normal Chaos of Love*. Polity Press, Cambridge

Benn M (1998) *Madonna and Child. Towards a New Politics of Motherhood*. Vintage, London

Berryman JC (1991) Perspectives on later motherhood. In: Phoenix, Woolett A, Lloyd, E, eds. *Motherhood: Meanings, practices and ideologies*. Sage, London: 103–22

Bewley S, Davies M, Braude P (2005) Which career first? The most secure age for childbearing remains 20-35. *British Medical Journal* **331**: 588–9

Botting B, Dunnell K (2003) Trends in fertility and contraception in the last quarter of the 20th century. *National Stat Popul Trends* **100**: 32–9

Boh K (1989) European family life patterns — a reappraisal'. In: Boh K, et al, eds. *Changing Patterns of European Life*. Routledge, London

Bobel C (1992) *The Paradox of Natural Mothering*. Temple University Press, Philadelphia

Boris E (1994) Mothers are not workers: Homework regulation and the construction of motherhood 1948–1953. In: Glenn EN, Chang G, Forcey LN, eds. *Mothering Ideology, Experience, and Agency*. Routledge, New York: 161–79

Buxton J (1998) *Ending the Mother War: Starting the workplace revolution*. Macmillan, London

Chodorow N (1978) *The Reproduction of Mothering: Psychoanalysisand the sociology of gender*. University of California Press, Berkeley

Collins PH (1994) Shifting the center: Race, class, and feminist theorizing about motherhood. In: Glenn EN, Chang G, Forcey LN, eds. *Mothering: Ideology, experience, and agency*. Routledge, New York: 45–64

Chesler R (1985) The rise of the neo-conventional family. *New Society*: 9 May

Crow G, Hardey M (1992) Diversity and ambiguity among lone-parent households in modern Britain.

Marsh C, Arber S, eds. *Families and Households: Divisions and change*. Macmillan, London

Dally A (1982) *Inventing Motherhood: The consequences of an ideal*. Burnett Books, London

Dixon M, Margo J (2006) *Population politics*. IPPR Report: *www.ippr.org.uk/ publicationsandreport*

Duden B (1993) *Disembodying Women: Perspectives on pregnancy and the unborn*. Harvard University Press, Cambridge, Massachusetts

Duncombe J, Marsden D (1995) Women's triple shift: paid employment, domestic labour and emotion work. *Sociology Review* **4**(4)

Earle S, Letherby G (2007) Conceiving Time? Women who do or do not conceive. *Sociology of Health and Illness* **29**(2): 233–50

Ehrenreich B, English D (1978) *For her Own Good: 150 years of the experts' advice to women*. Anchor Books, New York

Emisch J, Pevalin DJ (2003) *Does a 'Teen-Birth' have Longer Impacts on the Mother? Evidence from the 1970 British Cohort Study. ISER Working Papers Number 2003-28*. Colchester Institute for Social and Economic Research, Colchester

Engels F (1972, first published 1884) *The Origin of the Family, Private Property and the State*. Lawrence & Wishart, London

Eyer DE (1996) *Motherguilt: How our Culture Blames Mothers for what's Wrong with Society*. Times Books, New York

Ettorre E (2004) Comparing the practice of reproductive genetics in Greece, UK, Finland and the Netherlands: Constructing 'expert' claims while marketing 'reproductive 'time'. In: Stohr N, ed. *Biotechnology Between Commerce and Civil Society*. Transaction Books, New Jersey

Franklin S, Ragoné H, eds (1998) *Reproducing Reproduction: Kinship, power and technological innovation*. University of Pennsylvania Press, Phildaelphia, Pennsylvania

Friese C, Becker G, Nachtigal R (2006) Rethinking the biological clock: Eleventh-hour moms, miracle moms and meanings of age-related infertility. *Social Science and Medicine* **63**(6): 15550–60

Gatrell C (2005) *Hard Labour: The sociology of parenthood*. Open University Press, Oxford

Gavron H (1966) *The Captive Wife*. Routledge, London

Giddens A (1992) *The Transformation of Intimacy: Sexuality, love and eroticism in modern Societies*. Polity Press, Cambridge

Giddens A (2001) *Sociology*. 4th edn. Polity Press, Cambridge

Gough K (1972) An anthropologist looks at Engels. In: Glzer-Malbin N, Waehrer HY, eds. *Woman in a Man-made World*. Rand McNally, Chicago

Glen EN (1994) Social constructions of mothering. A thematic overview. In: Glen EN, Chang G, Forcey LN, eds. *Mothering: Ideology, experience and agency*. Routledge, New York: 1–29

Haralambos M, Holborn M (2008) *Sociology: Themes and perspectives*. 7th edn. HarperCollins, London

Hargreaves K (2006) Constructing families and kinship through donor insemination. *Sociology of*

Health and Illness **28**(3): 261–83

Hays S (1996) *The Cultural Contradictions of Motherhood*. Yale University Press, New Haven, Connecticut

Hochschild A (1983) *The Managed Heart: Communication of human feeling*. University of California Press, California

Hirst J, Formby E, Owen J (2006) *Pathways into Parenthood: Reflections from three generations of teenage mothers and fathers*. Sheffield Hallam University, Sheffield

Johnston DD, Swanson DH (2003) Invisable mothers: A content analysis of motherhood ideologies and myths in magazines. *Sex Roles* **49**: 21–33

Kalmijn M, Kraykaamp G (2005) Late or later? A sibling analysis of the effect of maternal age on children's schooling. Social Science Research **33**

Keller K (1994) *Mothers and Work in Popular American Magazines*. Greenwood Press, Westpoint, Connecticut

Laslett P (1982) In: Rapoport RN, Fogarty MP, Rapoprt R, eds. *Families in Britian*. Routledge & Keegan Paul, London: xi–xiv

Lasslett,P. (1983) Family and household as workgroup and kingroup. In: Wall, R, Robin J, and Laslett P, eds. *Family Forms in Historic Europe*, Cambridge University Press, Cambridge

Laslett P (1984) The family as a knot of individual interests. In: Netting RM, Wilk RR, and Arnold EJ, eds. *Households*, University of California Press, Berekerly, CA

Lavender T, Bedwell C (2006) Women in their sixties are too old to become mothers: Debate. *British Journal of Midwifery* **14**(9): 514–15

Letherby G (1994) Mother or not, mother or what? Problems of definition and identity. *Women's Studies International Forum* **17**(5): 525–32

Lewin E (1994) Negotiating lesbian motherhood: The dialectics of resistance and accommodation. In: Glenn EN, Chang G, Forcey LN, eds. *Mothering: Ideology, experience, and agency*. Routledge, New York: 333–354

Macionis JJ, Plummer K (1997) *Sociology: A global introduction*. Prentic-Hall, New Jersey

Martin E (1987) *The Woman in the Body*. Beacon Press, Boston

McKaughan M (1987) *The Biological Clock: Balancing marriage, motherhood and career*. Random, London

Millett K (1971) *Sexual Politics*. Sphere, London

Miller T (2007) Is this what motherhood is all about? Weaving experiences and discourse through transition to first-time motherhood. *Gender & Society* **21**(3): 337–58

Murdock GP (1949) *Social Structure*. Macmillian, New York

Murcott A (1980) The social construction of teenage pregnancy: a problem in the ideologies of childhood and reproduction. *Soc Health and Illness* **2**(1): 1–23

Nicolson L (1997) The myth of the traditional family. In: Marsh HL, ed. *Feminism and Families*. Routledge, New York

Oakley A (1974) *Sociology of Housework*. Basil Blackwell, Oxford

Oakley A (1979) *Becoming a Mother*. Harmondsworth Penguin, Oxford

Oakley A (1982) Cypriot families. In: Rapoport RN, Fogarty MP, Rapoport R, eds. *Families in Britain*. Routledge & Keegan Paul, London

Oakley A (2005) *The Ann Oakley Reader: Gender, women and social science*. The Policy Press, London

O'Brien M, Jones D (1996) Revisting family and kinship. *Sociology Review*: February

ONS (2003) *Fertility Assumptions for the 2002-based national population projections (winter)*: www.gad.gov.uk

Rapoport R, Rapoport RN (1982) British families in transition. In: Rapoport RN, Fogarty MP, Rapoport R, eds. *Families in Britian*. Routledge & Keegan Paul, London

Rapoport R (1989) Ideologies about family forms — towards diversity. In: Boh K et al, eds. *Changing Patterns of European Family Life*. Routledge, England

Rich A (1976) *Of Women Born: Motherhood as experience and institution*. Norton, New York

Risman B (1998) *Gender Vertigo: American families in transition*. Yale University Press, New Haven, Connecticut

Roseneil S (2005) Living and loving beyond the boundaries of the heteronorm: personal relationships in the 21st century. In: McKie and Chunningham-Butley, eds. *Families in Societies: Biundaries and relationships*. Policy Press, Bristol

Rothman BK (1994) Beyond mothers and fathers: Ideology in a patriarchal society. In: Glenn EN, Chang G, Forcey LN, eds. *Mothering: Ideology, experience, and agency*. Routledge, New York: 139–60

Parsons T (1959) The social structure of the family. In: Anshen RN, ed. *The Family: Its functions and destiny*. Harper & Row, New York

Phoenix A (1991) *Young Mothers?* Polity Press, Cambridge

Porter M, Bhattacharya S, Teijlingen van E (2006) Unfulfilled expectations: How circumstances impinge on women's reproductive choices. *Social Science and Medicine* **62**(7): 1757–67

Self A, Zealey L (2007) Fertility rates by age of mother at childbirth 1971–2005. *Social Trends* **37**

Sharpe S (1976) *Just like a Girl: How girls learn to be women*. Penguin, Harmondsworth

Silva EB, Smart C (1999) The 'new' practices and policies of family life. In: Silva and Smart, eds. *The New Family?* Sage, London

Stacey J (1996) *In the Name of the Family: Rethinking family values in the postmodern age*. Beacon Press, Boston. Massachusetts

Teenage Pregnancy Strategy (1999) *Teenage Strategy Practice*. Every Child Matters, London

Thompson C (2005) *Making Parents: The ontological choreography of reproductive technologies*. The MIT Press, Cambridge, Massachusetts

Throsby K (2004) *When IVF Fails: Feminism, infertility and the negotiation of normality*. Palgrave Macmillan, Basingstoke

Vincent C, Ball SJ, Pietikainen S (2004) Metropolitan mothers: Mothers, mothering and paid work. *Women's Studies International Forum* **27**: 571–87

Walkerdine V, Lucey H, Meldoy J (2001) *Growing up Like a Airl: Psychosocial explanations of gender and class*. Pagrave, Basingstoke

Weeks J, Donovan C, Heaphey B (1999) Everyday experiments: narratives of non-heterosexual relationships. In: Silva and Smart, eds. *The New family?* Sage, London

Willmott P (1963) *The Evolution of a Community: A study of Dagenham after forty years*. Routledge & Kegan Paul, London

Witz A (1992) *Professions and Patriarchy*. Routledge, London

Young M, Willmott P (1973) *Family and Kinship in East London*. Penguin, Harmondsworth

Zaretsky E (1976) *Capitalism, the Family and Personal Life*. Pluto Press, London

Zimmerman TS, Holm KE, Haddock SA (2001). A decade of advice for women and men in the best-selling self-help literature. *Family Relations* **50**: 122–33

CHAPTER 6

The maternal body

The purpose of this chapter is to introduce midwives to the ways in which our bodies are shaped by social influences. In recent years academic interest in the body has increased and the sociology of the body has emerged as a prominent sub-field within mainstream sociology. Davies (1997) identifies three explanations for current interest in 'the body'. First, she identifies authors who assert that the body has become a reflection of culture at large in late modernity (Turner, 1984; Featherstone, 1983). In other words, in contemporary societies where industrial capitalism is in decline and consumer culture dominates (i.e. late or high modernity) the meanings surrounding the body have changed. The body is no longer a given, it is malleable and central to an individual's identity (Giddens, 1991). The most obvious example of the centrality of the body in modern society is evident in popular interest in the shape, health and beauty of bodies and the burgeoning demand for cosmetic surgery.

The second explanation for current sociological interest in the body is that it is a theoretical development associated with the rise of post-modernism. This explanation owes a debt to Michael Foucault, who first identified the body as a site for the operation of modern forms of power, especially that of medicine (Foucault, 1976, 1977, 1978). Moreover, Frank (1990, 1991) has identified that the contradictions between modernist certainty and postmodernist uncertainty are particularly well illustrated when attention is turned to the body. In other words, for modernist theory the body is a constant, a hard fact, whereas for postmodernist theory cultural variations in bodies and bodily practices make the body an ideal starting point for challenging the universality of modernist theory.

According to Davies (1997) the third explanation for the emergence of sociological interest in the body is the influence of feminism(s). Davies (1997) states:

> '...whilst many of the "new", male body theorists seem somewhat reluctant to draw upon feminist scholarship on the body, they generally acknowledge the influence of feminism as a political movement on the emergence of the body as a topic'.

> Davies (1997: 4)

The body has been an omnipresent theme in feminist activism, theory and research for over a century. Consequently, this chapter draws heavily from feminist writings on the body and the maternal body in particular, where questions of reproduction, embodiment and gendered identify intersect. The chapter begins by outlining key perspectives on what the body is, drawing from the natural sciences and the emerging field of the sociology of the body. The focus then shifts to an overview of feminist perspectives on the body, before focusing specifically on the maternal body.

Defining the body

In the natural sciences, the body may be defined in terms of its anatomy and physiology. In medicine in particular, the body is viewed as the physical manifestation of corporeal existence that defines health, disease and illness. In midwifery too there is sometimes an emphasis on the body as biology and somewhat distinct from 'the woman'. For example, many student midwives are taught that the uterus is an involuntary muscle, whilst in practice they learn that a woman's uterine contractions respond to psychological or environmental stressors. Thinking about the anatomy and physiology of 'the body' as in some way distinct from 'the person' originates from the Enlightenment period and the mind/body dualism, otherwise known as the **Cartesian dualism** (or dichotomy).

In the seventeenth century, the French philosopher René Descartes was one of the key figures who founded modern science. Descartes established the assumption that humans comprise two separate entities, body and mind, linked during life but profoundly different. Descartes famously stated: '*I think, therefore, I am*', and taught that the body works like a machine (as introduced in chapter 3), whose structure and operations fall within the province of human knowledge. The Cartesian dualism provided the environment for the emergence of modern biomedical sciences, with successive generations of scientists focusing their efforts on explaining the functioning of the material (or corporeal) body, neglecting questions of the mind and, most significantly, the interconnectedness of the two. Today, whilst both medicine and midwifery champion consideration of the 'whole' person (mind and body) and their social environment, it is important to acknowledge the extent to which the legacy of Descartes mind/body dualism remains in shaping everyday attitudes and beliefs about the body.

The natural sciences' way of thinking about the body is also known as 'naturalistic', where the body is viewed as outside of society — a pre-social, biological basis of social relationships and inequalities. However in sociology the naturalistic view has been widely criticised as biological reductionism (a variant of such arguments is the feminist critique of biological determinism introduced in chapter five). Most sociologists, including feminist sociologists, recognise that the body is the site where gender, race and disability are physically and psychologically omnipresent. Consequently, a more sociological way of thinking about the body is to view the body as a corporeal entity fundamental to an individual's identity where adherence to social norms or the impact of social inequalities are played out.

Sociological perspectives and the body

According to some sociologists (Turner, 1992) classical sociology (as defined in chapter one) adopted a 'disembodied' approach influenced profoundly by the Cartesian dichotomy, which meant it focused exclusively on the mind as that which defines human beings. Shilling (1993) however, suggests that it may be more accurate to describe classical sociology as displaying a dual approach to the body, whereby it had something of an 'absent presence'. What he means by this is that whilst classical sociology rarely focused on the body as an area of investigation in its own right, its concerns with the structure and functioning of societies and nature of human action inevitably led them to deal with aspects of human embodiment.

Elias (1978, first published 1939) was the first male sociologist to take the body as an explicit focus in his book *The Civilising Process*. Elias (1978) developed the concept of the 'civilised body' as the product of three key social processes:

• Socialization
• Rationalization
• Individualization.

It was Elias (1978) who first documented how in developed societies people are encouraged to hide their natural bodily functions through the process of socialization, people are supposed to be able to control their feelings through the process of rationalization, and people learn to maintain an acceptable distance from each others bodies through individualization.

Other notable works by sociologists who have focused on the body and how it has come to assume such an important place in modern societies include Goffman's (1963) work on stigma, Bourdieu's (1984) work on the body as a form of physical capital, and the collective works of Foucault (1976, 1977, 1978). An accessible synopsis of Foucault's contribution to contemporary sociological thought and the body is provided by Nettleton (1995).

Nettleton (1995) identifies that a central theme across Foucault's work is that, as part of the transition from pre-modern to modern societies, there was a shift from sovereign power (residing in the body of the monarch) to **disciplinary power** (invested in the bodies of the wider population). Foucault's concept of disciplinary power relates to the way post-industrialization and post-Enlightenment (across Europe since the eighteenth and nineteenth centuries) bodies have increasingly become regulated, trained, maintained and understood, with disciplinary power particularly evident in social institutions such as schools, prisons and hospitals. Moreover, within such institutions knowledge of bodies is produced. For example, the observation of bodies in hospitals contributed to the knowledge base of medical science — a process Foucault refers to as power/ knowledge. According to Nettleton (1995) Foucault's concept of disciplinary power works on two levels: that of the individual and that of the population. In the first, individual bodies are trained and observed, whilst in the second (and concurrently) whole populations of bodies are monitored. Building on the concept of disciplinary power, Foucault developed his notions of 'the gaze' and 'surveillance', which we will return to later in the chapter when discussing the use of ultrasound technology in antenatal care. For now it is suffice to say that Foucault's interest in the body as a theoretical concern was seminal and has been particularly influential in some variants of feminism, as well as the sociology of the body that was to emerge later.

Foucault's writings on the body have been aligned with a particular variant of social constructionist thought and the body; a conception in which the body and disease are viewed as constructed by the discourses that describe them (i.e. the medical gaze). Other variants of social constructionist thought and the body include perspectives that recognize its material (corporeal) base but assert that this is shaped and altered by social practices and social context. For example, as women's diets have improved the height differential between men and women is no longer so marked.

It was during the 1990s that there was a proliferation of academic interest in the body and the sociology of the body first became known as a distinct field. Key texts associated with this period include Featherstone et al's (1991) *The Body: Social Process and Cultural Theory*, Turner's (1992) *Regulating bodies: Essays in Medical Sociology*, and Shilling's (1993) *The Body and Social Theory*.

Earlier chapters in this book have introduced the notion that within sociology there is a general consensus that we are amidst a period of fundamental social change. This social change has been conceptualised at one level as post-modernity or late/high modernity, and at another as post-Fordist (chapter three).

Turner (1992) introduces another term to conceptualise the current period: the **somatic society**. According to Turner (1992) the somatic society is a social system in which the body is central. In particular, Turner (1992) highlights the regulation of bodies as key. In an approach that draws from the earlier writing of Foucault, Turner examines the ways in which bodies are controlled in the somatic society, particularly by medicine, which he asserts serves a moral as well as a clinical function.

Both Turner (1992) and Shilling (1993) argue for a foundationalist view of the body where it is both: '*...concurrently socially constructed and organically founded*' (Turner, 1992: 17). In other words, there is a need to regard the body as a material, physical and biological phenomenon and acknowledge that our senses, knowledgeability and capability to act are integrally related to the fact that we are embodied beings. Thus, human bodies are taken up and transformed as a result of living in society, but they remain material, physical and biological entities. According to Shilling (1993) the body is best conceptualised as an unfinished biological and social phenomenon. From this starting point Shilling develops the notion of the *body as a project*, which is worked at and accomplished as part of an individual's self-identity and through their participation in society. The body as a project rests on the dual assumptions that the technological knowledge and ability to intervene and substantially alter the body exists, and people are aware of the body as an unfinished entity that is shaped partly as the result of lifestyle choices (Nettleton, 1995).

Chapter five also introduced Anthony Giddens' (1992) work on intimacy and the changing nature of personal relationships, which built on his notion of the reflective self that he first outlined in '*Modernity and Self-identity*' (Giddens, 1991). Central to his concept of the reflectively mobilised self is a view of the body in which people view their bodies from the outside and see them as things that can be altered and shaped according to fashion. Giddens argues that in high modernity (his term for late capitalist, industrialized societies): '...*the body is increasingly malleable — we become responsible for the design of our own bodies*' (Gidden's 1991: 102). Thus, in contemporary societies the body is increasingly a phenomenon of options and choices. However, we are also living in an age that has thrown into radical doubt our knowledge of what bodies are and how we should control them (Shilling, 1993).

Shilling (1993) identifies that the more that we as humans have been able to control and alter the limits of the body, the greater has been our uncertainty about what constitutes an individual's body, and what is natural about a body. Drawing on the examples of in vitro fertilisation (IVF) (which has enabled reproduction to be separated from the corporeal relations which have traditionally defined heterosexual experience) and heart surgery, Shilling (1993) demonstrates how the boundaries between bodies and the boundaries between bodies and technology are eroding what is natural. We will return to a similar line of argument in the context of IVF and related technologies later in the chapter so for now consider the example of heart surgery. Until very recently, humans were born and died with the same heart. Today this key organ in the human body may be modified by fitting a pacemaker (collapsing the boundary between medical technology and the body) or replaced in a heart transplant (collapsing the boundaries between bodies).

So far, this chapter has briefly introduced the emerging field of the sociology of the body. A field that demonstrates how twenty-first century bodies are located in age, gender, race, ethnic, able bodied and class ranked positions, while shaped simultaneously by the commodification of health, leisure, attractiveness, style and risk. Also it is a field that challenges the very foundations of what is natural (or not) about twenty first century bodies, which are reconstituted by medicine, science and technology. However, as previously identified such issues have long been at the heart of feminist scholarship.

Feminist perspectives and the body

There are many approaches to the body in feminist activism, theory and research, which are unified only by the theme that the body matters. On the one hand, the body has figured as a source of women's oppression, whilst on the other, it has been celebrated as the locus of a specifically female power (Andermahr et al, 2000). In addition, there are feminist approaches to the body (particularly those associated with post-modernism) that posit a textual corporeality that is fluid in its investments and meanings (Butler, 1993). It is worth pointing out that not only is the feminist literature on the body varied, it is also vast, therefore this chapter can only provide the most cursory of introductions for midwives (Price and Shildrick, 1999 provide a useful reader for midwives interested in knowing more).

As identified by Schiebinger (2000) early feminist scholarship on the body exposed the:

> '...privileged first born twins of modern science: the myth of the natural body and the myth of value-neutral knowledge.'
>
> *Schiebinger (2000: 4)*

In other words, from the late seventeenth century onwards feminists have simultaneously shown that what we think of as the natural body is constructed (not found) by science, and that science is guided by social priorities and cultural ideals that serve to subordinate not only women's biology in relation to men's, but also women in society. Feminists have shown how the biological body is represented as the 'natural' source of patriarchy, diverting attention away from socially constructed differences in gender roles. Arguably, no single author demonstrates the way in which cultural assumptions underlie contemporary perceptions of the body better than the collective works of the feminist anthropologist Emily Martin. These include *The Woman in the Body* (Martin, 1987) which highlights how metaphors of production shape sciences representation of childbirth (as described in chapter three), and *The Egg and the Sperm* (Martin, 1991) which demonstrates how male and female reproductive physiology is constructed according to prevailing gender roles. Martin (1991) argues that positive images are denied to the bodies of women through the application of gendered stereotypes in medical descriptions of reproduction. For example, the 'feminine' egg is represented as large and passive, whilst the 'masculine' sperm is streamlined, strong and active. According to Martin (1991) such representations not only reproduce patriarchal stereotypes but they also make them seem 'natural'. For Martin, an alternative (although not unproblematic) procreation story would be more egalitarian and use metaphors that characterise fertilisation as an interaction (rather than the sperm saving the egg from perishing).

Thus at one level feminist scholarship on the body replaces the argument that the inequalities between the sexes are derivative of nature and fixed in biology, with the argument that they are derivative of nurture and maintained by culture. Moreover, the distinction between nature and nurture has been further refined to identify how culture can shape and alter the physical body. For example, Bordo's (1993) study of thinness shows how culture inscribes itself on the bodily form, which is an issue that we will return to when considering the 'nature' of pregnant embodiment. However, at another level there has long been an appreciation of real sexual difference. In other words, irrespective of science's (mis)representations of the human female body as defective or subordinate to the males, women are, nevertheless, bodies in a way that men are not — they are in general, able to menstruate, develop another body within their own, give birth, and lactate.

How the female reproductive body is 'managed' at the level of society and the individual have long been concerns for feminist sociologists. Sandall (2005) identifies that the sub-field of the sociology of human reproduction (which is dominated by feminist work) initially focused on conception, pregnancy, birth and motherhood (as evident in the research agenda set out by MacIntyre [1977] and discussed in chapter one). At that time the two key concerns were the medicalization of childbirth, and drawing attention to the competing ideologies of childbirth (the medical model, natural childbirth, popular/lay ideas).

Oakley (1979; 1980), Kitzinger (1975; 1982), Graham (1977) and Cartwright (1979) were just some of the many feminist authors whose empirical studies demonstrate how overtly medicalized the British maternity care system of the 1970s was. For example, of the 66 women interviewed in Oakley's (1979) study of the transition to first-time motherhood 41% had induction or acceleration of their labour, 59% had their membranes artificially ruptured, 79% had epidurals, 98% had episiotomies, and 52% had forceps or ventouse deliveries.

Almost all of the second wave feminist literature on pregnancy and childbirth took a critical stance (Firestone, 1970, who was optimistic about the increased use of technology is a notable exception). On the one hand these authors acknowledge that there was no 'golden age' of childbirth, but on the other hand they argue that the increasingly routine use of obstetrics interventions, many of which had not been carefully evaluated at that time, were unnecessary, disliked by, and damaging to women. It was also as part of this 'medicalization of childbirth' literature that some feminists first began to chart the expropriation of women's tradition skills for managing childbirth by 'medical experts' (Donnison, 1977; Ehrenreich and English, 1978; Oakley, 1984;). This important strand of feminism drew attention to the ways in which women's reproductive bodies have long been regulated by the male-dominated medical profession, which in turn identified the body as a central focus for practical concerns that led to a more positive theorization. For example in the US the Boston Women's Health Book Collective's (1973) *Our bodies, Ourselves* encouraged women to regain control over their own bodies through greater access to knowledge; in the UK alliances between feminists and consumer groups forced the medicalization debate into the public arena. Rich's (1978) *Of Woman Born* theorized the uniquely female capacity to give birth as something to be celebrated and jealously guarded.

However, the medicalization of childbirth debates also gave rise to an alternative position that recognised how some women had gained from the process (Riessman, 1983). There was a shift from a 'cultural dope/just say no' approach advocated by some feminists to one that increasingly recognised women's agency and difference. Around the same time (early 1980s) the sociology of human reproduction widened its scope to encompass the new and emerging reproductive technologies. By the end of the 1980s a variety of feminist authors offered appraisals of women's interactions that appreciated their engagement with reproductive technologies. In 1987, the sociologist Michelle Stanworth edited a collection of papers by a variety of authors who shared concerns about the inadequacy of either an uncritical position that defers without question to the advances of science, or a pessimistic position that sees in contemporary reproductive technologies an unmitigated attack on women.

In feminist writing on reproduction, 'the maternal body' is a turn of phrase that is used in multiple ways with a variety of meanings. It is significant for feminist writers as diverse as Firestone (1970), Irigaray (1991), Chodorow (1978), Rich (1978) and Kristeva (1986) who have conceptualised the actual and potential variation of the relation between mother and child. It is not surprising therefore that contemporary technologies have stimulated new considerations for feminism and the body. What is at stake, as we shall see, is no longer simply the maternal body as such, but questions of what constitutes human beings, human individuals and human corporeality in general.

Reproductive technologies and the body

Stanworth (1987) defines four categories of reproductive technologies:

1. **Fertility control** which prevent conception, the implantation of an embryo, or terminate a pregnancy, most of which have been around for centuries (with the exception of the oral contraceptive pill)
2. **Management of labour and childbirth** which includes pain relief in labour, forceps and Caesarean sections
3. **Obstetric services in the antenatal period** which includes amniocentesis and other diagnostic, screening, scanning technologies that were a focus of development at the time
4. **Conceptive technologies** which are concerned with overcoming or bypassing infertility and they include in vitro fertilisation (IVF), which today provides a platform for a whole host of other new reproductive technologies (cloning, gestational surrogacy and other assisted fertility techniques, prenatal screening and diagnosis).

Sandall (2005) identifies that these **new reproductive technologies** (NRTs) are derived from a scientific approach to reproduction from which older technologies were also derived to 'manage' pregnancy and childbirth. Moreover, almost all of these technologies (old and new) centre on the bodies of women. Whilst in the field of childbirth this may seem obvious, in the arena of contraceptive and assisted conception technologies arguably more could take the male body as their focus. The complex reasons as to why this is not the case say much about women's position in society. Moreover, the consequences for women extend way beyond the routine application of such technologies in everyday medical practice.

First, we will consider the purported 'disappearance' of the maternal body. At one level, feminists draw attention to the use of terms such a 'artificial insemination' and 'test-tube baby' which deny the role of women's bodies in conceiving, gestating and giving birth to the babies 'created' by IVF and its associated technologies (Stanworth, 1987; Franklin, 1997). At another level feminists claim that the maternal body is rendered invisible in the increased use of visualising technologies during pregnancy, which range from endoscopes to ultrasound. Duden (1993) suggests that Lennart Nilsson's iconic photographic image of an 18-week old fetus that first appeared on the cover of *Life* magazine in 1965 has become part of the mental equipment of our time. In other words, we can no longer talk about pregnancy without visualising the life before birth that this image (and subsequent images of fetuses and embryos) conveys. These images serve to provide the unborn with an independent bodily presence even though they are totally dependent upon the body of the mother.

Historically, the status of personhood has only been attributed to infants after birth, whereas today many feminist analyses use the term **foetal-personhood** to conceptualise the personal and a public presence of the fetus in contemporary cultures (Petchesky, 1987; Gallagher, 1985 cited in Franklin, 1991). The notion of foetal-personhood has been used most extensively in the context of abortion politics, where an oppositional status between the interests of the woman and the interests of the fetus exists (Mitchell, 2001). Recently, however, there has been a move to explore the other ways in which the meanings and significance of the fetus are socially constructed more widely (Casper, 1998; Williams, 2005). For example, studies show that many pregnant women now expect to 'meet their baby' on the ultrasound screen (Mitchell and George, 1998). Nevertheless, it must be remembered that ultrasound grants access to the interior of a woman's body in a way that no other commonly used technology can. Whilst the benefits for individual women for whom this technology confirms everything is okay are apparent, the consequences for women for whom it does not are problematic (Rothman, 1986), and the routine use of such technologies for women as a social group are arguably less benevolent. The real-time visual and aural presence ultrasound conveys reinforces the fetus as independent with human needs that compete and often override those of the mother as the central concern during pregnancy. Moreover, women's embodied knowledge (e.g. date of conception, 'quickening') is increasingly discredited (Haraway, 1997). Thus whilst ultrasound currently holds a dual purpose with the simultaneous construction of 'the patient' and 'our baby' (Draper, 2002) it is first and foremost a tool for medical surveillance, which epitomizes the power of the medical **gaze** in contemporary society.

There are a number of feminist studies that focus specifically on the use of antenatal ultrasound as part of antenatal screening or diagnostic testing. These include a seminal study of amniocentesis in the US by Rayna Rapp (2000), as well as studies from the UK (Williams et al, 2005; Heyman et al, 2006). Williams et al (2005) report that the part played by the ultrasound scan in first trimester screening, particularly in relation to the higher-quality images now being obtained, has the potential to introduce new and novel ethical dilemmas for pregnant women. There is also a growing body of feminist work on the 'the new genetics', the term which refers to emerging knowledge and techniques following the invention of technology for identifying and manipulating DNA (Rothman, 1998; Ettorre, 2002; Webster, 2002). As identified by Ettorre (2002) the meeting point between surveillance medicine and the new genetics is a focus on the body, and that body is more often than not the pregnant female body, a point illustrated most poignantly in Franklin and Roberts's (2006) detailed ethnographic study of pre-implantation genetic diagnosis.

As alluded to earlier in this chapter there is a need to consider how reproductive technologies erode distinctions between what is natural and what is not about contemporary maternal bodies. At one level, the presence of such technologies is altering perceived notions of the boundaries between social and physical bodies. For example, the fact that women taking the contraceptive pill menstruate precisely every 28 days is representative of a social body shaped by technology (Oudshoorn, 1994). At another level, and perhaps most significantly for midwives, the assisted conception techniques associated with the new reproductive technologies are eroding distinctions between maternal bodies to such an extent they raise the question of who is the natural mother? A statutory distinction is now made between the biological mother (otherwise known as the genetic mother who provides the egg), the surrogate mother (otherwise known as the gestational mother who experiences pregnancy) and the social mother. However, as identified by Franklin (1997) the use of these technologies:

'...does not mean that reproduction is no longer seen as "natural": to the contrary, new forms of reproductive technology are ubiquitously re-naturalised'.

Franklin (1997: 10)

In other words, technology is seen as giving nature a helping hand and, in doing so, in various ways becomes perceived as part of nature. Thus the role of women's agency in debates about reproductive technologies must equally attend to consideration of how their bodies are used, altered and change as a result of their engagement.

The 'normative' maternal body

Feminist approaches to the body show us that there have always been bodies that fail to conform to normative standards (Dregar, 2000). These bodies include those of indeterminate sex, those which experience reproductive problems (i.e. infertility, miscarriage), are racially diverse, marked by social inequality, or different due to disability or disfigurement.

Many feminists, bioethicists, and disability rights activists report fears that the growing acceptance of prenatal diagnosis will lead to more intolerance of the disabled and the heightened stigma of families with disabled children (Kaplan, 1993). They assert that the increasingly routine offer of prenatal diagnostic screening implies that women should consider the possibility of disability for the fetus they are carrying, whilst at the same time clearly reinforcing support for the selective abortion of fetuses diagnosed with many types of disabilities. One study reports that 75% of consultant obstetricians interviewed said that they would only offer amniocentesis to women who agreed to terminate if an abnormality was found (Farant, 1985). This is a discourse that is not only problematic for families with disabled children, but raises complex issues concerning the nature of embodiment when women with disabilities are pregnant or desire a family themselves.

There has always been interest in the pregnant form (medical, personal and pornographic), but today pregnancy is a condition of hyper-visibility that was unimaginable less than 20 years ago. Images of the pregnant embodiment of women have become commonplace in western societies since Annie Leibovitz's photograph of the actress Demi Moore on the cover of *Vanity Fair* magazine provided a catalyst for a new visibility of pregnant women across a range of different cultural media (Tyler, 2001). It has been argued that this taboo breaking photograph:

> '...re-envelopes the foetus within the pregnant body and thus presents the opportunity to reject the mother/child dichotomy that monopolises discourses around reproduction'.
>
> *Tyler (2001: 81)*

However, it is a particular conception of the normative pregnant maternal body that prevails.

The new visibility of pregnant embodiment couples both the old ideology of motherhood (white, middle class, heterosexual) with new mothering discourse (combining intensive mothering with a career) as introduced in chapter five, whilst at the same time positing a new ideology of pregnant beauty. As highlighted earlier in the chapter culture can inscribe itself on the bodily form

(Bordo, 1993) and according to some feminist commentators this is increasingly becoming evident in the changing 'nature' of pregnant embodiment. According to Tyler (2005) a 'fit pregnancy genre' is emerging. This is evident in distinct pregnancy diets, keep-fit programmes, fertility control, fashion, and healthcare access (i.e. women requesting planned Caesarean sections and tummy tucks at 37 weeks before their bump gets too big), practices which are transforming pregnant embodiment.

Conclusion

This chapter has introduced midwives to sociological perspectives on the body and feminist perspectives on the maternal body in particular. It has highlighted that the current resurgence of sociological interest in the body owes much to the influence of feminism and post-modernism, which both consider the body as much shaped by its cultural context as a biological fact. On the one hand, this chapter has identified the need for theories of embodiment to take into account not simply sexual difference, but racial and class differences and differences due to disability; in short the specific contextual materiality of the body. On the other hand, this chapter has shown how individual agency means the body is increasingly an unfinished project; never fixed. Finally, this chapter has also served to highlight the centrality of images of the body in our culture; in particular it has drawn attention to importance of visual images of fetuses and pregnant embodiment in contemporary culture, which can be traced back to two iconic magazine covers (Life Magazine 1965 and Vanity Fair 1991). The next chapter considers the role of the media in society.

References

Andermahr S, Lovell T, Wolkowitz C (2000) *A Glossary of Feminist Theory*. Oxford University Press, New York

Bourdieu P (1984) *Distinction: A social critique of the judgement of taste*. Routledge, Kegen and Paul, London

Bordo S (1993) *Unbearable Weight: Feminism, western culture and the body*. University of California Press, Berkeley

Boston Women's Health Collective (1973) *Our bodies, Ourselves*. Boston Women's Health Collective, Boston

Butler J (1993) *Bodies that Matter*. Routledge, New York

Cartwright A (1979) *The Dignity of Labour? A study of childbearing and induction*. Tavistock, London

Casper M (1998) *The Making of the Unborn Patient*. Rutgers Press, New Brunswick

Chodorow N (1978) *The Reproduction of Mothering*. University of California Press, Berkeley

Davies K, ed (1997) *Embodied Practice: Feminist perspectives on the body*. Sage publications, London.

Donnison J (1977) *Midwives and Medical Men: A history of interprofessional rivalries and women's rights*. Heinemann, London

Draper J (2002) It was a real good show: the ultrasound scan, fathers and the power of visual knowledge. *Sociology of Health and Illness* **24**(6): 771–95

Dregar AD (2000) Doubtful sex. In: Schiebinger L, ed. *Feminism and the Body*. Oxford University Press, Oxford: 118–51

Duden B (1993) *Disembodying Women: Perspectives on pregnancy and the unborn*. Harvard University Press, Cambridge

Ehrenreich B, English D (1978) *For Her Own Good*. Anchor Books, London

Elias N (1978 first published 1939) *The Civilising Process. Volume 1: The history of manners*. Basil Blackwell, Oxford

Ettorree E (2002) *Reproductive Genetics, Gender and the Body*. London. Routledge, London

Farant W (1985) Who's for amniocentesis? The politics of prenatal testing. In: Homans H, ed. *The Sexual Politics of Reproduction*. Gower, London: 96–122

Featherstone M (1983) The body in consumer culture. *Theory, Culture & Society* **1**(2): 18–33

Firestone S (1970) *The Dialectic of Sex*. Jonathan Cape, London

Franklin S (1991) Fetal fascinations: new dimensions to the medical-scientific construction of fetal personhood. In: Franklin S, Lury C, Stacey J, eds. *Off-centre: Feminism and cultural Studies*. Harper Collins, London: 190-206

Franklin S (1997) *Embodied Progress: A cultural account of assisted conception*. Routledge, London

Franklin S, Roberts C (2006) *Born and Made: An ethnography of pre-implantation genetic diagnosis*. Princeton University Press, Massachussets

Foucault M (1976) *The Birth of the Clinic*. Tavistock Publications, London

Foucault M (1977) *Discipline and Punish: The birth of the prison*. Allen Lane, London

Foucault M (1978) *The History of Sexuality. Volume 1*. Pantheon, New York, Pantheon

Frank A (1990) Bringing bodies back in: A decade review. *Theory, Culture & Society* **7**: 131–62

Frank A (1991) For a sociology of the body: An analytical review. In: Featherstone M, Hepworth M, Turner BS, eds. *The Body. Social Process and Cultural Theory*. Sage, London: 36–102

Featherstone M (1983) The body in consumer culture. *Theory, Culture & Society* **1**(2): 18–33

Goffman E (1963) *Stigma: Notes on the management of spoiled identity*. Doubleday Anchor, New York

Giddens A (1991) *Modernity and Self-identity. Self and Society in the Late Modern Age*. Polity Press, Cambridge

Gidden A (1992) *The Transformation of Intimacy: Sexuality, love and eroticism in modern societies*. Polity Press, Cambridge

Graham H (1977) Images of pregnancy in antenatal literature. In: Dingwall R, Heath C, Reid M et al, eds. *Healthcare and Health Knowledge*. Croom Helm, London

Haraway D (1997) *Modest Witness Second Millennium. Female Man Meets Oncomouse: Feminism and Technoscience*. Routledge, London

Heyman B, Lewando-Hundt G, Sandall J, Spencer K, Williams C, Grellier R, Pitson L (2006) On being at higher risk: A qualitative study of prenatal screening for chromosomal anomalies. *Social Science and Medicine* **62**: 2360–2372

Kaplan D (1993) Prenatal screening and its impact on persons with disabilities. *Fetal Diagnosis and Therapy* **8**(supp 1): 64–9

Kitzinger S (1975) *Some Mothers' Experiences of Induced Labour*. National Childbirth Trust, London

Kitzinger S (1982) *Some Women's Experiences of Episiotomy*. National Childbirth Trust, London

Kristeva J (1986) *The Kristeva Reader*. Blackwell, Oxford

Irigaray L (1991) *The Irigaray Reader*. Blackwell, Oxford

Macintyre S (1977) The management of childbirth: a review of sociological research issues. *Social Science and Medicine* **11**: 447–84

Martin E (1987) *The Woman in the Body*. Beacon Press, Boston

Martin E (1991) The egg and the sperm: How science has constructed a romance based on stereotypical male-female roles. *Signs: Journal of Women in Culture and Society* **16**(31): 485–501

Mitchell L (2001) *Baby's First Picture: Ultrasound and the politics of fetal subjects*. University of Toronto Press, Toronto

Mitchell L, George E (1998) Baby's first picture: the cyborg fetus of ultrasound imaging. In: Davis-Floyd R, Dumit J, eds. Cyborg Babies: from techno-sex to tectno-tots. Routledge, London: 105–24

Nettleton S (1995) *The Sociology of Health and Illness*. Polity Press, Cambridge

Oakley A (1979) *From Here to Maternity: Becoming a Mother*. Penguin Books, Oxford

Oakley A (1980) *Women Confined: Towards a sociology of childbirth*. Martin Robertson & Co, Oxford

Oakley A (1984) *The Captured Womb: a history of the medical care of pregnant women*. Basil Blackwell, Oxford

Oudshoorn N (1994) *Beyond the Natural Body: An archaeology of sex hormones*. Routledge, London

Petchesky RP (1987) Foetal images: The power of visual culture in the politics of reproduction. In: Stanworth M, ed. *Reproductive Technologies: Gender, motherhood and medicine*. Polity Press, Cambridge: 57–80

Price J, Shildrick M (1999) *Feminist Theory and the Body*. Edinburgh University Press, Edinburgh

Rothman BK (1986) *The Tentative Pregnancy: Amniocentesis and the sexual politics of motherhood*. Viking, New York

Rothman BK (1998) *Genetic Maps and Human Imaginations*. WW Norton, New York

Rapp R (2000) *Testing the Woman, Testing the Fetus: The social impact of amniocentesis in America*. Routledge, London

Rich A (1978) *Of Woman Born: Motherhood as experience and institution*. WW Norton, New York

Riessman CK (1983) Women and medicalization: A new perspective. *Social Policy* **Summer**: 3–17

Sandall J (2005) Reproduction. In: Gabe J, Bury M, Elston M, eds. *Key Concepts in Medical Sociology*. Sage, London: 140-145

Schiebinger L, ed (2000) *Feminism and the Body*. Oxford University Press, Oxford

Shilling C (1993) *The Body and Social Theory*. Sage, London

Stanworth M (1987) *Reproductive Technologies: Gender, motherhood and medicine*. Cambridge, Polity Press

Turner BS (1984) *The Body and Society*. Basil Blackwell, Oxford

Turner BS (1992) *Regulating Bodies: Essays in medical sociology*. Routledge, London

Tyler I (2001) Skin-tight: Celebrity, pregnancy and subjectivity. In: Ahmed S, Stacey J, eds. *Thinking Through the Skin*. Routledge, London: 69–83

Tyler I (2005) *Pregnant beauty: The changing visual and cultural practices of pregnant embodiment*. Maternal Bodies Workshop. IAS, Lancaster Univeristy

Webster A (2002) Innovative health technologies and the social: redefining health, medicine and the body. *Current Sociology* **50**: 443–57

Williams C (2005) Framing the fetus in medical work: rituals and practices. *Social Science and Medicine* **60:** 2085-2095

Williams C, Sandall J, Lewando Hundt G, Grellier R, Heyman B, Spencer K (2005) Women as 'moral pioneers'?: Experiences of first trimester nuchal translucency screening. *Social Science and Medicine* **61**: 1983–92

CHAPTER 7

The mass media

The purpose of this chapter is to introduce midwives to the media as an important form of communication in contemporary society. Information now flows around the globe in unprecedented ways and at incredible speed, via television, mobile phones and the Internet. This chapter considers the role that the media plays in shaping popular knowledge and attitudes towards pregnancy and childbirth. Sociological interest in the media stems from the re-emergence of a consumerist society after the Second World War (post-1945) and the rise of television as an increasingly popular medium for communication. Later, during the 1960s and 70s the sociology of the mass media began to ask questions about what effects the various forms of media (radio, television, cinema) have on people generally, and whether or not they reflect the social, economic or political interests of certain groups at the expense of others in society. However, sociology is not the only discipline that offers important insights into the role of the media in contemporary society, consequently this chapter will also identify the work of authors who associate themselves more with cultural studies or media studies than with sociology. In addition, this chapter draws on research by feminist authors, medical sociologists and midwives who have questioned the impact of the media on contemporary women's beliefs about reproduction, pregnancy, childbirth and motherhood.

Defining the media

In sociology, 'the media' is a term that is used to refer to a variety of things, which according to Trowler and Burch (2008) include technologies (e.g. television, DVDs), modes of communication (e.g. print, visual, aural media), organizations (e.g. the British Broadcasting Corporation [BBC]), people who work in those organizations (e.g. BBC journalists) and specific methods of disseminating messages to audiences (e.g. the cinema). Most generally however, the media is said to comprise printed (e.g. newspapers, magazines, books), aural (e.g. radio, compact discs), audio-visual (e.g. television, cinema, video, DVD) and so-called new media (e.g. internet, mobile phones, e-mail). An important distinction is made between conventional media (the former) and newer media (the latter).

Many sociologists use the term **mass media** because more often than not media messages are conveyed from one point to a very large number of other points (i.e. a mass audience).

Forty years ago, Denis McQuail (1969) identified seven main characteristics of the mass media. First: they require complex organisations for them to be able to operate properly. Second: they are directed towards large audiences. Third: their content and distribution is open to all. Fourth: their audience is heterogeneous (it is made up of people living under widely varying cultures, and from different sectors of society. Fifth: they can establish simultaneity of contact with large numbers of people, at a distance from the source, and widely separated from each other. Sixth: the relationship between the communicator and the audience is impersonal in that an anonymous audience is being addressed by people known only in their public role as communicators. Seventh: and perhaps most significant the audience for mass communications is a phenomenon unique to modern societies.

The operation of the media can be either commercial or non-commercial. Non-commercial media are almost entirely publicly operated and may be classified into one of three types (Goulding, 1972 cited in O'Donnell, 1987). The first type is government-controlled media, whose explicit function is to convey government information (otherwise known as propaganda) and is found in modern totalitarian states (i.e. China) or developing societies. The second type of public mass media organisation is the semi-official statutory (established by parliament) body, of which the BBC is an example. The third type of non-commercial media is concerned with public regulation, such as the former Independent Broadcasting Authority, subsequently replaced by the Broadcasting Standards Commission and the Office of Communications (OfCom).

The commercial media includes newspapers, magazines, satellite television and Internet providers. O'Donnell (1987) identifies three important points to be made about the commercial media. First, it is run for profit, which raises the question as to what effect this has on its content. Second, the commercial media is concentrated in a few companies. Third, the commercial media has been through a process of diversification. This means that the companies behind commercial media also have business interests in other areas. Gidden's (2001) identifies that in the present day the commercial media is a multi-million pound business run by highly centralised conglomerates. For example, Rupert Murdoch's News Corporation's holdings include nine different media operations on six continents (including over 130 newspapers, Sky television and the film company Twentieth-Century Fox). According to some sociologists, the emergence of such large international media companies has done much to generate new international markets and promote new technologies that have no national boundaries (Herman and McChesney, 1997).

Somewhat ahead of his time, McLuhan (1964) recognised how electronic media (particularly television) creates a **global village** whereby people throughout the world can see major events unfold and hence participate in them. According to McLuhan (1964) the kind of media found in a society influences its structure much more than the messages it conveys. For example, everyday life is experienced differently in a society in which television plays a basic role compared with one that only has print. Perhaps most importantly, he asserts that developments in communication provide the main force for social change in human society, giving rise to the theoretical position known as media determinism. According to McLuhan (1964) when printing was invented and radio and television were developed, important social changes began to take place. Today, the relationship between new media (i.e. Internet, mobile phones, e-mail) and globalization forms a key area of sociological investigation. Moreover, many sociologists are concerned with the process of convergence, whereby the production, distribution and consumption of information are no longer self-contained. Convergence is evident both at the level of multi-national companies who produce television and digital media, and at the level of individual consumers who, for example, read newspapers, watch television and access the Internet.

Sociological perspectives and theories of media influence

The sociology of the media is a complex field that encompasses many different perspectives and approaches. Pluralist theories (which are associated with those working within the media as well as some sociologists) are concerned with how different parts of the media cater for various sections of society, suggesting that media content is principally dictated by audience demand. It is an approach that was most popular during the 1950s and 1960s, and emphasised the diversity of media content and its function for society. Classic studies associated with this perspective include Katz and Lazarsfield's (1955) investigation into how far the media influences people's political opinions, attitudes and voting behaviour. According to Katz and Lazarfield (1955) the degree of media influence is limited by variable exposure, dependent upon the type of media used to convey messages, the specific content and language used in messages, the pre-existing beliefs of individual audience members, and their immediate social network.

There are a number of variants of Marxist and neo-Marxist approaches to the media that share concerns about how the media serve the interests of **capitalism** and perpetuate the ideas of dominant groups in society by shaping our attitudes, beliefs and everyday taken-for-granted assumptions. Marxist perspectives suggest that it is the **logic of capitalism**, or in other words the pursuit of profit, which determines the content and effects of the media. Moreover, the production of **ideology** (a system of ideas that justifies or legitimates the subordination of one group over another) is key. According to Herbert **Marcuse** (1964) in advanced industrial societies (of the kind associated with late capitalism) the media replaces religion in diverting the masses attention away from awareness of their exploitation. Marcuse (1964) asserts that the trivial but amusing entertainment the media provides dulls the edge of any doubt about the social order (or in other words it suppresses radical, revolutionary tendencies) and promotes the idea that we can all hope to, and indeed should strive to, achieve material success. The relationship between the media, ideology and **cultural hegemony** is particularly important. Cultural hegemony is a concept that refers specifically to understanding ideology in terms of the process of making, maintaining and reproducing authoritative meanings and practices (Barker, 2000).

According to Hall (1982), inherent in the media are systems of signs that represent aspects of our cultures unique way of thinking about and understanding the world. The concept of signs originates from linguistics and refers to the production of meaning (signification). Hall (1982) argues that the media encodes (or in other words conveys) the meanings of the dominant interests in society through its signifying system.

The UK's **Glasgow University Media Group** provides a notable body of empirical research studies documenting the production, content and reception of media messages (see www.gla.ac.uk/centres/mediagroup). Their seminal studies 'Bad News' (1976), 'More Bad News' (1980), 'Really Bad News' (1982) and 'War and Peace' (1985) demonstrate the encoded and partial nature of news reporting, which they argue is ideologically loaded to serve the interests of the powerful. They also highlight how media professionals set the agenda for news reporting and legitimate particular understandings of them, whilst simultaneously excluding or downplaying other possible explanations, thereby narrowing the scope of public debate.

Another influential neo-Marxist body of work on the media originates from the **Frankfurt School**. As introduced in chapter one, the Frankfurt School is a group of sociologists and philosophers who revisited the writings of Marx with the aim of bringing them up-to-date. Amongst other things, they have drawn attention to the increasing influence of the culture industry and the media in modern capitalist societies. In particular, Jürgen **Habermas's** analysis of the development of the media from the 18th century to the late 20th century charts the rise and subsequent decline of what he terms the public sphere. According to Habermas (1989) the public sphere is an arena of public debate where individuals come together as equals and issues of general concern can be discussed and resolved. He argues that the public sphere originates from the meetinghouses of the 18th century and was central to the early development of democracy in western societies. However, in contemporary western democracies he asserts that the public sphere has become meaningless as the media suppresses public debate, politics is stage-managed and commercial interests dominate. He concludes that public opinion is formed not through open public debate, but through the manipulation and control of media audiences. An alternative view is offered by Thompson (1995) who demonstrates how the media increases critical thought and public debate by allowing audiences access to information that they have not had access to before. Thompson (1995) recognises that audiences are not passive recipients of media messages, which are typically discussed and re-interpreted by individuals and groups. According to Thompson (1995) the mass media has shifted the balance between the public and the private in our lives, with much more in the public domain than ever before.

As we have seen in previous chapters, some sociologists believe that developed western societies are in a period of social change best conceptualised as post-modernity. The media is fundamental to most conceptualisations of post-modernity because it is the media that principally provides access and meaning to the multiplicity of messages in circulation. Post-modernity is said to be media saturated. Moreover, the postmodernist **Baudrillard** (1988, 1995) argues that the media, particularly television, does not just represent the world to us, it increasingly defines what the world is. **Hyperreality** is the term Baudrillard uses to conceptualise how the distinction between reality and the words and images used by the media to portray it disintegrate. In other words, there is no longer a reality occurring in a particular time and place, but the reality is fluid created by television coverage of that occurrence and audience interpretation of the television coverage.

Since the post-war period, sociological thinking about the relationship between media messages and audience response has developed from simple cause-and-effect models to complex analyses of media texts, audiences and effects (Trowler and Burch, 2008). Trowler and Burch identify three examples of early cause-and-effect models. The hypodermic model uses an analogy of the media as the syringe, the media's message as what is injected and the audience as the patient. The social learning approach model suggests that people learn new behaviours through the observation of others and that this is more effective when the behaviour is reinforced in repeated media messages. The normative model highlights how a two-step process of media influence operates. The first step is when a media message reaches a member of an audience, whilst the second step is its interpretation and influence, which are affected by social interaction. Katz and Lazarfield's (1955) study discussed earlier in this chapter was one of those that informed the development of the two-step model.

The uses and gratification model is more complex. This model incorporates the audience as active interpreters of media messages and stresses how different people use the media in different ways. For example Denis McQuail (2000) identifies four motives for media usage. First, is the pursuit of information, which includes the seeking of advice, getting orientated about events in the environment and educational learning (for example, during pregnancy a woman may actively seek to watch television programmes about pregnancy, birth and parenting). Second, is the confirmation of personal identify, which includes gaining self-knowledge, finding models of behaviour, and using the media to reinforce personal values (to extend our example, a woman may draw on such television programmes to confirm her view that she is acting appropriately during pregnancy, e.g. avoiding certain foods or that the occasional glass of wine is okay). Third, McQuail (2000) identifies media usage as a means of integration and social interaction derived from finding out about others, relating to others and finding out how to play one's role and establish a basis for social interaction (therefore, through accessing media information about pregnancy, childbirth and parenting a woman is able to adapt and interact in accordance with her emerging social role as a mother). Fourth and finally, the media may be accessed as a source of entertainment, a means of relaxation, escaping from everyday problems or simply filling time.

However, people do not only use the media in different ways, they do different things with media messages. The interpretative model takes into account the ways in which audiences may actively interpret media messages. For example, they may read one media message in relation to others, they may use one media form to direct them to another, or they may move between different levels of engagement with the same media (Fiske, 1998). The structured interpretation model builds on the interpretative model, but suggests that there is a preferred meaning or dominant message. This means that whilst an audience may interpret media messages in different ways, one-way (the preferred meaning) is easier than others because of the way in which the story is presented and (intentionally or otherwise) reflects wider cultural norms.

To date, sociological research has not found convincing evidence of media influence in terms of uprooting the effects of primary socialization or the influence of family and social networks. However, health is one area where the media is increasingly being purported to be particularly influential.

The next section focuses on work from a range of authors working across the sociology of health and illness (also known as medical sociology), feminism(s), media and cultural studies who have studied aspects of health and the media.

The media and health

Interest in the media and health crosses many disciplines including sociology, cultural studies and midwifery. The production, nature and influence of media health messages, the role of the media in constructing and influencing illness experience, and the media's framing of expectations of healthcare are all important areas of investigation. According to Cartwright (2000):

> '...television, print media, cinema, on-line discussion groups and medical educational computer programmes are an important, if under considered, means through which health issues are taught, communicated and lived.'
> *Cartwright (2000:120)*

Thus rendering it impossible to understand health in society without acknowledging the crucial role of the media in the formation of health cultures.

Deborah Lupton (1998) identifies three important ways that medicine and healthcare dominate modern media. First, the popularity of medial dramas which include fictitious portrayals of doctors, other health professionals and patients. Second, the rise of docudramas portraying real life situations that include fly-on-the wall television series filmed in A&E departments, children's wards and maternity hospitals. Third, studies of news coverage of medical and public health stories show that they have a high level of prominence overall. Lupton (1998) argues that medical stories attract audiences because they strike at the fundamental concerns and uncertainties of modern life, in which birth and death are omnipresent; a theory that may account for why in soap operas, in particular pregnancy-related conditions (where the potential for birth and death loom simultaneously) provide vital and frequent themes for plots (Cassata et al, 1979).

According to some sociologists the media has become key to the process of medicalization in the 21st century (Moynihan, 2002). As introduced in chapter three, the term medicalization refers to the process of '...*defining a problem in medical terms, using medical language to describe the problem, adopting a medical framework to understand a problem, or using a medical intervention to treat it*' (Conrad, 1992). Whilst in the later decades of the 20th century and the first decade of the 21st century there has been a growing number of portrayals of doctors and scientific medicine as fallible (see Karpf, 1988; Bury and Gabe, 1994 for changes in portrayal of doctors over time), nevertheless, in both news and fictional portrayals, positive representations continue to outweigh those that are negative. Thus, doctors as characters continue to dominate over other professions and medical technology is singled out as the apotheosis of medical magic (Lupton, 2003).

Michelle (2007) asserts that among the voices most often amplified in media coverage of assisted reproductive and biogenetic technologies are those of medical specialists and consumers. Members of these groups are not only key sources for health reporters but, as identified by Michelle (2007), a symbiotic or concordance of interest exists between them. In other words, the reporters get cutting edge science that sells newspapers, the specialists get the opportunity to shape public opinion in their favour, and the public predominantly gets to hear the success stories of modern medicine.

Franklin (1990) identifies how media representations comprise an important source of both formal knowledge and commonsense understandings of developments in reproductive science and the experience of infertility. Moreover, Rapp (1998) reports that women frequently refer to the mass media for information about new reproductive technologies such as amniocentesis, incorporating this knowledge into the doctor-patient encounter.

We will now explore the relationship between media and health specifically in the context of media representations of pregnancy and childbirth.

Media representations of pregnancy, childbirth and early motherhood

This section explores how a variety of media forms exert influence over women's beliefs about pregnancy, childbirth and early motherhood in contemporary western culture. Specifically, it focuses on representations of pregnancy, childbirth and early motherhood as portrayed in books, magazines, newspapers, television and the Internet. Whilst this section deals with each of these media forms in turn, it is important to consider how these also interact together and the consequences of this (i.e. the relevance of the concept of convergence discussed earlier in the chapter).

Midwives should bear in mind that an individual woman's interpretation of media messages is dependent upon her immediate context (i.e. whether viewed alone or in a group), and is likely to be influenced by her social positioning (i.e. social class or ethnicity). Moreover, studies show that whilst some groups of pregnant women (and those planning a pregnancy) actively seek information from different media (i.e. the Internet and books), other groups depend more on information from their social environment (i.e. family and friends) and/or their midwives (Szwajcer et al, 2005).

Books

In recent years there has been a proliferation of self-help healthcare books, which include pregnancy, childbirth and parenting manuals (e.g. Gordon, 2002; Cooke, 2006; Stoppard, 2008). To date there is little published research concerning what women learn from such books. The American nurse-midwife Holly Kennedy is (at the time of writing) undertaking a study of 58 lay books on pregnancy and childbirth commonly found in US bookstores. Following analysis of both visual images and text the preliminary findings identify mixed messages about pregnancy, labour and birth, pain, the role of technology, and the role of midwives. According to Kennedy (2008) there are five continuums surrounding the portrayal of 'birth imagery' (from the body as beautiful and capable to the body as ugly and incapable), 'labour and birth' (from a normal life event to inherently risky and something to be feared), 'pain' (from having a purpose to being unacceptable), 'power and control' (from the woman having agency to the power presiding with healthcare professionals) and 'life preparation' (from a positive experience of pregnancy and birth as fundamental in the journey into motherhood to having the baby as the endpoint). This leads Kennedy (2008) to the tentative conclusion that lay pregnancy books send both overt and covert messages about childbirth which can affect women's perception of its safety and their ability to give birth (Kennedy, 2008). There is no systematic research evidence of the extent to which these findings are applicable to the top-selling UK pregnancy and childbirth books, however, even from the most cursory glance at such books it is possible to see how some of Kennedy's (2008) findings may have resonance beyond the US pregnancy book market.

Magazines

In contrast to the dearth of literature on pregnancy books, there exist numerous analyses of general women's magazines from both sociological and cultural studies perspectives. According to these analyses women's magazines create a particular cultural space through which understanding and the managing of human emotions are negotiated (Hermes, 1995; McRobbie, 1996). In other words, whilst women's magazines are generally read for pleasure and as a source of information, we must also recognise that they play a role in shaping both how we manage our emotions and how we act, thus contributing to who we are (our identity). At one level this is obvious (e.g. when we act on specific fashion, lifestyle or health advice from a magazine), but at another level it is not (e.g. when magazines covertly promote a particular ideology of womanhood in adherence with dominant cultural norms). There are a number of studies of representations of pregnancy and childbirth in general women's magazines. These include a study of Australian women's magazines over a one-year period, which reports that whilst many general women's magazines do provide a useful source of information a number of destructive themes are omnipresent (Handfield and Bell, 1996). These themes include weight gain in pregnancy, a lack of control in life as pregnancy progresses, the 'agony' of childbirth and the negative impact childbirth had on marital relationships and women's careers. Another study, undertaken in North America, analyses general women's magazines representations of pregnancy amongst women aged over 35 (Beaulieu and Lippman, 1995). This study also reports negativity in the portrayal of pregnancy, with the construction of women as principally to blame if a problem arises with either their own or their unborn baby's health.

When considering representations of pregnancy, childbirth and early motherhood in women's magazines it is, I suggest, important to make a distinction between general women's magazines and magazines aimed specifically at women who are pregnant. The increasing visibility of pregnancy in society (as identified in chapter six) has opened up a new market for pregnancy magazines and the advertisement of pregnancy products. To date, arguably the most notable study of pregnancy magazines is from the US. Dworkin and Wachs' (2004) analysis found that whilst 62% of the readership of the pregnancy magazine under investigation had full-time jobs during pregnancy, there was little mention made of getting back to work. Moreover, 81% of models were white, and fathers were only featured in 5% of articles. Single mothers or homosexual mothers were never shown or discussed. Thus they argue the underlying assumptions inherent in the portrayal of pregnancy and childbirth privileges whiteness, heterosexuality, stay-at-home motherhood, continual baby and self-care, and women getting their body back to a pre-pregnancy normative form. In other words, pregnancy magazines perpetuate the ideology of motherhood and modern motherhood discourse, as identified in chapter five.

In the UK, whilst the market for pregnancy magazines is in its infancy, it is not insignificant. The National Readership Survey (NRS) estimates readership of magazines targeted at pregnant women and new mothers during 2007 to be as illustrated in *Table 7.1*. The table also estimates the class, age and gender distribution of readers for the top four pregnancy and childbirth magazines.

Newspapers

Table 7.2 shows UK national newspaper circulation figures for February 2008. It is widely acknowledged that patterns of readership of print newspapers are declining (Giddens, 2001). Nevertheless, the influence of this media form remains significant. For example, consider the association between the phrase '*too posh to push*' and the rate of maternal request for Caesarean delivery. In January 1999, the phrase '*too posh to push*' first appeared in a newspaper article published in the *Daily Mail* (Moorhead, 1999). This article was published two months before the celebrity Victoria Beckham, also known as Posh Spice, delivered her first child by planned Caesarean section. This catchy phrase has also become synonymous with other celebrities and affluent women who allegedly wish to bypass labour and vaginal birth in favour of a planned Caesarean section. This has captured the imagination of British journalists for a decade and is now also used in the US (Declerq and Norsigian, 2006). Arguably, '*too posh to push*' is now as common a parlance in popular culture as '*test-tube babies*' was in the 1980s.

In my own research investigating women's views of vaginal and Caesarean childbirth, 89 women voluntarily used the phrase '*too posh to push*' when interviewed during pregnancy. Consequently, I undertook a retrospective study of newspaper articles on vaginal and Caesarean birth published whilst these women were pregnant to see whether or not they promoted the idea that women are increasingly 'choosing' planned Caesarean section (Kingdon, 2008). I identified 150 articles portraying vaginal birth and 6,440 on Caesarean section. I found no evidence to support the view that British newspapers were explicitly promoting the idea that women are demanding Caesarean delivery for maternal request. A random selection of all articles published in that period revealed that considerably less than one in every 20 articles on childbirth made any reference to maternal request, with the majority of articles that referred to Caesarean section reporting the advent of another birth by this method. Whilst both vaginal birth and Caesarean section are newsworthy, there are mixed messages about which is best for women, their babies and society, with neither method of birth portrayed particularly positively. Consequently, I conclude that it is how the media, in all its forms not just newspapers, implicitly promotes fear of childbirth *per se* that warrants further investigation.

A study by Henderson et al (2000) has previously demonstrated how the influence of newspapers and television converge to shape popular discourse surrounding bottle-feeding, rather than breastfeeding, as the norm in British culture. Henderson et al (2000) analysed portrayals of breast and bottle-feeding in 13 national newspapers and in television programmes during the month of March 1999. A total of 235 references to infant feeding were identified in the television sample (which included health and parenting series, news bulletins, soap operas and medical dramas) and 38 in the newspaper sample. Despite the known health benefits of breastfeeding, bottle-feeding was found to be shown more often, was portrayed as less problematic, and was associated with 'ordinary'

Table 7.1   Readership Estimates January–December 2007

Magazine	Total	ABC1	C2DE	15–44	45+	Women	Men
Mother & Baby	587,000	288,000	299,000	528,000	59,000	479,000	108,000
Practical Parenting	247,000	145,000	103,000	217,000	31,000	206,000	41,000
Pregnancy and Birth	191,000	90,000	101,000	184,000	8,000	165,000	27,000
Prima Baby & Pregnancy	171,000	86,000	85,000	167,000	4,000	153,000	18,000
Source: National Readership Survey (2007)							

Table 7.2   Readership Estimates for National Newspapers

	Newspaper	**Circulation**
Daily	*The Sun*	3,077,060
	Daily Mail	2,294,880
	Daily Mirror	1,500,543
	Daily Express	736,634
	Daily Star	723,905
	Daily Telegraph	866,693
	The Times	613,068
	Financial Times	448,342
	The Guardian	355,634
	The Independent	252,435
Weekly	*News of the World*	3,281,287
	Mail on Sunday	2,203,642
	Sunday Mirror	1,348,395
	Sunday Times	1,206,247
	Sunday Express	676,165
Source: Audit Bureau of Circulations (2008)		

families. Henderson et al (2000) conclude that the media rarely presents positive information on breastfeeding. Whilst they acknowledge that media coverage reflects the reality of what is publicly visible (i.e. many women do not breastfeed in public) and attention to the realities of breastfeeding may help prepare women, they also identify that these limited portrayals perpetuate a lack of acceptance of breastfeeding in public and may sustain the idea that breastfeeding is difficult and only an option for middle-class women.

Television

Beech (2000) and Clement (1997) draw attention to the power of television as a particularly influential media that shapes contemporary British women's views about the risks, pain and inconveniences associated with childbirth. Clement's (1997) analysis of 58 fictional and 32 genuine labours and births shown on British television reports that childbirth complications are more common in fictional accounts than in real life (Clement, 1997). Arguably, this is not surprising as television is a media form particularly geared to entertainment and voyeurism, which it could be said necessitates sensationalized, dramatic representations of childbirth. Shelia and Jenny Kitzinger (2001) comment:

> *'Television has produced a powerful mythology of birth. The drama of this myth is in the medical emergency, the speeding ambulance, the urgent bleep, and the struggles of a team of doctors and nurses to combat death. There are heart monitors on which the trace flattens out, Cesarean deliveries, massive hemorrhages, resuscitation of the baby. It is a drama that feeds the fears inherent in the dominant medical model of birth and, in this way, it conditions pregnant women to submit to its rituals.'*
>
> *Kitzinger (2001: 61)*

It is important to distinguish between the many different types of television programmes that may now include representations of childbirth (e.g. documentary programmes, fly-on-the-wall docusoaps, soaps, news reports and films). Haken's (2008) study of 85 television programmes screened during a one-week period on 15 channels demonstrates the increasing popularity of reality television (also known as fly-on-the-wall docusoaps); 90% of the programmes in her sample were of this genre. A total of 206 women were seen giving birth to 237 infants; 46% of births were 'normal' vaginal births, 9% were assisted vaginal births and 45% were Caesarean sections (emergency and elective). According to Haken (2008) the woman's voice is frequently silenced in favour of a professional voice-over and the majority of references in the script are to the unseen (i.e. the safety of the baby that is yet to emerge from the woman's body). These findings resonate with existing sociological research on media representations of pregnancy that have found that it is '*...generally portrayed as a time of considerable risk, in which the health and interests of the fetus loom large, if not larger than those of the woman*' (Seale, 2002: 198). Or in other words, the baby has a very real presence in the script even though it cannot be seen visually.

Thus whilst the proliferation of terrestrial, digital and satellite television channels in existence today means that it is possible to find alternative portrayals of childbirth to the dominant medical model, research evidence suggests the dominant portrayal of pregnancy, childbirth and early motherhood on television remains a negative one. This is particularly important to highlight because successive sociologists suggest that the influence of television was (before the invention of the Internet) the most important development in the media (Giddens, 2001). This is because television is a form of mass media that is increasingly available across the developing world and in the countries of the developed world is a resource that is open to almost everybody. For example, in 1999, in the UK only 1% of households were without a television. Consequently, there is little variation in ownership between socio-economic groups (ONS, 2001). Watching a lot of television is however associated with lower socio-economic groups. *Table 7.3* illustrates that, on average in the UK, people aged 4 years and over spent 26 hours a week watching television, with women spending more hours watching television than men, and individuals aged 65 and over watching the most television. Whilst we know television typically represents pregnancy, childbirth and early motherhood in a negative way, further research is needed to investigate the responses of different audiences to such portrayals.

Internet

The Internet is a global multimedia library that allows individuals not only to search for information, but to download documents, video and audio files, or to upload their own information. Figures from the UK show that in 2006, over 50% of households had Internet access (Social Trends, 37), although the trend towards rapid year-on-year increase in the proportion of households with Internet access has slowed since 2000/1. Moreover, whilst one in every two people do have access to the Internet, it is important to stress that it is not currently a media available to all and may not be in the future. In particular, the old and those from lower socio-economic groups have limited Internet access (Wong, 2004).

In sociology, **cyberspace** is the term used to describe the space of interaction formed by the global network of computers that compose the Internet (Giddens,

**Table 7.3   Television viewing by age and gender
(hours per person per week)**

Age in years	Male	Female
4–15	18.6	17.9
16–24	17.7	22.8
25–34	21.6	26.5
35–44	22.5	25.4
45–54	25.3	26.9
55–64	28.8	32.1
65 and over	36.4	36.5
All aged 4 and over	24.1	27.0
Source: Social Trends 31		

2001). Most sociologists agree that the Internet is transforming the contours of daily life and is one of the main contributors to and manifestations of globalization. However, according to Giddens (2001), opinion on the effects of the Internet fall into two broad categories. First, some observers see the online world as fostering new forms of electronic relationships that either enhance or supplement existing face-to-face relationships. Second, other observers suggest that the Internet technology is leading to increased social isolation as it encroaches on time previously spent with family and blurs the boundaries between home and work. To date, the impact of the Internet on midwives and women's knowledge about pregnancy, childbirth and motherhood has been studied little.

The Internet has opened up access to a broad range of information about pregnancy, birth and early motherhood, of varying scientific creditability and produced for vastly different purposes. There are the sites for pregnant women and new mothers financed by commercial advertising (for example, http://www.babycentre.co.uk/pregnancy) that provide women with week-by-week guides to pregnancy. There are also sites developed and run by consumers (for example, http://www.birthchoiceuk.com) that offer women statistics to inform their choice of place of birth. In addition there are personal pregnancy websites where women up-load their pregnancy diaries and photos. Finally, women can also access a plethora of professional sites (for example, http:///www.rcm.org.uk) to obtain information about childbirth. However, one key issue raised by the increasing use of the Internet is the quality of information available and whether or not users have the skills to evaluate the validity of the information they can now access.

A focus group study of pregnant women and young mothers in the US reports that they use the Internet to '...*confirm their beliefs or reassure themselves that their perceptions were correct*' (Bernhardt and Felter, 2004). These women were relatively well educated and voiced their scepticism of sites selling baby-related products, but liked the sites that were tailored to their stage of pregnancy and presented personalised messages (which are paradoxically sponsored by businesses selling baby-related products).

Another study has surveyed Australian obstetricians about their perceptions of sources of information commonly accessed by pregnant women (Handfield et al, 2006). Three quarters of obstetricians who returned the questionnaire (152/1999), reported patients had either mentioned or brought printed website information to show them during consultations. This indicates that women are accessing websites for information about pregnancy and birth, and in Australia at least they are telling their obstetricians about it. Earlier research by the same team interviewed 14 women pregnant for the first time, all of whom talked about accessing the Internet daily to seek health information relating to pregnancy and childbirth (Handfield, 2005). However, most of these women were self-selected, affluent, and accessing private maternity care in Australia.

Little is known about patterns of Internet access and influence amongst pregnant women in the UK. In the field of oncology, studies show patients use web to verify their doctor's opinion and to access second opinions in the context of anonymity (Ziebland et al, 2004). However, whilst access to the Internet was found to increase patients understanding of their illness, it also increased levels of anxiety and confusion (Newnham et al, 2005).

Conclusion

This chapter has introduced midwives to the sociology of the media. It has highlighted how contemporary society is saturated with media messages, and how they serve to perpetuate dominant discourse, including the medical discourse. In addition it has identified that audience response models suggest different people engage with media messages in complex ways. Midwives familiarity with the media is not a routine part of contemporary practice; nevertheless greater appreciation of the importance of the media in contemporary society could be translated into action for more positive portrayals of pregnancy, birth and early motherhood in popular culture. Moreover, this chapter demonstrates the dearth of research into women's responses to media representations of childbirth. This is a fertile area for future research that requires sociological research skills. The next chapter introduces sociological research.

References

Barker C (2000) *Cultural Studies: Theory and Practice*. Sage, London

Baudrillard J (1988) *The Ecstasy of Communication*. Semiotext, New York

Baudrillard J (1995) *The Gulf War did Not Take Place*. Power Publications, Sydney

Beech B (2000) Journalism and other influences. *RCM Midwives Journal* **3**(2): 53

Bernhardt J, Felter E (2004) Online paediatric information seeking among mothers of young children: Results from a qualitative study using focus groups. *J Med Internet Res* **6**(1) : e7

Bury M, Gabe J (1994) Television and medicine: Medical dominance or trial by media? In: Gabe J, Kelleher D, Williams G, eds. *Challenging Medicine*. Routledge, London

Beaulieu AF, Lippman, A (1995) Everything you need to know. How women's magazines structure prenatal diagnosis for women over 35. *Women and Health: A multidisciplinary Journal of Women's Health Issues* **23**(3):

Cassata M, Skill T, Boadu S (1979) In sickness and in health. *Journal of Communication* **29**(4): 73-80

Cartwright L (2000) Community and the public body in breast cancer media activism. In: Marchessault J, Sawchuk K, eds. *Wild Science: Reading feminism, medicine and the media*. Routledge, London

Clement S (1997) Childbirth on television. *Br J Midwifery* **5**(1): 37–42

Cobb J (1995) Birth on the Box. *New Generation* **December**: 3–4

Cooke K (2006) *The Rough Guide to Pregnancy and Birth*. Rough Guides Ltd, London

Cottle S (1998) Ulrich Beck, risk society and the media: a catastrophic view? *European Journal of Communication* **13**(1): 5–32

Conrad P (1992) Medicalization and social control. *Annual Review of sociology* **18**: 209–32

Conduit CM (1994) Hegemony in a mass-mediated society: Concordance about reproductive technologies. *Critical Studies in Mass communications* **11**(3): 205–30

Corner J, Richardson K, Fenton N (1990) Textualising risk: TV discourse and the issue of nuclear energy. *Media, Culture & Society* **12**(1): 105–24

Davidson R, Kitzinger J, Hunt K (2006) The wealthy get healthy, the poor get poorly? Lay perceptions of health inequalities. *Social Science and Medicine* **62**: 2171–82

Declerq G, Norsigian J (2006) Mothers' aren't behind a vogue for Caesareans. *The Boston Globe* **3 April**

Dworkin S, Wachs F (2004) Getting your body back. Post-industrial fit motherhood in shape fit pregnancy magazine. *Gender & Society* **18**(5): 610–24

Fiske J (1998) *Television Culture*, Methuen, London

Franklin S (1990) Deconstructing 'desperateness': The social construction of infertility in popular representations of new reproductive technologies. In: McNeil M, Varcoe I, Yearley S, eds. *The New Reproductive Technologies*. Macmillian, Basingstoke: 200–9

Giddens A (2001) *Sociology*. 4th edition. Polity Press, Cambridge

Gitlin T (1980) *The Whole World is Watching*. University of California Press, Berkeley

Gordon Y (2002) *Birth and Beyond: The definitive guide to your pregnancy, your family from minus 9 to plus 9 moths*. Vermilion, London

Handfield B, Bell R (1996) What are popular magazines telling young women about pregnancy, birth, breastfeeding and parenting? *ACMI Journal*

Handfield B (2005) *Imagining Childbirth*. Proceedings of the 27th Congress of the International Confederation of Midwives 4–5 July, Brisbane

Handfield B, Turnbull S, Bell RJ (2006) What do obstetricians think about media influences on their patients? *Australian and New Zealand Journal of Obstetrics and Gynaecology* **46**: 379–83

Hall S (1982) The question of cultural identity. In: Hall S, Held D, McGrew T, eds. *Modernity and its Futures*. Polity Press, Cambridge

Habermas J (1989) T*he Structural Transformation of the Public Sphere: An inquiry into a category of bourgeois society*. Polity Press, Cambridge

Haken C (2008) *Staging Labour: Representations of childbirth on contemporary British television*. International Confederation of Midwives, SECC, Glasgow, Scotland, June 2008

Henderson L, Kitzinger J, Green J (2000) Representing infant feeding: content analysis of British media portrayals of bottle feeding and breast feeding. *BMJ* **321**(7270): 1196–8

Herman ES, McChesney RW (1997) *The Global Media: The new missionaries of global capitalism.* Cassell, London

Hermes J (1995) *Reading Women's Magazines: An analysis of everyday media use.* Polity Press, Cambridge

Haran J, Kitzinger J, McNeil M, O'Riordan K (2007) *Human Cloning in the Media: From science fiction to science practice.* Routledge, London

Hughes E, Kitzinger J, Murdock G (2006) Risk and the media. In: Taylor Gooby P, Zinn J, eds. *Risk in Social Science.* Oxford University Press: 250–70

Katz E, Lazarsfield P (1955) *Personal Influence: The part played by people in the flow of mass communication.* Free Press, Glencoe

Kennedy H (2008) *Childbirth Discourse: Interpreting media messages.* International Confederation of Midwives, SECC, Glasgow, Scotland: June 2008

Kingdon C (2008) Do British newspapers promote the idea that women are demanding Caesarean birth? *New Digest* **41**: 17–18

Kitzinger S, Kitzinger J (2001) Childbirth and Breastfeeding in the Media. *Birth* **28**(1): 60–3

Lupton D (1998) Medicine and healthcare in popular media. In: Peterson A, WAddell C, eds. *Health Matters: A sociology of illness, prevention and care.* Open University Press, Buckingham

Lupton D (2003) *Medicine as Culture.* Sage, London

McQuail D (1969) *Towards a Sociology of Mass Communications.* Collier-McMillan, London

McQuail D (2000) *Mass Communication Theory.* 4th Edition. Sage Publications, London

McLuhan M (1964) *Understanding Media: The extension of man.* New American Library, New York

McRobbie A (1996) More! New sexualities in girls' and women's magazines. In: Curran J, Morley D, Walkerdine V, eds. *Cultural Studies and Communications.* Arnold, London: 172–94

Marcuse H (1964) *One Dimensional Man*: Studies in the ideology of advanced industrial society. Sphere, London

Michelle (2007) Human clones talk about their lives: Media representations of assisted reproductive and biogenetic technologies. *Media, Culture and Society* **29**(4): 639–33

Moorhead J (1999) Are you too posh to push? The way you give birth has become a status symbol of our times. And by 2010 half of all women will refuse to endure the pain of natural birth. *Daily Mail* **26 January**: 36-37

Moynihan R, Heath I, Henry D (2002) Selling sickness: the pharmaceutical industry and disease mongering. *BMJ* **324**(7342): 886–91

Newnham GM, Burns WI, Snyder RD et al (2005) Attitudes of oncology health professionals to information from the Internet and other media. *Med J Aus* **183**: 197-200

O'Donnell M (1987) A new introduction to sociology.

ONS (2001) *https://www.ons.gov.uk*

Rapp R (1998) Refusing prenatal diagnosis: The uneven meanings of bioscience in a multicultural world. In: Davis-Floyd R, Dumit J, eds. *Cyborg Babies: From techno-sex to techno-tots.* Routledge, London: 143–67

Seale C (2002) *Media and Health.* Sage, London.

Stoppard M (2008) *Conception, Pregnancy and Birth: The childbirth bible for today's parents.* Dorling Kindersley Publishers, London

Szwajcer EM, Hiddink GJ, Koelen et al (2005) Nutrition-related information seeking behaviours before and throughout the course of pregnancy: consequences for nutrition communication. *European Journal of Clinical Nutrition* **59**(1): S57–65

Thompson JB (1995) *The Media and Modernity: A social theory of the media.* Polity Press, Cambridge

Trowler P, Burch S (2008) Communication and the media. In: Haralambos M, Holborn M, eds. *Sociology: Themes and perspectives.* HarperCollins, London: 710–41

Wong G (2004) Internet access is a socio-economic issue. *BMJ* **328**: 1200–201

Ziebland S, Chapple A, Dumelow C et al (2004) How the internet affects patients' experience of cancer: a qualitative study. *BMJ* **328**: 564–69

CHAPTER 8

Sociological research

No introduction to sociology would be complete without a discussion of sociological research. The purpose of this chapter is to provide an overview of the different approaches used by those engaged in sociological enquiry. It should be clear from the studies discussed in earlier chapters that there is no single method or approach associated with research in sociology. It may also have become apparent that the methods of data collection used by sociologists are not dissimilar to those used by midwives who undertake research. Indeed, many of the underpinning traditions informing the principles of research design in midwifery today have been adopted from sociology.

This chapter serves to inform midwives of the distinctiveness of sociological research, discuss commonly used methods, and to highlight key considerations for midwives who may be considering undertaking research. This chapter should also be of interest to midwives who are not planning to undertake any research of their own, but need to be able to read sociological research papers with confidence. Having said that, this chapter is not a definite guide to undertaking sociological research. For this midwives will need to consult a range of texts that focus exclusively on research. In both sociology and midwifery there are many excellent books devoted entirely to research (for example Burgess, 1991; Gilbert, 1995; Hicks, 1996; Robson, 2002; Rees, 2003; Cluett and Bluff, 2006; Alasuutari et al, 2008), and throughout this chapter midwives will be directed to further reading pertaining to specific aspects of sociological enquiry (i.e. feminist research, qualitative research methods).

Defining research

In midwifery, knowledge about research has been an integral part of training and practice since the mid 1990s. Every midwife employed by the NHS is now expected to continuously update their practice in accordance with the best available research evidence (Department of Health, 1998; Royal College of Midwives, 2000; Nursing and Midwifery Council, 2008). Moreover, an increasing number of midwives are actively engaging in research. Colin Rees (2003) defines research in midwifery as:

> '...a process that extends knowledge and understanding through the systematic collection of information that answers a specific question as objectively and accurately as possible'.
>
> Rees (2003: 9)

Similarly, Carolyn Hicks (1996) states:

'Research is about asking questions and finding answers to those questions in a systematic way. Midwives should routinely challenge the effectiveness of their own practice in order both to improve the quality of care and to support their choice of treatment. Knowing how to question practice in a scientific way is the first stage in the research process'.

Hicks (1996: 4)

Both of these definitions emphasize the importance of collecting information in a systematic way. All good research is systematic, or in other words, it follows a predefined process and adheres to accepted standards. However, the use of the term 'objectively' and the phrase 'a scientific way' alludes not to the prerequisites of all research, but to the association between research in midwifery and research in obstetrics. Obstetric research is a branch of medical science, which values experimental research and the principals of the scientific method. Whilst many midwives have successfully embraced a range of research approaches, from both the natural and the social sciences, until very recently their efforts were principally judged according to the dictates of the former. Consequently, by introducing midwives to the dictates of 'social' research this chapter may challenge midwives existing beliefs about what research is.

Broadly speaking, in sociology there are those who advocate the same research approach as that used in the natural sciences, who have been called *positivist* or *quantitative sociologists* (all terms in italics are discussed in more detail later in this chapter). There are also those who believe that the unique subject matter of sociology (i.e. human action and societal institutions) requires a different approach to that of the natural sciences; these are known as interpretivist or qualitative sociologists. In addition, there are those who are less concerned with whether either of the former approaches can bring you closer to 'the truth', and more with understanding the world better to bring about social change. This group of sociologists study the experiences of oppressed social groups and are sometimes known as *critical social researchers*; they include feminist researchers. Finally, there are post-modernists, some of whom utilise an eclectic mix of research traditions in the pursuit of multiple truths. The lack of a single research approach (as is found in the natural sciences), coupled with a copious amount of research jargon ('*-isms*' and '*-ologies*' abound) makes understanding sociological research difficult at times. Nevertheless, it is hoped that this chapter will serve as an enlightening and useful introduction for midwives.

The distinctiveness of sociological research

Arguably the boundaries between sociological, midwifery and medical research are increasingly becoming blurred in terms of their focus. For example, studies of practitioner-patient interactions are no longer exclusively the domain of medical sociologists, with midwives, obstetricians and gynaecologists increasingly turning a sociological lens on themselves (i.e. Harris and Greene, 2002; Kirwan et al, 2003; Hunt, 2004). Today sociological research retains its distinctiveness, not by being the sole preserve of sociologists, but in the kinds of questions it asks and its reliance on (as well as contribution to) sociological theory.

Giddens (2002) identifies at least four kinds of questions sociologists may ask in their research. First, there are factual questions. An example of a factual question would be: '*What proportion of pregnant women, from different social-economic groups, who plan a home birth, actually deliver at home?*'. Second, there are comparative questions, which relate one social context within society to another, or contrast examples from different societies. For example: '*Why do rates of home birth vary so significantly in different communities around the UK, or in comparison to other countries?*'. The third kinds of questions sociologists may ask are developmental questions. These kinds of questions require sociologists to not only look at societies in relation to each other, but also to consider their past and present. For example, in order to understand more about rates of home birth today you could look at the history of home birth in the UK since the industrial revolution. The fourth kinds of questions sociologists pose are theoretical questions. These are the questions that enable them to interpret their data because it is theory, not data that defines patterns and gives meaning; thus it is theory that enables us to see things differently. An example of a theoretical question would be: '*To what extent do concepts of social class explain the relationship between home birth and socio-economic status in the UK today?*'.

Another way in which sociological research may be distinct is if it is undertaken with the political aim of changing aspects of society for the better. As already highlighted, feminist research is a variant of critical social science. It is principally undertaken to improve the position and experiences of women in society. Over the course of the last 40 years a distinctly feminist research agenda has evolved in response to 'malestream' research. The term **malestream** refers to the absence of gender issues in mainstream sociological research (Abbot et al, 2005). In contrast to malestream research, feminist research centres on gender issues and focuses on the everyday aspects of women's lives. Seminal examples of distinctively feminist sociological research into childbirth include Ann Cartwright's (1979) '*The dignity of labour? A study of childbearing and induction*' and Ann Oakley's (1979) '*From here to maternity: Becoming a mother*'. These studies pioneered an approach to researching womens' everyday experiences of childbirth that has inspired countless researchers since and led to the implementation of a philosophy of 'woman-centred care' in NHS maternity services (DH, 1993).

However, arguably the most distinguishing feature of all sociological research, compared to midwifery or medical research, is the conscious relationship between **methods, methodology, theoretical perspective** and **epistemology**. In social research texts the bulk of discussion and much of the terminology relate to these four distinct elements, all of which are essential to the research process (see *Box 8.1*).

Crotty (1998) defines methods as 'the techniques or procedure used to gather and analyse data related to some research question or hypothesis.' In sociology observation is an example of a research method. Crotty (1998) defines methodology as: '...*the strategy, plan of action, process or design lying behind the choice and use of particular methods and linking the choice and use of methods to the desired outcomes*'. A sociologist using observation as a method would most likely be using ethnography as their methodological approach. Crotty (1998) defines theoretical perspective as: '...*the philosophical stance informing the methodology and thus providing a context for the process and grounding its logic and criteria*'. Therefore to extend the example, a sociologist using observation as a method, within an ethnographic methodological approach, would most likely be aligned with symbolic interactionism as a theoretical perspective. Finally, Crotty (1998) defines epistemology as: '...*the theory of knowledge embedded in the theoretical perspective and thereby in the methodology*'.

The epistemology embedded in symbolic interactionism is interpretivism (also known as 'interpretive' sociology). So observation is an appropriate method, as part of an ethnographic methodological approach, which stems from symbolic interactionism as a theoretical perspective and is underpinned by an interpretivist epistemology.

Figure 8.1 represents the complex relationship between epistemology, theoretical perspective, methodology, and research methods in a simple schema.

Box 8.1 Four elements in social research design (Crotty, 1998: 3)

• **Methods** are the techniques or procedure used to gather and analyse data related to some research question or hypothesis.

• **Methodology** is the strategy, plan of action, process or design lying behind the choice and use of particular methods and linking the choice and use of methods to the desired outcomes.

• **Theoretical perspective** is the philosophical stance informing the methodology and thus providing a context for the process and grounding its logic and criteria.

• **Epistemology** is the theory of knowledge embedded in the theoretical perspective and thereby in the methodology.

An easy way to think about the relationship between methods, methodology, theoretical perspective and epistemology is to ask the following questions:

- What methods do you propose to use?
- What methodology governs your choice and use of methods?
- What theoretical perspective lies behind the methodology in question?
- What epistemology informs this theoretical perspective?

The top layer of *Figure 8.1* represents epistemological considerations. As previously stated, in sociology there is no single research paradigm (unlike in the natural sciences where objectivism prevails). In sociology, objectivism and interpretivism are both dominant theories of knowledge. Moreover, since the 1970s they have existed alongside feminist epistemologies and post-modernism and its variants (i.e. post-structuralism and post-constructivism).

Objectivism is the belief that knowledge has an objective existence independent of human study. Put simply, the world around us exists independently of us and we 'discover' facts that are already out there. In contrast, interpretivism is underpinned by the belief that knowledge is culturally derived and representative of historically situated interpretations of the world. In other words, human understanding of the world is constructed by us; we make meaning through interpretation and action. Hence, variants of interpretive sociology are also known as **constructivism**. In sociological enquiry the epistemological perspective you adopt ultimately depend on your research question. Studies that ask why, or want to explore human attitudes, beliefs and meaning are best addressed by an interpretive epistemological approach, whilst studies that seek to explore incidence or establish causation typically adopt an objectivist epistemological approach.

Arguably the most influential of feminist epistemologies is standpoint epistemology. Feminist standpoint epistemology asserts that feminist knowledge can only come from examining the unique experiences of women as an oppressed social group. The philosophical arguments for standpoint epistemology are associated with the work of Sandra Harding (1986, 2004). However, more sophisticated, post-modern variants of standpoint epistemology have since been developed (i.e. Haraway 1988, 1991). There are many variants of **post-modernist** epistemology. Jean-François **Lyotard** (1984) asserts that all knowledge is essentially stories about the world and is therefore critical of the 'meta-narratives' (grand stories) that claim objective knowledge is possible. Thus some variants of post-modern epistemology confine themselves to critiquing existing knowledge about the world (i.e. Lyotard, 1984; see Kamuf, 1991 for a discussion of Derrida), whilst others engage in empirical research to advance post-modern theory. In sociology, certain epistemological approaches are associated with specific theoretical perspectives.

The second layer in *Figure 8.1* represents theoretical considerations. Typically (although not exclusively) structural theoretical perspectives are aligned

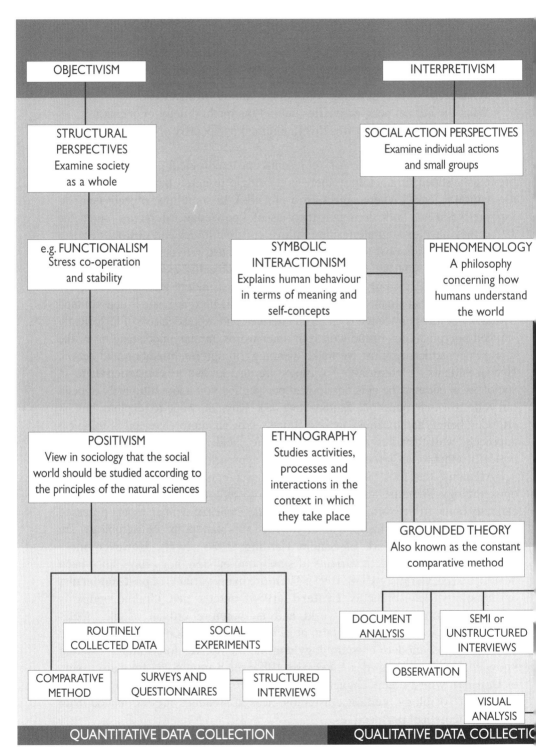

Figure 8.1 Relationship between epistemology, theoretical perspective, methodology

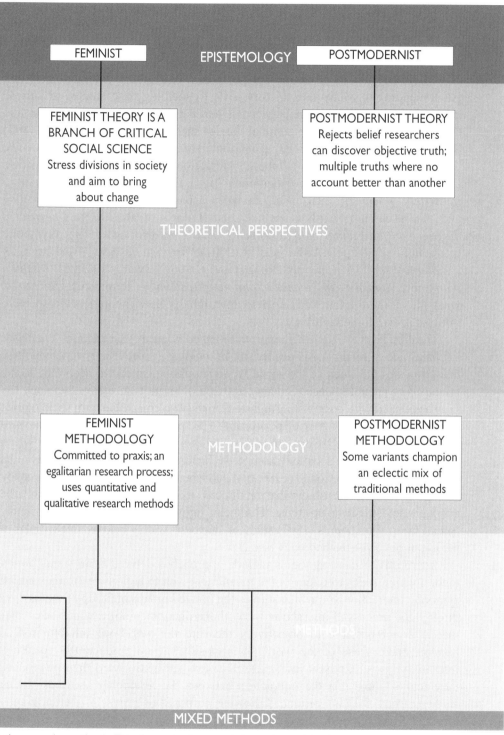

and research methods. This figure is discussed throughout this chapter.

with objectivist epistemology, whilst social action perspectives are aligned with interpretivist epistemology. Notable exceptions to this dichotomy include the many variants of feminist and postmodernist theory. Chapter one introduced key theoretical perspectives in sociology including structuralism (i.e. functionalism and Marxism) and social action perspectives (i.e. symbolic interactionism and phenomenology). Many introductory texts to sociology use studies of suicide to illustrate the relationship between a particular theoretical perspective and sociological research. These seminal studies include Emile Durkheim's (1897) *'Suicide: a study in sociology'* (functionalism), Jack Douglas's (1967) *'The social meaning of suicide'* (symbolic interactionism) and Maxwell Atkinson's (1978) *'Discovering suicide'* (phenomenology). Examples of studies relevant to midwifery where the relationship between a particular theoretical perspective and the research is explicit include Joan Lalor's et al (2007) *'Unexpected diagnosis of fetal abnormality: Women's encounters with caregivers'* (symbolic interactionism), Angela Arthur's et al (2007) *'Teenage mothers' experiences of a maternity services'* (phenomenology) and Nadine Edwards's (2005) *'Birthing autonomy: Women's experiences of planning homebirth'* (feminism). Ultimately, what all of these examples serve to highlight is how theoretical perspective informs research methodology.

The third layer in *Figure 8.1* represents methodological considerations. On the far left hand-side of *Figure 8.1* is **positivism**. In sociology, positivism is a methodology that advocates the study of the social world should be conducted according to the principals of natural science (Giddens, 2002:695). From its inception sociology has been associated with positivism. Auguste Comte (who coined the term sociology) is credited as being the 'father of positivism'. His 'positive philosophy' was devised to equip sociology, the 'science of society', with a methodological approach which he believed would see sociology ascend the hierarchy of the natural sciences to its pinnacle. According to Comte (1986, first published in the 1840s) sociological study should be confined to observable or directly measurable phenomena. Similarly, although not strictly a positivist, Durkheim argued that sociology should study 'social facts'. Durkheim's (1897) study of suicide is widely held as an exemplar of the use of positivist methodology (see *Box 8.2*).

Interpretivist methodologies include approaches derived from social action theory, which seeks to interpret the meanings given to actions by human actors; symbolic interactionism, which studies the image humans build up of themselves through the process of interaction with others; phenomenology, which advocates that it is not possible to objectively measure the world we inhabit, instead humans make sense of the world by imposing meaning. Generally speaking, interpretivist sociologists view research as less straightforward than positivists; they acknowledge that the interaction between the researcher and those being studied affects the data produced. For the purposes of *Figure 8.1*, ethnography (derived from symbolic interactionism) provides an illustrative example of an interpretive methodology.

The ethos of ethnography is to emerge oneself in the culture under study, an approach that has its origins in late nineteenth century anthropology. In sociology, the development of ethnography as an influential methodology is credited to the University of Chicago's Sociology Department (also known as the 'Chicago School') who combined the development of interpretative theory with the ethnographic study of Chicago residents during the first half of the 20th century. As a methodology ethnography is unique '*in that it studies activities,*

Box 8.2: An example of positivist methodology: '*Suicide: A study in Sociology*' (Durkheim, 1897)

In '*Suicide: A study in sociology*', Emile Durkheim (1951, first published in 1897) demonstrates how suicide rates can be explained within the framework of society, rather than the psychological state of the individual. Durkheim uses the term social facts '*to describe elements of society which can be studied independently of individual disposition*' (Morrison, 2004: 394). Arguably, the first way in which his study of suicide was positivist is in the parallels between this conceptualisation of 'social facts' and the positivist belief (advocated by Comte) that sociologists should only study phenomena that can be objectively observed and classified.

The second and less controversial way in which Durkheim's study of suicide is an exemplar of positivist methodology is in its use of statistical data. Durkheim studied the suicide rates of different countries along with other forms of numerical data (i.e. counts of educational achievements, religious affiliations and marriage rates) all of which he regarded as social facts. In so doing he was looking for relationships that could account for rates of suicide outside of the individual. Relationships (and varying strengths of relationships) in statistical data are known as correlations. Having identified correlations the next stage in positivist methodology is to establish causal connections. However, Durkheim realised that whilst a relationship may be observed between two social facts (i.e. suicide rate and level of education) it does not necessarily follow that one is causing the other to take place. Thus Durkheim developed the statistical technique known as multivariate analysis to assess the relative importance of different variables. He used multivariate analysis to identify the most important social facts and determine whether causal relationships existed between them. The most important causal relationship he found was between suicide rates and religious affiliation.

The final stage in positivist methodology is to establish laws of human behaviour. Whilst few sociologists today would describe themselves as positivists, nevertheless many continue to use positivist principles in their analysis and interpretation of statistical data. Neo-positivist is the term used to describe contemporary sociologists who believe that the use of objective scientific methods can produce factual data that meaningfully explains social phenomena.

processes and interactions in the context in which they take place and not in artificial situations constructed for the purpose' (Hunt and Symonds, 1995: 41). Irving Goffman's (1961) *'Asylums'* provides a widely cited seminal example of the use of ethnographic methodology in sociology (see *Box 8.3*). However, in recent years there has been debate around a precise definition of ethnography and whether or not it is a methodology or a method (Atkinson and Hammersley, 1994; Denzin and Lincoln, 1994). Ethnography is not the only approach to social research where controversy exists as to whether it is a methodology or method.

In-between the methodology and the methods layer in the interpretivist branch of *Figure 8.1* is grounded theory. Grounded theory, like ethnography, is one of many qualitative approaches in sociological research, but it is perhaps the one that most midwives have heard of. Examples of midwifery research that have employed a grounded theory approach include Carlsson et al (2007) and Schneider's (2002) research. Grounded theory originates from the work of the sociologists Barney Glasner and Anselm Straus (1967). Having said that, a number of different variants of grounded theory have emerged since the original, see for example Anselm Strauss and Juliet Corbin (1997, 1998). Broadly speaking, **grounded theory** aims to produce theories that are grounded in in-depth data and the real social world. At the heart of grounded theory is the idea of the constant comparative method, where concepts or categories emerging from one stage of data collection and analysis are compared with concepts emerging from the next, thus fuelling assertions that it is principally a method, not methodology.

Feminist methodology does not share the concern of positivist and interpretive

---

Box 8.3: An example of ethnographic methodology:
'Asylums: Essays on the social situation of mental patients and other inmates' (Goffman, 1961)

Erving Goffman's (1961) *'Asylums'* is principally written around his observations at the National Institute of Mental Health in Washington, USA, where he sought employment and as a consequence was able to observe the naturally occurring interactions between staff and patients. His use of 'covert' observation raises significant ethical considerations today; nevertheless the study remains an exemplar of how emerging oneself in the culture under study can reveal hitherto unquestioned aspects of human behaviour and social action. Goffman famously observed how upon admission to 'total institutions' such as asylums and prisons individuals are stripped of their previous sense of self by the removal of personal possessions, by the clothing the are required to wear, by the assignment of a number and by the restriction of contact with their social network through designated visiting times only. Goffman observed numerous responses by patients to this process, from complete withdrawal to outright resistance and 'acting the part.'

methodologies with how best to access 'the truth' about the social world. The essence of **feminist methodology** is to minimise harm to those being researched and to diminish the control exercised by the researcher; underpinned by a commitment to produce research of value to women and improve their lives (DeVault, 1999). Thus the dictates of feminist methodology infuse feminist theory and activism into how feminists actually do research. There are many seminal feminist methodology papers (e.g. Finch, 1984; Graham ,1983; Oakley, 1981; Roberts, 1992a). Helen Roberts (1992b) edited collection '*Women's Health Matters*' and the sister volume '*Women's Health Counts*' (Roberts, 1990) provide two excellent starting points for midwives interested how feminist methodology has been employed in health research. Collectively this body of literature serves to highlight the variety of methods that can be employed in feminist methodology.

The fourth layer in *Figure 8.1* includes examples of research methods associated with different methodologies, theoretical perspectives and epistemological approaches. Remember that Crotty (1998: 3) stated that '*methods are the techniques or procedure used to gather and analyse data related to some research question or hypothesis*'. Examples of research methods commonly used in sociology include accessing routinely collected data (i.e. official statistics), or undertaking surveys, interviews and observations. The use of routinely collected data, social experiments, surveys and structured interviews are typically associated with positivist methodology, whilst semi-structured or unstructured interviews (also known as in-depth interviews) and observation or document analysis are most commonly associated with interpretivist methodologies. Before discussing these commonly used sociological research methods in more detail, it is important to highlight a key distinction between the type of data generated by the research methods on the left hand side of *Figure 8.1* (*quantitative*) and the type generated by the methods to the right of these, which appear in the centre of the flow diagram (*qualitative*).

Quantitative and qualitative data

In sociology, a distinction has long been made between **quantitative** and **qualitative** approaches. Quantitative research approaches are defined as 'any research that results in the data being expressed in numerical form (Jary and Jary, 1991). Quantitative research is typically associated with objectivism and positivism. Examples of quantitative study designs and methods include social experiments, surveys and randomised controlled trials where questionnaires and proformas are used. When reading a research paper in a journal one of the easiest ways of determining whether or not a quantitative approach was used is to look at how the results section is presented. If the results section includes tables and charts it is most likely a quantitative piece of research, whereas if it includes quotes, diagrams or visual images a qualitative research design was used.

Qualitative research approaches are generally associated with interpretivism. They rely on sociologists' skills as empathetic interviewers or observers to collect unique data, which is considered to be 'rich' in detail and close to the informants' perceived world (Jary and Jary, 1991). Qualitative approaches are much more than simply the antithesis of quantitative approaches, they focus on the complex and broad; that is the words, images, actions and meaning that 'make' the world we live in. Examples of qualitative study designs include exploratory studies, ethnographic studies and studies using grounded theory. Data collection methods for qualitative studies include observation, interviews, diaries and visual methods. Qualitative methods such as photo-elicitation, participant observation, diaries, narrative and life histories can all facilitate in-depth understanding and insights into aspects of society and ourselves.

At this point in the chapter, it should be clear to midwives that in sociology certain epistemological approaches, theoretical perspectives, and methodologies are typically associated with particular methods. Moreover, those adopting a structural theoretical approach typically use quantitative methods, whilst the kinds of research questions asked by interpretivist sociologists are most typically suited to qualitative research methods. Having said that it is equally important to highlight that the need for such rigid divide between quantitative and qualitative research approaches has long been questioned and many contemporary sociologists now mix methods. The next section discusses commonly used methods in social research in more detail and what is to be gained by mixing quantitative and qualitative methods.

Sociological research methods

As already highlighted, studies that ask why, or want to explore human attitudes, beliefs and meaning are best addressed by the interpretive branch of *Figure 8.1*, whilst studies that seek to explore incidence or establish causation are best addressed in the objectivist branch. Thus it is the nature of your research question that determines your epistemological approach, theoretical and methodological considerations and which methods you use for collecting data.

In sociology, the field of investigation is inevitably broad. This means that what qualifies as data is inevitably broader than traditionally used in medical and midwifery research. In sociological research data may be either 'found' in the everyday world (e.g. newspaper articles, television interviews) or manufactured (e.g. questionnaires, interviews) (Silverman, 2007). A distinction is made between methods for obtaining data from primary and secondary sources. Primary data is data collected by the sociologists (or their teams) own effort and with a specific purpose in mind. Secondary data is material collected or produced by other people (for quite different purposes) that sociologists re-interpret and analyse for their research. Official statistical records are an example of secondary data. A further distinction may also be made between public and private documents as sources of data (Denzin, 1970). Examples of public documents include newspapers and advertisements, whilst examples of private documents include letters, diaries, and autobiographies (Burgess, 1991).

Figure 8.1 identifies social experiments, the comparative method, routinely collected data, surveys and structured interviews as key methods for quantitative data collection. This section discusses each of these methods in turn.

Experiments

Sociologists rarely carry out laboratory experiments. This is because laboratory experiments involving humans (such as those undertaken in psychology for example) confine individuals to artificial situations where the knowledge that they are under study is known to affect behaviour and distort result. Moreover, many of the issues sociologists are interested in cannot be recreated in a laboratory setting (i.e. communities, social change).

Thus the kinds of experiments typically undertaken by sociologists are field experiments. However these experiments have proved no less problematic as evident in the infamous study by Elton Mayo (1933) at the Hawthorne works of the Western Electricity Company in Chicago. A social experiment was designed to test aspects of worker productivity. However, irrespective of the intervention, productivity increased throughout the study period. This effect, where humans modify their behaviour by virtue of knowingly being studied in a social setting, has subsequently become known as the **Hawthorne effect**. The only way to avoid the Hawthorne effect is if participants are unaware a social experiment is taking place, which raises often insurmountable ethical issues. Nevertheless, an example of a sociologist who has successfully employed experimental designs in the field of health and social care research is the feminist Ann Oakley. Oakley has employed experimental designs in studies of social support and motherhood (1990) and sex education in schools (2004). She has also argued for greater recognition of the value of social experiments and the inclusion of qualitative components in trial design (Oakley, 1998; 2004a,b; 2005).

Comparative method

The comparative method involves the comparison of different societies, or the comparison of different groups in a single society, or the comparison of the same group or society at different time-points. The comparative method is most useful in examining social change. Examples of sociological studies using the comparative method already alluded to in this book include classic works by Durkheim, Marx and Weber (see chapter one) and more recent studies such as O'Brien and Jones (1996, see chapter five) that compared contemporary families and kinship in east London with the findings of Wilmott (1963). An example of a midwifery research study that utilised the comparative method is Jo Green et al (2003) '*Greater expectations*', which was designed specifically to facilitate comparison with the earlier findings of '*Great expectations: A prospective study of women's expectations and experiences of childbirth*' (Green et al, 1988).

Statistics

Official statistics are the most important type of routinely collected data used by sociologists. In the UK the government produces a vast range of official statistics that are published by the Office for National Statistics (ONS). The ONS is responsible for the registration of vital events (i.e. births, marriages, deaths) through the General Register Office, the census and other large surveys (for example the national crime survey, the general household survey), which provide important information about our society (ONS, 2008). Of particular relevance to midwives are Birth Statistics (ONS, 2007) and NHS Maternity Statistics 2005-6 (ONS, 2007). The latter is an annual bulletin that summarises information relating to all NHS maternity units and includes some comparisons with similar data from earlier years. Other bulletins such as Social Trends, which is published annually, or Health Statistics Quarterly also provide valuable information.

The value of official statistics in sociological research has been much debated, particularly in the field of crime and deviance, where official statistics have been shown to be unreliable. However, even if the limitations of using routinely collected data are acknowledged, official statistics can be very useful. Moreover, they are easily accessible and cost sociologists nothing to produce (Haralambos, 1991). *Table 8.1* summarises the strengths and limitations of using routinely collected data compared with other commonly used sociological research methods.

Surveys

Sociologists regard surveys as an invaluable source of data. Newell (1995) lists four main categories of information that can be obtained from a survey:

- Attributes (i.e. personal characteristics or circumstances)
- Behaviour
- Attitudes
- Beliefs.

Surveys involve the completion of a predetermined list of questions (i.e. a questionnaire). They can be conducted over the internet, the telephone, via postal services or face-to-face and completed either on a hard (paper) copy or electronically. Surveys where a researcher administers a questionnaire to a

Table 8.1 Strengths and weaknesses of the main methods used in sociological research

Research method	Strengths	Weaknesses
Routinely collected data	• Already gathered therefore cannot be influenced by researcher • Generalisations can be made • Cheap and quick to use • Seen by positivists as being objective	• The information gathered may not be accurate • Does not explore individuals' meaning of the situation • Imposes meanings and realities where they may not exist • Static and does not explore processes
Surveys, structured interviews and questionnaires	• Can be used to collect large quantities of data from considerable numbers of people, relatively cheaply and in a short period of time • Requires little personal involvement with respondents • Relatively quick to analyse • Produces 'objective' data	• Researcher imposes their assumptions on respondents in a predetermined framework • May lack validity if a questionnaire is poorly designed or respondents give inaccurate or incomplete responses • Postal surveys typically have low response rates • Responses may not be what people actually believe but what they which to be seen to believe in
Semi or unstructured interviews	• Flexible and adaptive way of finding things out • Face-to-face interviews offer the possibility of modifying one's line of enquiry, following up interesting responses or investigating underlying motives • Rich, in-depth responses can be gained • Participation van be gained from a wide range of people	• Quality of the data generated is determined by the skills of individual interviewers • Interviewer influence may lead to acceptable responses • Often generate huge amounts of data • Data collection and analysis can be very labour intensive for the researcher • Can be expensive • Findings will be neither replicable, nor generaliseable
Observation (overt, covert or non-participating)	• Gets close to 'reality' • Does not change the behaviour of the subject of study, specially if observation is covert • Allows close, small scale study • Is not static, therefore allows subjects of study to develop and change over time	• Covert observation raises substantial ethical issues • Overt observation could change the behaviour and attitudes of subjects of study • Generalisations cannot be made • Too small scale • Danger of discovery if observation is covert • Time-consuming and expensive

respondent are known as structured interviews. Surveys are a relatively cheap and easy way to access data from large numbers of people. However, the value of any survey is ultimately dependent upon the quality of the questions asked (see Oppenheim, 2001) and the representiveness of respondents (see Aldridge and Levine, 2001).

There are two forms of question that may be used in a survey. Open questions are those that allow individuals to respond in any way they wish, whilst closed questions are drafted in advance, complete with all the possible answers which could be given. The use of closed questions generates statistical data that can be analysed quantitatively, whilst the answers to open questions may be grouped for quantitative analysis or if particularly lengthy, analysed qualitatively. However, structured interviews (that use questionnaires to generate quantitative data for surveys) should not be confused with semi-structured or un-structured interviews that use interview schedules to generate qualitative data.

Figure 8.1 identifies semi-structured interviews, observation, documentary analysis and visual methods as important methods for qualitative data collection. A semi-structured interview is where the interviewer has a pre-defined list of open questions to ask the interviewee (for example: '*What do you enjoy about being a mother?*'. '*Who has influenced your perceptions of motherhood?*'). An unstructured interview does not have a formal interview schedule, instead the interviewer begins by posing a general question and the ensuing conversation is led entirely by the response of the interviewee (for example: '*Can you tell me about motherhood?*'). In some variants of social research (i.e. grounded theory) it is usual for an interview schedule to develop as the project progresses.

Observation

All sociological research involves some sort of observation, however the specific form of observation referred to here is the observation of social phenomena in the setting where it naturally occurs. This kind of in-depth observation is used by ethnographers and phenomenologists as a key source of data and is known as participant observation. There are several types of participant observation:

- Overt
- Covert
- Non-participant.

Overt participant observation is where those studied know why the researcher is there and s/he engages in interactions with them. Covert participant observation is where the researcher conceals their 'true' identify from those under study. Non-participant observation is where a researcher observes events without getting involved. Using observation as a method involved taking copious field notes. This means you need to make detailed descriptions of events, people, conversations and setting. It is also important to record your personal impressions and feelings as the observation unfolds.

In sociology there are many examples of participant observation studies (e.g. Humpreys, 1970; Young, 1971; Sanders, 2004). However, participant observation in a healthcare setting is problematic because you must get the informed consent of everyone you observe. This makes covert participant observation impossible. However, non-participant observation has been used successfully in a number of recent studies. For example, Julia Simpson successfully used observation as a method to access naturally occurring talk between medical teams in an obstetric theatre (Simpson, 2004). Denis Walsh fruitfully observed daily events in a free-standing birth centre (Walsh, 2006).

Documentary analysis

In addition to interviews and observation, ethnographers will often use some form of qualitative documentary analysis in their research. This may involve analysing contemporary documents (i.e. governments reports or newspapers as they become available), or examining historical documents such as letters or diaries. One example of an ethnographic study that does just this combining documentary analysis, observations and interviews is Rayna Rapp's (2000) *'Testing women, testing the fetus: The social impact of amniocentesis in America'*. Sometimes documentary analysis will require a form a visual analysis.

Visual methods

This is an umbrella term for a range of techniques and tools that are used to collect and analyse visual data. Examples of visual data include almost everything that we can see: a photograph depicting a particular scene, children's drawings (Prosser, 2008), speech and thought bubbles (Wall et al, 2007), concept maps (Georghiades, 2000) or 'shooting back' — where respondents are given cameras and invited to record aspects of their life that are important to them. Since the early 1980s increasing numbers of sociologists have studied imagery and there are now many excellent texts on the subject (see Prosser, 1998; Banks, 2001; Van Leewen and Jewitt, 2001; Pink, 2007). There is no one particular way of conducting visual research and studies may utilise multiple media (i.e. video, still cameras, camera phones), adopt a particular perspective (i.e. semiotics, socio-semiotics, critical theory), or be aligned with a particular discipline (i.e. sociology, cultural studies, visual anthropology). Moreover, whilst an association is often made between visual methods and qualitative research, it is important to note that not all visual methods are qualitative; content analysis for example is a quantitative approach. Arguably, the most widely used visual method is photo-elicitation, where photographs (which may be researcher found, research generated or respondent generated) are used to explore the significance or meaning evoked by a particular image. In sociology, photo-elicitation is used in mediated interviews with varying degrees of success. In midwifery, Lesley Briscoe has highlighted some of the pitfalls of using respondent generated photos that where intended to promote discussion about aspects of asylum women's experiences of maternity care (unpublished MPhil thesis). The usefulness of visual research to midwifery is currently being explored by, amongst others, Clara Haken (2008), Cathie Melvin (2008) and Holly Kennedy (2008). Moreover, if midwives reflect only on the images used in this book it should be apparent how important the visual is in how humans make sense of the social world we inhabit. Visual research is an exciting field, however, even the most experienced and passionate visual researcher would not argue that the visual should be prioritised over all other forms of social research. Consequently, most visual research is undertaken as a component of studies using other methods as well.

Mixed methods

This is the term used when multiple methods of data collection are combined in the same study. For example, ethnography typically includes observation, documentary analysis and interviewing, thus combining the assets and weakness of different qualitative methods (Reinharz, 1992). Mixed methods may also refer to the mixing of quantitative and qualitative methods. For example, as discussed in chapter four, the feminist sociologist Hilary Graham (1990) demonstrates the value of using statistical and qualitative data in an exemplar study that sought to explain the complexity of identifying and pursuing patterns of behaviour that promote health. An association is often made between mixed methods and the concept of **triangulation**.

The qualitative researcher, Norman Denzin (1970, 1978) defines triangulation as the combination of methodologies in the study of the same phenomenon. He identifies four variants; method triangulation (where different methods are used to address the same phenomenon); data triangulation (where different data sources are used to address the same phenomenon); investigator triangulation (where different investigators are used in the same study); theoretical triangulation (where different theoretical models are used in the same study). More recently, other authors have added 'analysis triangulation' and 'interdisciplinary triangulation' to this list (Janestick, 1994). Denzin's (1970) notion of triangulation is based on capturing a more reliable picture of social reality. In other words, the findings of one method are compared with the findings of another to confirm the accuracy of each. An alternative view on the usefulness of combing methods is offered by the qualitative sociologist David Silverman (1985). He asserts that the use of multiple sources of data can be helpful in overcoming the partiality of data drawn from a single source, but does not believe that the intention should be to judge between the accuracy of each method used. An example of a study that mixes methods in this way is my own (Kingdon, 2007). Routinely collected data (hospital records), questionnaires and interview data where all collected to gain a richer picture of the multiple realities of women's first experiences of childbirth.

The intention was never to judge which method reflected reality most accurately; they all captured different, but no less important realities.

The first section in this chapter identified what is distinct about sociological research, whilst this section has highlighted commonly used sociological research methods. The next section introduces the actual process of 'doing' research. However, before outlining key stages in the research process, there is one final point to make about the relationship between epistemology, theoretical perspective, methodology, methods, quantitative and qualitative data; they determine how the credibility of your research is judged.

Assessing quality

There are a number of different ways of judging quality in research. Positivist research has traditionally been judged in relation to notions of generalisability, validity and reliability. In the social sciences as in the natural sciences, the generalisability of your research relates to what degree of confidence you can say your findings are applicable to the general population. Reliability refers to the extent to which another researcher could replicate the same methodology and produce the same results. Data is considered valid if it is considered to provide a 'true' picture of what is being studied. A number of criteria exist for judging quality in qualitative research including credibility, dependability, confirmability and transferability (Lincioln and Guba, 1985), relevance and validity (Mays and Pope, 2000), and relevance, validity and reflexivity (Malterud, 2001). Central to each of these criteria is the view that the findings of good qualitative research should resonate beyond the setting in which it was undertaken, the research process must be undertaken in accordance with the highest methodological standards, and researchers must acknowledge their own preconceptions before exploring the meanings of social phenomena as experienced by those studied. The role of researcher in the processes of knowledge production is considered particularly important in qualitative research, therefore in all qualitative research papers there should be some discussion of reflexivity. Reflexivity refers to the processes associated with researchers' self-awareness of how they impact and transform the research they undertake. However, just as the notions of generalisability, validity and reliability have been used to judge quantitative and qualitative research; there is no reason why credibility, dependability, transferability and reflexivity may not be used to judge qualitative and quantitative research. For an accessible summary of reflexivity and its application beyond qualitative research midwives may refer to Kingdon (2005).

Carrying out sociological research

When undertaking research, a series of predefined steps, known as the research process, is generic across many disciplines (including sociology and midwifery).

Each of these key steps is illustrated in *Figure 8.2*. When undertaking an actual research project you may find each of these steps does not succeed each other in such a linear fashion, nevertheless you should find each of these steps present. For example, a researcher using grounded theory would not review the literature in any depth prior to collecting their data; they would do this after data collection. Thus midwives planning to actually undertake a piece of research should read this section as an introduction and consult more detailed research methods books for the specific steps, and the order undertaken, for further guidance.

As identified in *Figure 8.2*, the research process begins with the identification of the research focus, or in other words, defining the area that you wish to research. Once you have identified this, the next step is to establish what is already known about the area. This is achieved by speaking to experts and systematically reviewing existing literature. You must undertake a comprehensive literature search. This can be done particularly effectively using the electronic databases widely available through university and NHS libraries. The actual databases to be searched will depend on your individual research focus. Two important databases to identify relevant literature from sociology are Sociofile and the Social Science Citation Index (SSCI). In addition library catalogues should be searched because many sociological studies are published as monographs (books). It is also a good idea to 'berry pick' from the reference lists of particularly relevant literature. When searching the literature a good search strategy is of the utmost importance. Colin Robson's (2002) chapter entitled '*Developing your ideas*' provides an excellent overview of how to search the literature and formulate research questions.

Once you have established what is already known about your planned area of investigation you are in a position to finalise your research question, select an appropriate research design and methods. An example of a research design is a longitudinal study, or in other words a study that follows the same group of individuals over an extended period of time. Other examples of study designs include exploratory studies or randomised controlled trials.

Having selected your research design you must them make decisions about your sample. A sample is the actual individuals to be studied. In sociology there are a number of different ways of selecting a sample. If you need to access large numbers of people (i.e. in a survey) the simplest way to select a large sample is to use random sampling (also known as probability sampling). For example, if you have a list of all the nulliparous women attending NHS antenatal booking clinics in a one-month period, if you use random sampling each woman on the list has an equal chance of being chosen to participate in your study. A number would be assigned to each woman's name and then you would use a random number table (found in most statistics books, for example Campbell and Machin, 1995: 182) to select which women will be approached to take part. Random sampling relies on statistical probability to ensure the representativeness of the sample and therefore requires large samples to be confident that the sample is genuinely representative

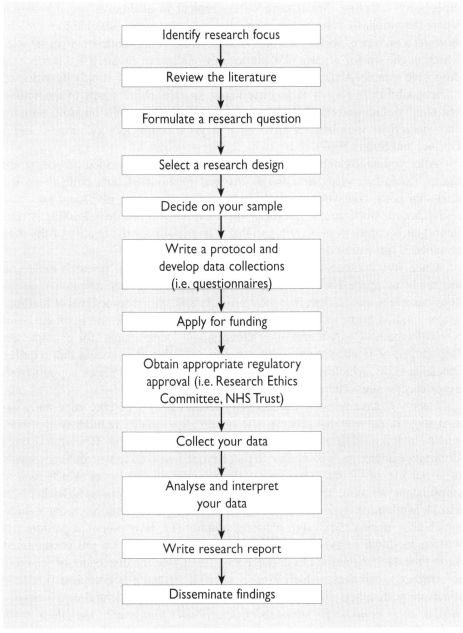

Figure 8.2 The research process

of the population. Systematic sampling is where you would select every 10th or 20th woman on the list so it is not strictly speaking random. In quantitative social research other sampling techniques included stratified random-sampling (involves the division of the sampling frame into groups in order to ensure the sample is representative), quota sampling, multi-stage sampling and nonprobability sampling. Small samples are typical in qualitative social research where the emphasis is on accessing as diverse a sample as possible to represent as wider a picture of social phenomena as possible. A non-representative sample, which is chosen for a particular purpose in qualitative research is known as a purposive sample. A sample that is available to a researcher simply by virtue of its accessibility is known as a convenience sample. Other forms of qualitative sampling include snowball sampling (where personal contacts build up sample) and theoretical sampling as advocated in grounded theory (Charmez, 1983; Glasner and Straus 1967).

After you have established your focus of enquiry and decided on your study design (including your sampling frame and methods of data collection), the next step is to write your research protocol (your research plan) and pilot any research tools (for example questionnaires, interview schedules). Piloting is very important because, as already highlighted, in any survey the quality of the data obtained is ultimately dependent upon good questionnaire design.

Once your protocol is written and you have all of your research tools you are ready to apply for research funding. Undertaking any research requires considerable resource, therefore most projects will require some level of funding. Major funding bodies of social research in the UK include the Economic and Social Research Council and other Government Departments (for example the Department of Health). Applying for funding is a lengthy process that requires specialist skills, which means that novice researchers should seek support from experienced teams when applying for funding.

Once you have secured the necessary resources to undertake your study the next stage in the research process is to obtain all necessary regulatory approval, which includes organisational management approval and Research Ethics Committee approval. It is inevitable that anyone involved in researching aspects of social life or human behaviour will encounter ethical issues which require careful consideration, irrespective of their methodological approach (Richardson and McMullan, 2007). Examples of common ethical considerations include those which arise during the design phase of a study (i.e. how potential participants will be recruited to avoid any undue coercion), those which are encountered during the data collection phase (i.e. how to deal with the disclosure of sensitive information), and those which remain after the research is complete (i.e. how to ensure participants anonymity in publications and confidential data storage). Whilst '*there is no single set of rules or practices that govern the ethics, truth and politics of a research project*' (Soobrayman, 2003: 107), there are a number of regulatory committees and professional codes of conduct that set the standards by which your research may be deemed 'ethical' or 'unethical.' The NHS has a National Research Ethics Service (NRES) with a centralised application system. Any research that involves NHS patients (or their data), staff or premises requires a favourable review by an NHS Research Ethics Committee. A useful overview of the history and principles underpinning NHS RECs, as well as discussion of some of the particular ethical considerations raised by qualitative research, can be found in Manning (2004).

In sociology, a number of projects generated furious debate during the 1970s concerning issues of sponsorship (Horowitz, 1967), secrecy and deception (Humphreys, 1970) and the anonymity of respondents in published data (Vidich and Bensman, 1958, 1968). This led the British Sociological Association to produce a statement of ethical practice in 1970; the 2002 version of which can be accessed at the Association's website. As reflected in the most recent British Sociological Association statement of ethical practice, contemporary ethical debates in sociology are complex and diverse, encompassing issues of personal integrity, responsibilities to research participants and obligations to research funders. There are numerous sociological papers that focus exclusively on the ethical issues — papers that midwives may find useful include Corrigan (2003), Miller and Boulton (2007) and Malone (2003) whose insights into researching 'in your own back yard' may be transferable to midwives undertaking research in their own sphere of practice.

Finally you reach the point where you are ready to collect your data. This is often the most rewarding part of a study where you get to interact with research participants and begin to get a feel for what your study will add to existing knowledge on a subject.

Once all your data is collected the next step is to analyse and interpret your data. Quantitative data analysis typically involves the use of statistics. The Statistical Package for Social Scientists (SPSS) is a software package designed to help in this process. Descriptive statistics are used to summarise your data, whilst inferential statistics are used to infer relationships between different variables (as highlighted in *Box 8.2*) or explore the strength of relationships between different variables. One excellent introduction to statistics written specifically for midwives is Hick's (1996). Qualitative data analysis is a lengthy and complex process that requires significant skill on the part of the researcher. Moreover, there are at least 40 different qualitative research traditions (Tesch, 1990) each with their own 'recipes' for analysis. Consequently, in addition to midwifery research text books that have individual chapters on qualitative data analysis (i.e. Lavender et al, 2004; Rees, 2003), there are many texts devoted entirely to the subject of qualitative data analysis (see Bryman and Burgess, 1994; Miles and Huberman, 1994; Richards, 2005; Silverman, 2006).

The processes associated with qualitative data analysis can be done entirely by hand or with the assistance of a computer programme designed specifically to manage qualitative data. These packages include Atlas–Ti, MAXqda, NVivo (also known as Nudist), HyperRESEARCH, QDA Miner and QUALRUS. Irrespective of the kind of research you undertake, all researchers should have a clear idea about how they plan to analyse their data long before they collect it. Research Ethics Committees and other regulatory bodies now require details of proposed analysis (quantitative or qualitative).

The research process does not end until you have produced a research report and disseminated your research findings to all appropriate audiences. Moreover, you may find that the end of one project leads into another.

Conclusion

This chapter has introduced midwives to sociological research. It has identified a number of key approaches (i.e. positivist, interpretivist, feminist, post-modernist) and highlighted the explicit relationship between methods, methodology, theoretical perspective and epistemology in sociological research. In addition, it has highlighted important differences between quantitative and qualitative research approaches, the value of mixed methods and a number of key stages and considerations in the research process, thus providing midwives with the necessary knowledge to read sociological research papers with confidence and a starting point for those who may be contemplating undertaking their own sociological research.

References

American Sociological Association (2007) *The Health of Sociology: Statistical Fact Sheet*. Available at http://www.asanet.org/galleries/Research/SocHealthsheet_Funding.pdf. Accessed: 22 February 2008

Abbot P, Wallace C, Tyler M (2005) *An Introduction to Sociology: Feminist Perspectives. 3rd edn*. Routledge, Abingdon

Alasuutari P, Bickman L, Brannen J (2008) *The Sage Handbook of Social Research Methods*. Sage, London

Aldridge A, Levine K (2001) *Surveying the Social World: Principles and Practice in Survey Research*. Open University Press, Buckingham

Arthur A, et al (2007) Teenage mothers' experiences of a maternity services: a qualitative study. *Br J Midwifery* **15**(11): 672–7

Atkinson J (1978) *Discovering Suicide*. Macmillan, London

Atkinson P, Hammersley M (1994) Ethnography and participant observation. In: Denzin NK, Lincoln YS, eds. *Handbook of Qualitative Research*. Thousand Oaks, Sage: 248–61

Banks M (2001) *Visual Methods in Social Research*. Sage, London

Bluff R (2006) Grounded Theory. In: Cluett and Bluff, ed. *Principles and Practice of Research in Midwifery*. 2nd Edition. Churchill Livingstone, London

Briscoe L (2006) *Women asylum seekers and refugees' experience of midwifery*. University of Central Lancashire: unpublished MPhil thesis

British Sociological Association (1970) Statement of ethical principles and their application to sociological practice. *Sociology* **4**(1): 114–17

Bryman A, Burgess RG, eds (1994) *Analysing Qualitative Data*. Routledge, London

Burgess RG (1991) *In the Field: An introduction to field research*. Routledge, London

Campbell MJ, Machin D (1995) *Medical Statistics: A common sense approach*. John Wiley and Sons, Chichester

Carlsson IM, Hallberg L, Odberg Pettersson K (2007) Swedish women's experiences of seeking care and being admitted during the latent phase of labour: A grounded theory study. *Midwifery*: In Press

Cartwright A (1979) T*he Dignity of Labour? A study of childbearing and induction*. Tavistock, London

Charmez K (1983) Loss of self: a fundamental form of suffering in the chronically ill. *Sociology of Health and Illness* 5: 168-95

Comte (1986 first published in 1840s) *The Positive Philosophy*. Bell & Sons, London

Corrigan O (2003) Empty ethics: The problem with informed consent. *Sociology of Health and Illness* **25**(3): 768–92

Cluett E, Bluff R (2006) Principles and Practice of Research in Midwifery. 2nd edn. Balliere Tindall, London

Crotty M (1998) *The Foundations of Social Research: Meaning and perspective in the research process*. Sage, London

Denzin NK (1970) *The Research Act in Sociology*. Butterworth, London

Denzin NK (1978) *Sociological Methods: A source book*. 2nd edn. McGraw-Hill, New York

Denzin NK, Lincoln YS, eds (1994) *Handbook of Qualitative Research*. Thousand Oaks, Sage

DH (1993) *Changing Childbirth. Part 1: Report of the Expert Maternity Group*. Stationary Office, London

DH (1998) *A First Class Service: Quality in the New NHS*. NHS Executive, Leeds

DH (2006) *Health Survey for England*. Stationery Office, London

DeVault M (1999) *Liberating Method: Feminism and social research*. Temple University Press, Philadelphia

Durkheim E (1951, first published 1897) *Suicide*. The Free Press, New York

Douglas,JD. (1967) *The Social Meaning of Suicide*. Princeton University Press, Princeton

Edwards NP (2005) *Birthing Autonomy: Women's experiences of planning home births*. Abingdon, Routledge

Finch J (1984) It's great to have someone to talk to: The ethics and politics of interviewing women. In: Bell C, Roberts H. eds. *Social Researching: Politics, Problems and Practice*. Routledge and Kegan Paul, London

Georghiades P (2000) Beyond conceptual change learning in science education: focusing on transfer, durability and metacognition. *Educational Research* **42**(2): 119–39

Glaser BG, Strauss AL (1967) *The Discovery of Grounded Theory: Strategies for qualitative research*. Aldine, Chicago

Giddens A (2002) *Sociology*. Polity Press, Cambridge

Gilbert N (1995) *Researching Social Life*. Sage Publications, London.

Goffman E (1961) *Asylums: Essays on the social situation of mental patients and other inmates*. Doubleday, New York

Graham H (1983) Do her answers fit his questions? Women and the survey method. In: Gamarnikow et al, eds. *The Public and the Private*. Heinemann, London

Graham H (1990) Behaving well: Women's health behaviour in context. In: Roberts H, ed. *Women's Health Counts*. Routledge, London: 195–219

Green JM, Coupland VA, Kitzinger JV (1998) *Great Expectations: A prospective study of women's expectations and experiences of childbirth*. 2nd edn. Books for Midwives Press, London

Green JM, Baston HA, Easton SC, McCormick F (2003) *Greater Expectations: The inter-relationship between women's expectations and experiences of decision making, continuity, choice and control in labour, and psychological outcomes. Summary report*. Mother & Infant Research Unit, University of Leeds

Haken C (2008) *Staging Labour: Representations of childbirth on contemporary British television*. International Confederation of Midwives, SECC, Glasgow, Scotland, June 2008

Harding S (1986) *The Science Question in Feminism*. Cornell University Press, New York

Harding S, ed (2004) *The Feminist Standpoint Theory Reader: Intellectual & political controversies*. Routledge, New York

Haraway D (1988) Situated knowledges: the science question in feminism and the privilege of partial perspective. Feminist Studies, 14 (2), pp.583-590.

Haraway D (1991) Situated knowledges: the science question and the privilege of partial perspective. In: Haraway D, ed. *Simians, Cyborgs, and Women: The reinvention of nature*. Routledge, New York: 183–201

Harris M, Greene KR (2002) *How Good Communication and Support – or their Absence – Affect Labour Outcomes. The Rising Caesarean Section Rate: From audit to action*. Royal College of Physicians, London

Hicks CM (1996) *Undertaking Midwifery Research: A basic guide to design and analysis*. Churchill Livingstone, New York

Horowitz IL, ed (1967) *The Rise and Fall of Project Camelot*. MIT Press, Cambridge, Massachussets

Humphreys L (1970) *Tearoom Trade*. Duckworth, London

Hunt S, Symonds A (1995) *The Social Meaning of Midwifery*. Macmillan Press, Basingstoke

Haralambos M, Holborn M (1991) *Sociology: Themes and perspectives*. Collins Educational, London

Hunt S (2004) *Poverty, Pregnancy and the Health Professional*. Books for Midwives, London

Janestick VJ (1994) The dance of qualitative research design: Metaphor, methodolatory, and meaning. In: Denzin NK, Lincoln YS, eds. *Handbook of Qualitative Research*. Sage, Thousand Oaks: 209–19

Jary D, Jary J (1991) *Dictionary of Sociology*. Harper Collins, Glasgow

Jupp V (2006) *The Sage Dictionary of Social research Methods*. Sage, London

Kamuf P, ed (1991) *A Derrida Reader: Between the blinds*. Columbia University Press, New York

Kennedy H (2008) *Childbirth Discourse: Interpreting media messages*. International Confederation of Midwives, SECC, Glasgow, Scotland: June 2008

Kingdon C (2005) Reflexivity: Not just a qualitative methodological tool. *Br J Midwifery* **13**: 622–7

Kingdon C (2007) *Re-visioning Choice through Situated Knowledges: Women's preferences for vaginal or caesarean birth*. Unpublished PhD thesis, Lancaster University

Kirwan JM, Tincello DG, Lavender T, Kingston RE (2003) How doctors record breaking bad news in ovarian cancer. *Br J Cancer* **88**: 839–42

Lalor JG, Devane D, Begley CM (2007) Unexpected Diagnosis of Fetal Abnormality: Women's Encounters with Caregivers. *Birth: Issues in Perinatal Care* **34**(1): 80–8

Lavender T, Edwards G, Alfirevic Z, eds (2004) *Demystifying Qualitative Research in Pregnancy and Childbirth*. Quay Books, London

Lincoln YS, Guba EG (1985) *Naturalistic Inquiry*. Sage Publications, London

Lyotard JF (1984) *The Postmodern Condition*. Manchester University Press, Manchester

Manning D (2004) What are the ethical considerations? In: Lavender T, Edwards G, Alfirevic A, eds. *Demystifying Qualitative Research in Pregnancy and Childbirth*. Quay Books, London: 35–47

Malterud K (2001) Qualitative research: standards, challenges, and guidelines. *The Lancet* **358**: 483–88

Mays N, Pope C (2000) Quality in health research. In: Pope CP, Mays N, eds. *Qualitative Research in Health Care*. 2nd edn. BJM Books, London: 89-101

Miles M, Huberman A (1994) *Qualitative Data Analysis*. Sage. London

Miller T, Boulton M (2007) Changing constructions of informed consent: Qualitative research and complex social worlds. *Social Science & Medicine* **65**(11): 2199-2211

Malone S (2003) Ethics at home: Informed consent in your own backyard. *Qualitative Studies in Education* **16**(6): 797–815

Mayo E (1933) *The Human Problems of an Industrial Civilization*. Macmillan, New York

Newell R (1995) Questionnaires. In: Gilbert N, eds. *Researching Social Life*. Sage, London: 94–114

Morrison K (2004) *Marx, Durkheim, Weber: Formations of Modern Social Thought*. Sage Publications, London

NMC (2008) *The Code: Standards of Conduct, Performance and Ethics for Nurses and Midwives*. NMC, London

Oakley A (1979) *From Here to Maternity: Becoming a Mother*. Penguin Books, Oxford

Oakley A (1981) *Interviewing Women: A contradiction in terms?* In: Roberts H, ed. Doing Feminist Research. Routledge, London

Oakley A, Rajan L, Grant A (1990) Social support and pregnancy outcome: report of a randomised controlled trial. *Br J Obstetrics and Gynaecology* **97**: 155–62

Oakley A (1998) Experimentation and social interventions: a forgotten but important history. *BMJ* **37**: 1239–42

Oakley A, Strange V, Stephenson J, Forrest S, Monteiro H, and the RIPPLE study team (2004a) Evaluating processes: a case study of a randomised controlled trial of sex education. *Evaluation* **10**(4): 440-62

Oakley A (2004b) Qualitative research and scientific enquiry. *Australian and New Zealand Journal of Public Health* **28**(2): 102–4

Oakley A (2005) Whose afraid of the randomised controlled trial? Some dilemmas of the scientific method and 'good' research practice. In: *The Ann Oakley Reader: Gender women and social science*: 233–43

O'Brien M, Jones D (1996) Revisiting family and kinship. *Sociology Review*: February

Oppenheim AN (2001) *Questionnaire Design, Interviewing and Attitude Measurement*. Continuum, London

Pink S (2007) *Doing Visual Ethnography*. Sage, London

Prosser J, ed (1998) *Image-based Research: A source book for qualitative researchers*. Falmer Press, London

Prosser J (2008) *Introducing visual methods: A roadmap. In: ESRC Researcher Development Initiative. Building Capacity in Visual Methods: Introduction to visual methods handbook*. University of Manchester

Rapp R (2000) *Testing the Woman, Testing the Fetus: The social impact of amniocentesis in America*. Routledge, London

Rees C (2003) *Introduction to Research for Midwives*. 2nd edn. Books for Midwives, Edinburgh

Reinharz S (1992) *Feminist Methods in Social Research*. Oxford University Press, Oxford

Richardson S, McMullan M (2007) Research ethics in the UK: What can sociology learn from health? *Sociology* **41**(6): 1115–32

Robson C (2002) *Real World Research*. 2nd edn. Blackwell Publishing, Oxford

Richards L (2005) *Handling Qualitative Data: A practical guide*. Sage, London

Roberts H (1990) *Women's Health Counts*. Routledge. London

Roberts H (1992a) Answering back: The role of respondents in women's health research. In: Roberts H, ed. *Women's Health Matters*. Routlegde, London: 176–92

Roberts H (1992b) *Women's Health Matters*. Routlegde, London

Sanders T (2004) *Sex Work*. Willan Cullompton, Devon

Silverman D (1985) *Qualitative Methodology and Sociology*. Gower, Aldershot

Silverman D (2006) *Interpreting Qualitative Data: Methods for analysing talk, text and interaction.* Sage, London

Silverman D (2007) *A Very Short, Fairly Interesting and Reasonably Cheap Book about Qualitative Research.* Sage, London

Simpson J (2004) Negotiating elective caesarean section: An obstetric team perspective. In: Kirkham M, ed. *Informed Choice in Maternity Care.* Palgrave Macmillan, Basingstoke: 211–34

Schneider Z (2002) An Australian study of women's experiences of their first pregnancy. *Midwifery* **18**(3): 238–49

Soobrayman V (2003) Ethics, truth and politics in constructivist qualitative research. *Westminister Studies in Education* **26**(2): 107

Strauss AL, Corbin J (1997) *Grounded Theory in Practice.* Sage, London

Strauss AL, Corbin J (1998) *Basics of Qualitative Research: Techniques and Procedures for Developing Grounded Theory.* 2nd edn. Sage, Thousand Oaks

Tesch R (1990) *Qualitative Research: Analysis types and software tools.* Falmer, Bristol

Van Leewen T, Jewitt C, eds (2001) *Handbook of Visual Analysis.* Sage Publications, London

Vidich AJ, Bensman J (1958) *Small Town in Mass Society.* Princetown University Press, Princeton, New Jersey

Vidich AJ, Bensman J (1968) *Small Town in Mass Society.* 2nd edn. Princetown University Press, Princeton, New Jersey

Wall K, Higgins S, Packard E (2007) *Thinking and Talking about Learning: Using templates to find out pupils' views.* Southgate Publishers, Devon

Walsh D (2006) *Improving Maternity Service. Small is Beautiful: Lessons for maternity services from a birth centre.* Radcliffe Publishing, Oxford

Wilmott P (1963) *The Evolution of a Community: A Study of Dagenham after Forty Years.* Routledge & Kegan Paul, London

Young J (1971) The role of the police as amplifiers of deviancy, negociators of reality and translators of fantasy. In: Cohen S, ed. *Images of Deviance.* Penguin, Harmondsworth

CHAPTER 9

Future challenges
for sociology and midwifery

The International Confederation of Midwives (ICM) statement on competencies for midwifery practice requires that all:

> '...midwives have the requisite knowledge and skills from the social sciences and ethics that form the basis of high quality, culturally relevant, appropriate care for women and childbearing families'.
>
> *ICM (2002: 4)*

Sociology is one of the disciplines that comprise the social sciences. This book has been written with the explicit aim of enhancing midwives' knowledge of sociology and their appreciation of its relevance to everyday midwifery practice. It has tried to achieve this by focusing on substantive issues relevant to midwives — including the role of the midwife, the family, the body and the media — employing a sociological lens to the familiar, all too often taken-for-granted aspects of the world that we inhabit.

The purpose of this chapter is to bring the issues raised throughout the book together, reflect on why sociology may hitherto have been perceived by some midwives as 'difficult' or 'just common-sense', and to speculate as to the future for a sociology that midwives could more easily identify with. This chapter is also where I reflect on why writing this book proved problematic.

The problem of defining sociology today

As introduced in chapter one, contemporary social theory comprises of perspectives that can be traced back to the founding fathers alongside the newer approaches associated with the numerous variants of feminist and post-modernism thought. None of these approaches are mutually exclusive and they each have multiple variants. Consequently, and as widely acknowledged by other commentators, any introduction to sociological theory today represents a challenging and somewhat formidable task.

A second problem faced when introducing sociology today arises from the fact that society is itself in the midst of a period of social change. Consequently sociological debates concerning the nature of that change are not only complex and varied, but they are emergent.

Another reason why this book has been such a challenge for me personally is that it has not been possible to do justice to the range of feminist work highlighting the importance of differences between women according to their class, age, geography, ethnicity, sexuality or disability. I hope that by drawing attention to this here it reinstates the importance of such issues for both sociology and midwifery.

Shared concerns across sociology and midwifery

The defining features of sociology (i.e. how society is organised and how we experience life) means that in one sense every sociologist studies issues that have relevance to us all. However, the purpose of this book is to introduce midwives to what, in particular, sociology can offer to how you think about your everyday experiences as midwives.

Challenges facing the profession

Chapter two introduced historical and contemporary sociological analyses of the role of the midwife, whilst chapter three highlighted that we are currently in a period of significant organisational change within the British National Health Service. At ground-floor level midwives recognise the pressures arising from insufficient recruitment, retention and skill-mix. There are also concerns about the diversification of midwifery roles that are perceived as representing both an opportunity (in terms of the expansion of midwives skills and continuity of care for women) and a threat (as the traditional role of the midwife is not only eroded, but devalued in favour of high-technology midwifery). Moreover, the increased use of maternity support workers is sparking mixed responses. The significance of the processes of globalization is a key concern in contemporary sociology. Processes that are particularly relevant to midwives at the level of the media (because as introduced in chapter seven it is the medical model of childbirth that dominates a global stage), but also at the level of everyday labour ward practice with the international recruitment of midwives to work in the British NHS, midwives increasingly caring for migrant women from other cultures, and evidence-based guidelines that are standardising global 'best-practice'. For example, studies show that the publication of the term breech trial in October 2000 transformed obstetric practice worldwide, almost overnight, to routine planned Caesarean section for term breech babies (Steen and Kingdon, 2008). Collectively, all of these issues represent challenges to the midwifery profession, but they also present exciting opportunities for extending sociological analyses and bringing about positive change.

Challenges from the 'delivering choice' agenda

Policy documents including '*Maternity Matters*' (DH, 2007) mean individual midwives, Trusts and commissioning bodies are all responsible for delivering the present UK government's agenda around choice. What choice means, who has choice, and how choice is it enacted are important issues for contemporary sociology. As introduced in chapter three, the particular model of consumerism currently employed in the NHS is congruent with enterprise culture and the market (which determines what we may choose between), coupled with an emphasis on the rights of the individual (with which comes responsibility for the choices made).

Chapters four, five and six highlighted the centrality of notions of choice in relation to (un)healthy lifestyle choices, 'chosen' families (in particular the increasing number of women who 'choose' to delay childbirth until aged over 35 years), and the body as an unfinished project.

Chapter six also highlighted how increased fetal surveillance may limit the choices available to mothers who are increasingly expected to make the 'right choice' for their unborn 'baby'. However, perhaps most significantly is the medicalization literature (from sociology) that suggests some women have gained from this process and papers (principally from obstetrics) that report women are now 'choosing' planned Caesarean section for maternal request. Further analysis of all of these issues can only benefit from trans-disciplinary working that marries sociological, midwifery and medical perspectives in the pursuit of understanding why women make the choices they do and how they impact on maternal and neonatal outcomes.

Challenges from medicalized birth as the norm

As introduced in chapter one norms are the rules of behavior that reflect or embody a culture's values. Chapter three introduced the rise of hospital birth, the industrialization of birth and the medicalization debates, whilst chapter four identified a number of different ways of conceptualizing health, although as we saw in chapter seven, it is the (bio)medical model of childbirth that dominates the media. Thus, medicalized birth is the norm in our society. Additionally, across many of the chapters, Beck's (1992) notion of risk society is omnipresent because at its heart lies an '...*insatiable appetite for medicine*' (Beck, 1992: 211). What is more, as identified in chapter six one consequence of increased medical surveillance during pregnancy is the formation of heightened awareness of risk amongst healthy, pregnant women. Thus, sociology offers some important insights into understanding how medicalized birth as the norm operates in our culture, which is the first step in challenging it.

This section has picked up threads of earlier chapters, reiterating the relevance of sociology to midwives in past, the present and the future. Yet to date, the relevance of sociology to midwives is all too often overlooked or dismissed and it is a subject few midwives are keen to pursue. The purpose of the next section is to reflect on why sociology may hitherto have been perceived by some midwives as 'difficult' or 'just common-sense'.

Disciplinary misconceptions

I suggest that one of the principal reasons sociology may be perceived as difficult by some midwives is because its resonance to the everyday world is all too often lost by the use of overly complicated language in 'theory rich' journal articles and books. It is my intention that this book in general, and that chapter's one and eight in particular, go some way to explain the importance of theory for sociologists. Moreover, the glossary that follows this chapter should re-acquaint midwives with the key terms and concepts introduced throughout the book. Another reason why I believe that sociology can sometimes get a bad press amongst midwives is that many of its strands are overtly critical in their theoretical underpinning and empirical conclusions. In other words, many sociologists go looking for conflict and can be particularly critical when they find it. Consequently, there is an observed tendency for some sociologists to be too critical and overstate their case. At best a critical stance can promote positive social change, but at worst it can mean work looses its empirical resonance, leading to charges of irrelevance.

In contrast to assertions that sociology is too difficult or not relevant is the claim that it is just 'common-sense'. This is particularly interesting because on the one hand sociology is nothing like common-sense, whilst on the other, arguably the best sociology does indeed come to be thought of as 'common-sense'. At one level sociology differs from common sense because it challenges the everyday taken-for-granted assumptions that are 'common-sense'. For example, in chapter one we began challenging the common-sense assumptions behind the notion all women should have an antenatal booking scan. We asked whose interests does this common-sense assumption serve and what are its consequences. Moreover, phenomenology and some variants of social constructionism have been specifically concerned with the processes whereby we as humans construct common(sense) perceptions of reality. However, at another level seminal pieces of sociology illuminate aspects of our lives that come to be thought of as obvious and thus become part of our common-sense understanding of the world. For example, the sociological concepts of stigma and gender.

Advancing a collaborative agenda

As evident throughout this book there is a strong tradition of midwives and sociologists (particularly those from feminist perspectives and/or medical sociology) working together, which dates back to the 1970s. Additionally, there are also monographs (research books) and many papers reporting the findings of research that are co-authored by midwives and sociologists.

Today, a growing number of midwives are also trained as sociologists. An increasing number of midwives are publishing in social science journals and many sociologists work within academic departments of midwifery (and nursing) or medicine. Equally, if not more significant for the future, some of the barriers for obtaining funding for collaborative research are receding with the introduction of schemes such as the Economic and Social Research Council's (ESRC) Innovative Health Technologies Programme (*www.york.ac.uk/res/iht/introduction.htm*).

Collectively this all amounts to an exciting time for the future of the sociology *of* midwifery and sociology *in* midwifery. Moreover, future collaborative research efforts, coupled with more widespread teaching of the issues identified in this book, could ultimately lead to a 'new' sociology of childbirth; one that many more midwives can identify with.

References

Beck U (1992) *Risk Society*. Sage, London

DH (2007) *Maternity Matters*. DH, London

ICM (2002) Essential competencies for basic midwifery practice. *www.ckpa.cz/download/zahranicni–okenko/009.pdf*

Steen M, Kingdon C (2008) Vaginal or caesarean delivery? How research has turned breech birth around. *Evidence-Based Midwifery* **6**(3): 95–9

Glossary

A

Absolute poverty: Refers to the minimum requirements necessary for basic subsistence.

Acheson Report: Published in 1998, found evidence of widening health inequalities in Britain. The report recommended reducing health inequalities amongst women of childbearing age, expectant mothers and young children as a national priority.

Adorno, Theodor (1903-1969): German sociologist and a leading member of the Frankfurt School of Critical Theory.

Agency: Fundamental concept in sociology, which refers to the power of individuals or groups to operate independently of the determining constraints of social structure.

Agrarian societies: Primarily based on agricultural production.

Alienation: Sociological concept first employed by Karl Marx. In its broadest sense it refers to an individual's feelings if estrangement from a situation, group or culture.

Althusser, Louis (1918-1990): French sociologist and leading proponent of Marxism.

Anthropology: The study of human beings with social/cultural anthropology focusing specifically on the structures and cultures produced by human beings.

B

Biological determinism: The notion that the female sexes role in reproduction determines the role of women in society. Different variants of this notion are known as biological reductionism and essentialism.

Black Report: Published in 1980, is a seminal study that shows striking evidence of the extent of health inequalities in Britain. It found men and women in the lowest occupational class had a two and a half time greater chance of dying before retirement age than those in the highest. Moreover, evidence of class inequalities in mortality was found at birth, during the first year of life, in childhood, adolescence and adult life.

Blumer, Herbert (1900-1987): American sociologist who worked in the symbolic interactionist tradition.

Bourgeoisie: Karl Marx's term for the capitalist class who own the means of production.

Baudrillard, Jean (1929-2007): French sociologist who was influential in developing post-modernist perspectives.

British Sociological Association (BSA): This is the professional association for sociologists in the UK.

C

Capitalism: Is a system of economic enterprise where the goal of production is to make profit via the sale of goods in a competitive market. The capitalist mode of production is principally associated with industrial societies.

Cartesian dualism: Refers to the notion that humans comprise two separate entities: body and mind, linked during life but profoundly different. It originates from the work of the 17th century French philosopher René Descartes who was one of the key figures that founded modern science and medicine.

Chicago School: Refers to work emanating from the Department of Sociology, University of Chicago. Most notably, during the 1920's and 1930's the Chicago School pioneered an approach to urban sociology and was at the centre of the development of symbolic interactionism.

Chosen families: Are the diverse kinds of families evident today within which it is argued that individuals play a greater role in their creation and dissolution. Examples of chosen family structures include same-sex parent families and step-families.

Class: Is a key concept in sociology, which can be traced back to the work of

Karl Marx and Max Weber. However, there is no single accepted way of defining social class. At one level it may be defined as segments of the population sharing broadly similar types and levels of resources, with broadly similar styles of living and some shared perception of their collective condition, or at another level simply in terms of an individual's occupation.

Classical sociology: Encompasses the works of key figures in the development of sociology during the eighteenth, nineteenth and early twentieth century.

Comte, Auguste (1798-1857): Frenchman who coined the term sociology and developed positivism.

Communism: Is a set of political ideas derived from the work of Karl Marx and associated with the societal structures of China, the former Soviet Union and Eastern Europe. It is based on socialist principles communist societies aim to eradicate private productive property and inequalities between social classes.

Consumption: Is a sociological concept that refers to the process in which goods or services are used to satisfy needs.

Consumerism: Can be defined in many different ways. It may be used to refer to social movements that aim to protect or promote the rights of consumers. Alternatively it may be used to refer to the cultural dominance of marketing and the consumption of goods and services. In the NHS, since the reforms of the early 1990s, a model of consumerism congruent with enterprise culture and the market, coupled with an emphasis on the rights of the individual and a notion of patient choice has prevailed.

Cultural hegemony: Is a sociological concept associated with the work of the Italian Marxist Antonio Gramsci. It refers to the ideological domination of one class by another through the dominant class's control of cultural forms (i.e. the media).

Culture: Refers to the ways of life of members of a society — the values, ceremonies and shared meanings — that are characteristic of their particular social grouping.

D

Deprofessionalization theory: Asserts that medicine is losing its monopoly over knowledge, public belief and expectations of autonomy and authority as members of the public become increasingly well-educated and informed.

Deviance: Is the term used to describe actions that do not conform to a society's accepted norms which may be considered deviant in one society may not be so in another temporal or cultural context.

Disciplinary power: Is a concept developed by Michael Foucoult to describe how post-industrialization and post-enlightenment human bodies have increasingly become regulated, trained, maintained and understood (in particular by medicine).

Discourse: Refers to the framework that shapes how we think about specific areas of social life. For example, much of the language and imagery that shapes how we think about childbirth and how individuals act when they encounter pregnancy is shaped by medical discourse.

Division of labour: Refers to the division of tasks or occupations that create interdependence. For example, in the NHS healthcare division of labour midwives, obstetricians, healthcare assistants and clerical staff are all required to provide seamless care for women during pregnancy and childbirth.

Durkheim, Emile (1858-1917): French sociologist who was fundamental in founding the discipline and was the first Professor of Sociology.

E

Economic base: Is a term used by Karl Marx to demonstrate how the system of social relations is derived from economic production.

Economic determinism: Refers to any approach that emphasises the importance of the economy in shaping society.

Emotion work: Is a concept developed by Arlie Hochschild (1983) to conceptualise the previously undocumented work done by airline cabin crew when trying to keep airline passengers happy.

Enlightenment: Is the period of intellectual ferment leading up to the French Revolution that was characterised by the application of reason and rationality. It marked the transition from traditional to modern forms of thought and social organisation.

Epidemiology: Is the branch of medicine that involves the study of the prevalence and incidence of disease.

Epistemology: Is the branch of philosophy concerned with the theory(ies) underpinning the production of knowledge.

Essentialism: Is a term used in feminist writing to refer to a particular variant of biological determinism. Specifically, essentialism is where the essential qualities attributed to women turn out to be biological in origin. More generally the term essentialism may be used to convey the view that science is able to represent absolute truths.

Ethnicity: May be defined as the cultural values and norms that distinguish the members of a given group from others.

Ethnocentrism: Is the practice of judging other cultures by comparison with ones own. It is particularly discouraged in sociology where comparison with other societies and cultures has shown that the world created by modern societies is not necessarily to be equated with progress.

Ethnography: Is a research approach that involves emerging oneself in the culture under study. It usually involves observation as a research method.

Ethnomethodology: Is a specialist branch of interpretive sociology that involves the study of the methods and social competence individual's' employ when constructing our sense of reality.

Extended family: Refers to family units that extend beyond the nuclear family. Extended families may include grandparents (i.e vertical extensions of the nuclear family) and/or additional wives (i.e. horizontal extensions of the nuclear family).

F

Family cycle: Refers to the cylindrical process whereby most individuals leave home, get married, move in with their spouse, have children, children leave home and the cycle starts again.

Feminism(s): Constitutes both a political movement and an academic field. Its origins can be traced back to pre-Enlightenment. However today, it is not a unified field; arguably the only things all feminisms share is a central concern with gender and a commitment to improving the lives of those disadvantaged by gender inequality.

Feminist methodology: Derived from feminist theory, aims to minimise harm to those being researched and to diminish the control exercised by the researcher, coupled with a commitment to produce research of value to women.

Foetal-personhood: Is a term that conceptualises the personal and a public presence of the fetus in contemporary visual cultures, which serves to ascribe personhood on the unborn.

Fordism and post-Fordism: The former refers to a pattern of work organization based around the notion that management needs to control the work force by specifying in some details what is to be done, how it is to be done, and in what quantity it is to be done. In contrast, post-Fordism is centred around the premise that workers can be more productive if they are encouraged to use all their abilities in a relatively free rather than closely monitored way and where responsibility is directed downwards to the point of contact with clients.

Foucault, Michel (1926-1984): French philosopher who is particularly influential in contemporary sociology where his writings on knowledge, power and the body have been associated with variants of structuralist and post-structuralist thought.

Frankfurt School: Refers to work emanating from the Frankfurt Institute for Social Research (established in 1922 and disbanded in 1969) where a group of sociologists and philosophers revisited the writings of Marx with the aim of bringing them up to date. The continued influence of the Frankfurt School is evident today in the writings of Jürgen Habermas.

Functionalism: Is a key perspective sociology that explains societal institutions (i.e. the judicial system, the family, the church) in terms of the function they perform for society. The origins of functionalism as a distinct sociological theory are credited to Emile Durkheim. However, it was Talcott Parsons structural functionalism that was to prove particularly influential in sociology up until the late 1960s.

G

Garfinkel, Harold (1917-): American sociologist who first developed ethnomethodology as a distinct sociological approach.

Gaze: Is a concept associated with the work of Foucault (i.e. the medical gaze) and feminist writers (i.e. the male gaze). It refers to the power manifest in a particular line of vision or dominant way of seeing. For Foucault the gaze is fundamentally liked to his notions of surveillance, power, discipline and control with 'the gaze' serving to reduce deviancy by means of self-conformity. Some feminist conceptions of the gaze highlight how the male gaze promotes a certain bodily form as the feminine ideal, whilst others show how the medical gaze serves to promote conformity and uniformity through visual surveillance techniques (which include antenatal ultrasound scans).

Gender: Refers to the culturally prescribed differences between men and women. It is a sociological concept first developed by the British feminist sociologist Ann Oakley. The contemporary utility of the sex/gender distinction is currently up for debate reflecting developments in sociobiology (that challenge the two-sex model) and the rise of post-modernism (which rejects such binary distinctions).

Giddens, Anthony (1938-): British sociologist who has made multiple contributions to contemporary sociology, including the formulation of structuration theory and arguments emphasizing the reflexive nature of late modernity.

Glasgow University Media Group: Refers to the work of a group of sociologists whose critical studies of television news have received wide acclaim. The group was established in 1974 and its work continues today.

Goffman, Erving (1922-82): North American sociologist who conducted a number of seminal ethnographic studies of face-to-face interactions and is associated with the symbolic interactionist tradition.

Globalization: Refers to the process that is intensifying worldwide social and economic relations creating interdependence for societies and individuals.

Global village: Refers to the process whereby electronic media (particularly television) means people throughout the world can see major events unfold and hence participate in them together.

Grounded theory: In its broadest sense refers to any sociological theory that is built up gradually from detailed observation of a social phenomenon. The development of grounded theory as a distinct methodology can be traced to the work of Barney Glasner and Anselm Straus, however a number of different variants now exist.

H

Habermas, Jürgen (1929-): German sociologist who is arguably the leading contemporary proponent of an approach to radical social theorizing originating from the Frankfurt School of Critical Theory.

Hawthorne effect: Refers to the process whereby humans modify their behaviour by virtue of knowingly being studied in a social setting.

Hyperreality: Is the term Jean Baudrillard uses to conceptualise how the distinction between reality and the words and images used by the media to portray it disintegrate. In other words, there is no longer a reality occurring in a particular time and place, but the reality is fluid created by television coverage of that occurrence and audience interpretation of the television coverage.

I

Iatrogenesis: Refers to the increased levels of illness and social problems caused by what Ivan Illich perceived as unnecessary medical intervention resulting from medicalization.

Ideal types: Are conceptual models that represent a phenomenon in its purest form. As a sociological concept the 'ideal type' originates in the work of Max Weber who advocated actual situations in the real world could be understood better by comparing them to an ideal type.

Ideology: Refers to shared ideas or beliefs that serve to justify the interests of dominant groups, legitimising their subordination of others. For example, Karl Marx recognised the power of ideology in legitimising and therefore maintaining the power of the bourgeoisie over the proletariat.

Ideology of motherhood: Refers to the system of ideas that posits a white, middle class, stay-at-home, heterosexual, biological mother, who delivers constant care and attention to her children as the feminine ideal. The ideology of motherhood serves to enforce women's primary role as in the domestic (private) sphere and men's as in the public (as breadwinner). This conventional ideology of motherhood has been widely criticised by feminist writers.

Industrialization: Refers to the emergence of machine production based on the use of inanimate power resources (e.g. steam or electricity). The industrialized societies of the modern world originated in Europe at the end of the eighteenth century, however industrialization is a process that continues today.

Intensive mothering: Refers to the process whereby individual mothers are increasingly expected to invest heavily (time, energy, money and emotion) to enhance their child's intellectual, physical, social and emotional development. It is an emergent discourse first discussed in the sociological literature by Susan Hays in the 1990s who describes it as child-centred, expert guided, emotionally absorbing, labour intensive and financially expensive.

Interpretive sociology: Is underpinned by the belief that knowledge is culturally derived and representative of historically situated interpretations of the world. In other words, we construct human understanding of the world; we make meaning through interpretation and action. Examples of sociological perspectives using an interpretive approach include symbolic interactionism, phenomenology, and ethnomethodology.

Inverse care law: Was first described by Julian Tudor Hart in the 1970s. Based on his experience as a general practitioner (GP) he asserts that those who have the most need of NHS health care services actually obtain them later, and in smaller amounts, whilst those who have less need use more, and often better health services. Subsequent sociological research offers support for this assertion, as have studies reporting an inverse relationship between need and provision of antenatal care.

L

Legitimated authority: Refers to the occupational self-control, over the terms and conditions of work, which are crucial to sociological conceptualisations of medicine as a profession.

Life-course explanation for health inequalities: Is based on research that suggests the consequences of socio-economic disadvantage accumulate from conception, through childhood and adolescence to adulthood and in later life.

Logic of capitalism: Refers to the pursuit of profit inherent in capitalist societies.

Logic of subordination: Refers to the process whereby medicine ensures its continued position at the top of the healthcare division of labour by demarcating other clinicians' (including midwives) sphere of practice.

Lyotard, Jean-François (1925-1998): French philosopher and proponent of post-modernism, in particular the human condition in post-modernity and the rejection of meta-narratives.

M

Macro sociology: Is concerned with society as a whole.

Malestream: Is a term found in feminist scholarship that refers to the absence of gender issues in mainstream sociological theory and research.

Marcuse, Herbert (1898-1979): German sociologist and member of the Frankfurt School of critical theory.

Martineau, Harriet (1802-1876): First translated Comte's founding work into English.

Marx, Karl (1818-1883): German and key figure in sociology. He developed a body of ideas and theory that encompasses the whole of the social sciences and the humanities, and was the inspiration for the communist societies of the twentieth century.

Marxism: Is the body of work that aims to develop, amend or revise the ideas put forward by Karl Marx.

Mass media: Refers to any system of communication aimed at mass public audiences. Most generally the media is said to comprise printed (i.e. newspapers, magazines, books), aural (i.e. radio, compact discs), audio-visual (i.e. television, cinema, video, DVD) and so-called new media (i.e. internet, mobile phones, e-mail).

Materialist explanations: For inequalities in health emphasize the role of socio-economic factors (i.e. low and insecure income, poor housing). Neo-materialist explanations of health inequalities emphasise the importance of an unequal social structure.

McKeown thesis: Recognises the contribution of medicine to bringing relief from illness but asserts that non-medical factors (including improvements in public health) are more significant in reducing mortality rates.

Mead, George Herbert (1863-1931): American sociologist based at the University of Chicago who was central to the development of symbolic interactionism.

Means of production: Is a term associated with Karl Marx and Marxism that refers to the tools, machinery and buildings used in the production of goods in capitalist economies.

Medical model: Is based around the notion that specific aetiology underlies specific diseases (which alter anatomy and physiology, giving rise to specific symptoms). It is also commonly associated with the notion of science as objective (or in other words value-free), mechanical metaphors (as evident in chapter three), the mind-body dualism and a doctor-patient interaction based on individualism and intervention. It is the dominant approach to disease in Western medicine, which was established during the nineteenth and early twentieth century.

Medicalization: Is the process whereby medicine's control in society is increased as non-medical problems become defined and treated as medical conditions. The sociological origins of the concept can be traced to the work of Eliot Freidson, Irving Zola and Ivan Ilich in the 1970s. A substantial body of work documenting the medicalization of childbirth emerged during the 1970s and 1980s. Contemporary debates recognise the benefits of medicalization as well as the problems, focus on the growing influence of biotechnogy, the role of the media in the new medicalization debates and the notion of de-medicalization.

Meso sociological analyses: Are found in the sociology of organisations and focus on the intermediate layer (between the macro and micro level) where policy and organizational and managerial processes tend to be concentrated.

Meta-narratives: Are broad over-arching theories or beliefs about societal structure and social change. The term is associated with post-modernism's rejection of grand or meta-narratives.

Methods: Are the techniques or procedure used to gather and analyse data related to a particular research question.

Methodology: Refers to the strategies associated with a particular epistemology that inform a researchers choice of methods.

Micro sociology: Is concerned with individual interaction.

Mills, Charles Wright (1916-1962): Influential American sociologist.

Mode of production: Is a term used by Marx to show how economic production shapes the system of social relations and the class system arising from it.

Modernity: Refers to the modern age, that is societies post-industrialization.

N

National Health Service (NHS): Came into existence on the 5th of July 1948 offering free medical care to the population of Britain.

National Statistics Socio-Economic Classification (NS-SEC): Is the scheme used to report differences between social classes in Britain. The NS-SEC is designed to facilitate a variety of analytical class breakdowns. The three-class breakdown is the one currently used to define the Department of Health's target for infant mortality.

Neo-conventional family: Is a notion based on research suggesting that there is now no single British family, but a rich variety of forms, states, traditions, norms and usages.

New reproductive technologies: Refers to technologies for preventing conception, facilitating antenatal screening, managing labour and childbirth, and promoting assisted conception.

Norms: Are the rules of behavior that reflect or embody a culture's values.

Nuclear family: Refers to a family unit consisting of a husband, wife and their dependent children.

O

Objectivism: Is the belief that knowledge has an objective existence independent of human study

Q

Quantitative research approaches: May be defined as any research that results in data being expressed in numerical form. Quantitative research is typically associated with objectivism and positivism.

Qualitative research approaches: Are generally associated with interpretivism. Qualitative research focuses on the broad and complex where data may comprise words, images, observations or documents.

P

Parsons, Talcott (1902-1979): American sociologist who was a leading proponent of structural functionalism and fundamental to the development of sociology during the twentieth century.

Patriarchy: Is a term that is used to refer to a societal wide system of gender relations of male dominance and female subordination, and the ways in which male power is institutionalised within different sites in society (i.e. in the family). Many feminists argue patriarchy is most evident in industrial societies.

Phenomenology: May broadly be defined as the descriptive study of experiences and the meanings we as humans attach to phenomenon. Phenomenology is a branch of philosophy that was developed into a sociological theory by Alfred Schutz.

Political economy: Refers to a number of perspectives (not unique to sociology) that emphasise the importance of economic factors in shaping society, which are politically charged. For example political economy perspectives have highlighted the tension between the pursuit of profit and the pursuit of health.

Positivism in sociology: Is a methodology that advocates the study of the social world should be conducted according to the principals of natural science

Post-modern family: Refers to a notion of the family where the existence of a dominant culture is contested, ambivalent and undecided and family relationships are diverse, dynamic and unresolved.

Post-modernism: Is variously defined. Most generally it is a position that purports a shift beyond modernity, with theorists rejecting the meta-narratives of the modern period, highlighting instead how the post-modern world is in a constant state of flux.

Post-structuralism: Developed out of critique of structuralism and is principally associated with the work of a group of French philosophers in the late 1960s, 1970s and 1980s. It is a perspective that rejects linear, holistic or binary ways of thinking (hence it is sometimes conflated with post-modernism), which has been particularly influential in feminist thinking.

Poverty: May be defined exclusively in terms of health (i.e. malnutrition), or more widely in terms of an individual's general standard of living, their access to consumer durables, leisure activities and social participation (all of which undoubtedly have an impact on general health status). The concept of absolute poverty is based around ideas of basic subsistence requirements; whereas, the concept of relative poverty relates to the standards of a particular society at a particular time.

Pre-modern societies: Include hunting and gathering societies, pastoral/agrarian societies and traditional civilisations (also known as empires).

Profession: Refers to an occupation accorded high status and a high degree of autonomy over its work. Whilst this definition does not necessarily preclude the occupation of midwifery in Britain today, law, medicine and the church are the occupations that have been traditionally used as examples of 'the professions' in sociology.

Professional project: Refers to the more or less conscious efforts of members of an occupation to work collectively to improve their status and their economic prospects.

Professional socialization: Is the processes through which new entrants to an occupation acquire their professional identities.

Professionalization: Refers to the process of achieving the status of a profession.

Proletariat: Is Karl Marx's term for the working class who do not own the means of production.

Proletarianization theory: As advocated by John Mckinlay and colleagues, asserts that medicine is loosing some of its power and control in advanced capitalist societies.

Psychology: Is the study of behaviour.

Psycho-social explanations for health inequalities: Are based on research that suggests contemporary ways of life impact on the lower social classes disproportionately. According to this perspective high workload, job insecurity, poor promotion and low control combine to produce social stresses that affect mental well-being and physical health.

Public health: Is the branch of medicine that shares concerns with medical sociology about the social determinants of disease, inequalities in health and structural barriers to improving health and health care. It has origins in the nineteenth century reforms for improved sanitation. The 'new public health' refers to the re-emergence of public health medicine since the late 1980s and a renewed focus on the social causes of illness and disease and community participation to improve health.

R

Reconstituted family: Is the term used to describe a family in which at least one of the adults has children from a previous marriage or relationship (stepfamilies in other words).

Reflectively mobilised self: Is a concept developed by Anthony Giddens to capture how individuals in late capitalist societies increasingly alter and shape their lives (including their bodies) according to a range of options and choices.

Registrar Generals' Social Class (RGSC) scheme: Has proved particularly useful in the study of health inequalities in Britain. It originates from 1913 and was used to classify occupations into one of six social classes. It was replaced by the National Statistics Socio-Economic Classification (NS-SEC) scheme in 2001.

Risk society: Is a concept developed by Ulrich Beck to capture how society has come to reflect upon modernity itself and the problems it creates. According to Beck at the heart of risk society is the phenomenon of health and an insatiable appetite for medicine.

Role: Refers to the way in which society expects a person who occupies a given position to behave. Roles carry duties and obligations and they may also confer rights, privileges and status

S

Schutz, Alfred (1899-1959): Developed phenomenology into a branch of sociological theory.

Self: Is a key concept in interpretive sociology. The 'self' refers to the mental construction of the person by the person, which occurs through interaction with other human beings.

Sick role: Is a concept that was originally developed by Talcott Parsons, which distinguishes illness as a social role from illness as a biomedical category. Parson saw the sick role as a socially sanctioned form of deviance that inferred certain obligations and behaviour.

Socialization: Refers to the processes by which children, or other new members of society, learn the way of life of their society. Primary socialization occurs in infancy when children learn language and basic behavioral patterns, usually from their families, whilst secondary socialization takes place in later childhood and into maturity.

Social action theory: Was developed by Max Weber. It takes human individuals, their ideas, and their actions as a starting point for sociological analysis

Social exclusion: Refers to people who, through no inherent failing, do not have access to rights or resources taken for granted by the majority. Some strands of work into social exclusion focus on poverty, equality and material deprivation, whilst others propose that ideas of social cohesion, belongingness and integration are central.

Social model of health: Is constructed around the notion that health is a state of complete physical, mental and social well-being and not merely the absence of disease or infirmity.

Social facts: Is a term associated with Emile Durkheim who used it to describe elements of society which can be studied independently of individual disposition.

Society: May be defined as the totality of human relationships.

Somatic society: Is a notion developed by the sociologist Bryan Turner, which highlights the body, and the regulation of bodies in particular, as central to contemporary society.

Spencer, Herbet (1820-1903): British social theorist whose work has been associated with structural functionalism.

Stereotype: Refers to a set of inaccurate, simplistic generalizations about a group of individuals that enables others to categorize individuals who are members of that group and treat them according to pre-defined expectations

Stigma: Is a concept that refers to any negatively defined physical or social condition, attribute, trait or behaviour that confers deviant status.

Stratification: Is the term used to describe the division of society into levels that form a hierarchy with the most powerful at the top.

Structure: Is a fundamental concept in sociology, which is typically used to describe any relatively enduring pattern or interrelationship of social elements. For example, in British society the judicial, educational and occupational structures are surface social structures, whilst the rules that reproduce social systems such as language provide examples of deeper social structures.

Structuration theory: Was developed by the British sociologist Anthony Giddens and asserts the importance of recognising the duality of structure and action in shaping society.

Surveillance: May be defined most simply as to keep a close eye. In sociology it is a concept most notably associated with the work of Michael Foucault. Foucault developed the notion of 'institutional surveillance' (evident in prisons, hospitals and schools) from Bentham's panoptican model of a prison where a single warden can stand in one place and view all prisoners. Central to Foucault's concept of surveillance is the notion of the gaze.

Symbolic interactionism: Is a key perspective in sociology that recognises the role of symbols and language in human interaction.

T

Theoretical perspective: Provides the underpinning framework for sociological analysis.

Triangulation: Refers to the combining of different perspectives or methods in the same research study to enhance reliability or go some way to addressing the partiality of data drawn from a single source.

W

Weber, Max (1864-1920): German sociologist who is credited with establishing the interpretive branch of sociology.

INDEX

V

W